Presented to

_____

on the occasion of

_____

date

_____

First published in the United States in 1989 by
Ideals Publishing Corporation
Nashville, Tennessee
Copyright © 1989 by World International Publishing Limited
Manchester, England
Printed and bound in Yugoslavia.
ISBN 0·8249·8355·6

Children's BIBLE in Story

Retold by James F. Couch, Jr.
Illustrated by Michael Codd

IDEALS CHILDREN'S BOOKS
Nashville, Tennessee

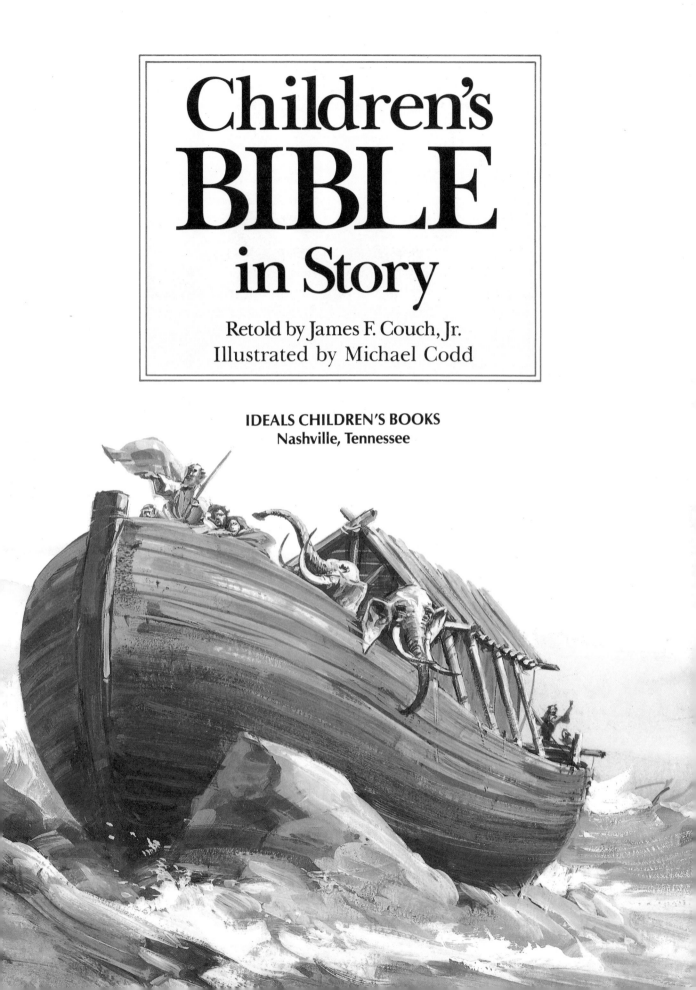

Advisory Board

MICHAEL CODD began his career as an artist at the age of thirteen when he was accepted into art school. After completing his training in design and graphic arts, Codd expanded his work to include painting and illustration. Although he specializes in the illustration of children's books, he has also illustrated encyclopedias, informational books, and works with a historic background. Codd currently teaches fine art and drawing in a college in the south of England.

PREFACE

Throughout the years of my ministry in the church and in special ministries and my years in publishing the Scriptures, I have found the Bible to be a unique source of inspiration and encouragement. When I was approached by Ideals Publishers about this *Bible in Story*, I was immediately enthusiastic.

For twelve years I worked with youth from preschoolers to graduate students. In every case, I found the overwhelming need to understand the truth of the Scriptures. For most, the Bible is a collection of separate and confusing books. My great desire is for people, especially children, to understand that the Bible is the story of God and his marvelous love for us. The Bible is filled with thousands of stories illustrating how God cares for individuals.

I have found in my years of editing reference and study Bibles that the Scriptures are accurately conveyed only if they are understood by the reader. Therefore, rather than a literal rendering of the text, at times I have chosen to retell the story using the simple language of a child. The purpose is to always remain faithful to the Scriptures while focusing on the central truth.

To help the child become familiar with the Scriptures, the stories follow the same order as they appear in the Bible. They begin with creation in Genesis and move on through the Epistles in the New Testament. The stories have been divided into Old and New Testaments like the Bible. Since the life of Christ is found in four different Gospels, the stories of Christ are in chronological order to harmonize the Gospels.

I would like to thank the three excellent scholars who consented to read and comment on the *Bible in Story*. There is no adequate way in which I can thank these men who took time from their busy schedules to help and advise.

Most of all, I pray that the children who read these stories begin to realize that the people of the Bible were not superheroes, nor did they have, for the most part, extraordinary faith or intelligence. They were only people like you and me who chose to either follow God or turn away from him. Their success or failure was dependent on their response. It is the same with us. I pray that we learn as they did to follow God wherever he leads.

James F. Couch, Jr.

Contents

THE OLD TESTAMENT

THE NEW TESTAMENT

THE
OLD
TESTAMENT

Genesis 1:1-31; 2:1-3

Creation

In the beginning there was no earth, no sky, and no universe. But there was always God.

Then God created heaven and earth. At first he made only darkness and water and swirling mists. God said, "Let there be light," and there was light. God saw that it was good. God separated the light from the darkness to create day and night, morning and evening, and that was the first day.

Next God separated the waters into some above and some underneath. The space between them he called "sky," and that was the second day.

Then God gathered together the waters under the sky so that dry land appeared. Some of the water formed into great, wide seas with sandy beaches or rocky shores. Some of the water formed into streams, pools, and waterfalls. And there were deep rivers, flowing down to the sea.

On the land God made trees and plants grow. He made tall forests and brightly colored flowers. He made trees for fruit and shade. He made plants that were good to eat and beautiful to see. In each one God put seeds so that as the first trees and plants died, others of the same kind would grow in their places. That was the third day. God was pleased with the world he was making.

To mark the days, the months, and the seasons, God made the sun, the moon, and the stars. That was the fourth day, and God saw that it was good.

Except for the sighing of the wind in the trees and the splashing of the waves on the empty shores, the world was silent and still. So God made creatures to go in the sea. He made great whales and tiny fish and all sorts and sizes in between. The seas were filled with life.

Then God made birds to fly in the sky. He made birds that swooped and soared, birds that perched on the rocks and nested in the trees. God blessed all the creatures and said, ''Have young, each of your own kind, and fill the seas and the sky.'' That was the fifth day.

Then God made creatures to go on the land. He made animals of all kinds and sizes. God blessed them so they would multiply and fill the earth. God saw that all he had made was good.

But there was still no one to help care for the earth and its creatures. There was no one to love God and to talk to him. So God made people. He made man and woman in his own likeness. God blessed them and said, ''Have many children to live on the earth and rule wisely over it.'' That was the sixth day. God saw everything he had made, and it was very good.

The work of creation was finished, so on the seventh day God rested. He blessed the seventh day so that it was set aside as a special day.

In the Garden of Eden

God planted a garden in the east, and there he put Adam, the first man he made.

The garden was very beautiful, full of flowers and trees. In the middle of the garden, God planted two special trees, the Tree of Life and the Tree of the Knowledge of Good and Evil. And God said to Adam, ''You may eat the fruit of any tree in the garden except the fruit of the Tree of the Knowledge of Good and Evil. If you eat from that tree, you will die.''

So Adam lived in the garden, which was called Eden, and he cared for it. But God could see that Adam was lonely. I'll make someone to help him, thought God.

God brought every living creature to Adam in turn, and Adam gave them names. None of them was just right to share Adam's life. So God made Adam fall into a deep sleep. While he slept, God took out one of Adam's ribs and closed the wound. He had made Adam from dust, but now he made a woman from Adam's rib. Then God brought her to Adam.

Adam named her Eve, and they were very happy together.

But in the garden lived a serpent, a cunning serpent.

One day the serpent came up to Eve and whispered, ''If you eat from the Tree of the Knowledge of Good and Evil, you won't really die. You will understand everything and be as wise as God.''

Eve looked at the serpent. Then she looked at the tree. Until that moment she'd not thought much about it. Now the more she looked at it, the more she longed to know what the fruit would taste like. And she wanted to be as wise as God.

She looked around her; then she stretched out her hand, picked a fruit, and ate it. It was delicious.

"Adam!" she called. "Try this fruit!" And he did.

Immediately the happy peacefulness they had always felt was destroyed. They became anxious because they were naked. So they hurried to make some sort of clothing for themselves from fig leaves.

By then it was evening, and God was walking in the garden in the cool of the day. Now they heard him coming. Feeling afraid and guilty, they hid among the trees. God called to Adam, "Where are you?"

It was no use trying to hide. Trembling, Adam and Eve came out. "I heard your voice and I was afraid because I was naked, so I hid," Adam admitted.

"Who told you that you were naked?" asked God. Then he asked, "Have you eaten from the forbidden tree?"

Adam trembled still more and tried to escape blame. "You put a woman here with me. She made me do it," he said.

God looked at Eve. "Why did you do it?" he asked.

"The serpent made me!" cried Eve.

Then God was very angry. He commanded that the serpent would have to crawl on the ground from that moment on and that people would always be its enemy. To Eve, God said, "From now on, when women have children, they will suffer pain." And to Adam, he said, "For as long as they

live, men will always have to work hard to get a harvest from the earth.''

Then God looked at the clothes which Adam and Eve had tried to make from fig leaves, and he made clothes for them himself from the skins of animals. But Adam and Eve could no longer be trusted to live in the Garden of Eden because they might eat from the other special tree, the Tree of Life. Because they had disobeyed God and had eaten from the Tree of the Knowledge of Good and Evil, they would one day die.

So God sent them out from the garden where he had meant them to live happily, and an angel and a flaming sword guarded the way to the Tree of Life. Adam and Eve could never return.

Two Brothers

Now life was different for Adam and Eve. The work of cultivating the ground was hard. But God still loved and cared for them. Eventually Eve had two sons, Cain and Abel. As the boys grew up, they helped with the work. Cain became a farmer and Abel became a shepherd.

In those days offerings were made to God. Cain and Abel would build an altar of stones and light a fire on it. Then they would take their best lamb, kill it, and burn its body on the fire so that the smoke rose, making a sweet aroma to God. Or they might offer some of their best fruit or grain. They made the offerings gladly to show their love for God and to thank him for his love for them.

One day Cain and Abel made an offering to the Lord. Cain brought some of the harvest from his fields. He didn't bring it out of love and thanks. He didn't want to make the offering at all.

But Abel brought the best from his freshly killed sheep, and he gladly offered it to God.

God accepted Abel's gift, but he refused Cain's.

Cain was furious. God said to him, "Why are you so angry? If your thoughts and actions are right, then your gifts will be acceptable. But if your thoughts are wrong and you do not overcome them, sin will control your life, and things will get worse for you."

Cain was too angry to take any notice of God's warning. And he was furiously jealous of his brother. Pretending to be friendly, Cain said to Abel, "Let's go out into the fields." Abel went with Cain unsuspectingly. But once they were alone, Cain suddenly and violently hit Abel, killing him.

Thinking no one would find out, Cain left his brother's body where it lay and came home as if nothing had happened.

But God said to him, "Where is your brother, Abel?"

Feeling defensive, Cain replied, "How should I know? Am I my brother's keeper?"

Then God said, "Your brother's blood cries out to me from the ground." And Cain realized nothing can be hidden from God.

God said, "Never again will you get a harvest from the ground. You will leave here and wander the earth for the rest of your life."

Cain cried out, "That punishment is too hard for me to bear. I'll never see you again. And anyone who finds me will attack me and kill me."

"No," said God. He put a mark on Cain. Now no one would harm Cain, but everyone would know he had killed his brother.

So Cain left the place where he had been born and moved toward the east. Adam and Eve had another son, Seth, and were comforted a little for the loss of their son Abel.

And in his turn, Seth married and had children. And their children had children, and so on, until there were many people living on the earth.

Noah

God looked at the world he had made and the people he had made. He saw people killing each other, robbing each other, cheating each other, quarreling with each other. He saw they were thinking less and less about him, and they were thinking more and more about themselves. They had grown wicked and God became sorry he had made them.

Only one man was different— Noah. Noah still loved God and God loved him.

One day God spoke to Noah. "I am going to destroy these people. My world is full of violence because of the way they are behaving. I am going to send a great flood on the earth. All life under the skies will be destroyed."

Noah was afraid, but God said, "Do not fear. You are a good man. I will not destroy you or your family. I will make a covenant, an agreement, with you. You must do as I tell you, then your lives will be saved."

God told Noah to build an Ark. It was to be made of gopher wood and covered with tar inside and out so that it would be waterproof. It was to measure about four hundred and fifty feet long, seventy-five feet wide, and forty-five feet high. It was to have three decks and be divided into rooms. In one side it was to have a door, and there was to be a window.

Noah listened, puzzled. With his wife, his three sons, and their wives, there were eight people in his family. Why did the Ark need to be so huge?

God continued, "You must bring into the Ark pairs of all the creatures that live, one male and one female. You must keep them alive with you. And you must take all the different kinds of food that will be needed and store it in the Ark."

The task was enormous! But Noah trusted God, so he and his family set to work. Soon there was much hammering, sawing, bending, and shaping of wood going on outside his home. The people who lived nearby jeered.

"He's building a boat. Here, miles from the sea. It probably won't even float. Floods? What floods? He must be mad!"

Noah simply believed God's words and went on building. At last the Ark was finished. Noah and his family started to gather the food. When the leaves, hay, fruit, and grains were stored in the Ark, it was time to collect the animals. How was that to be done?

As Noah wondered, a strange thing happened. Animals, birds, and insects of all varieties came to Noah. It was an amazing sight. God told Noah to collect seven pairs of some of them. Of others, he was told to collect two each, a male and a female. Noah led the way into the Ark, and two by two, the animals, birds, and insects followed. Noah and his family led them all to the place specially prepared for them.

When the last one was inside, God closed the door.

The watching people were astonished, but they still jeered. It had already begun to rain. Now rain poured down like water from a bucket. All the springs overflowed and added to the flood. The water rose higher than the mountaintops. Every living thing on the earth was destroyed as God had said. But the Ark floated safely on the water with Noah and all the creatures snug and dry inside.

For forty days and forty nights, it rained. During the day, Noah cared for the animals. At night he lay listening to the rain beating on the roof of the Ark. And then one morning when he awoke, something was different.

The rain had stopped.

"Hurrah!" cried Noah's sons, Shem, Ham, and Japheth. "Now we can get out."

"Wait!" warned Noah. He ran to look out of the window at the top of the Ark. There was nothing to see but water. No one could leave the Ark yet.

For one hundred and fifty days, the waters covered the earth. But God hadn't forgotten Noah and all the creatures that were with him in the

Ark. God sent a strong wind to blow The wind helped to dry up the water.

And as the wind blew and the sun shone, ever so slowly the floods went down. Still the Ark rocked gently on the water until one day, with a grind and a bump, it settled onto solid ground.

"Surely we can get out now," said Shem, Ham, and Japheth. But from the window, there was still nothing to be seen but water.

"We must be on a mountaintop," said Noah. "We shall have to wait longer yet." And they went on with their task of keeping the animals alive.

For over two months more, they waited. Now other mountaintops were showing. Noah took a raven and let it fly from the window.

"If there is dry land, the raven will find it, and he will not return to the Ark," Noah said.

Anxiously they watched the bird until they could see it no longer. Noah also sent forth a dove. The raven flew to and fro until the earth was dry, but the dove returned to the Ark, having found no place to rest.

"The floods still cover the earth," Noah said.

Seven days they waited. Once more Noah let the dove fly from the window. Once more it returned. The dove flew to Noah's hand, and he brought it inside the Ark. "See," said Noah, "the dove has an olive leaf in its beak. Olive trees grow mainly in the valleys. There must be dry land."

Then everyone laughed and cheered. Seven more days they waited before Noah let the dove fly again. This time it did not return.

Cautiously, Noah opened the door of the Ark. He saw that the ground was dry. Then God said to him, "It is time for you to come out of the Ark: you, your family, and all the creatures."

So out came Noah. And out came all the animals, stretching and blinking in the sunshine before flying, galloping, hopping, scampering, and crawling away to make their own homes. They began to make new families and to have young.

What a relief it was to see them go!

The world was clean, shining, and beautiful again. Noah and his family built an altar, and Noah made a special thanksgiving offering to God for saving their lives.

God was pleased. He blessed Noah and his family and said, "You must have many children and fill the earth with people once more. Never again will I bring a great flood on the earth to destroy everything."

And then across the sky, Noah and his family saw an arc of beautiful colors shining against the dark clouds. There were brilliant red, orange, yellow, green, blue, indigo, and violet.

"See," said God. "This is a sign of my covenant. I will put a rainbow in the sky. And whenever you see it, you can remember my promise. And my promise will last forever."

Tower of Babel

After the flood Noah's sons and daughters-in-law soon had children, and their children had children, and so on, until Noah, who was by now a very old man, had a very large family with many great-great-grandchildren. The families spread out a little, but they still all spoke the same language. They wandered east looking for a good place to settle, and they came to the plain of Shinar. This was it. They would stop here.

They decided to build a splendid city with a huge tower at its center, for they had discovered how to make bricks out of clay. It would be a tower so high, it would reach right up to heaven. A tower which would help the people to stay together and united. A tower which would show everybody what an important nation this was.

So the people started to build. Everyone helped and the tower soon began to rise high. God came down to see what they were doing. He saw they were growing proud and arrogant. They had left him out of their lives and were trying to reach heaven by their own work. God knew they could never succeed. And if they went on leaving him out, they would soon be no better than the people before the flood had been. He had to stop them. So he did.

One morning when the people came to start work on the tower, they found they couldn't understand what anyone else was saying. God had confused their language. The sounds came out all mixed up. At first the people were puzzled, angry, and afraid. No matter how much they shouted or stamped their feet, they couldn't make themselves understood.

Work on the tower stopped. So many mistakes were being made, it wasn't safe to go on.

After a while each person discovered there were a few others speaking a language which he or she could understand. These groups got together and moved away from the rest.

So God's purpose was fulfilled. The people were scattered over the earth. The people of each group had their own language, and they sought to live apart with those they understood.

The unfinished tower became known as the Tower of Babel because in Hebrew "Babel" meant "confusion."

Abram

Abram was a brave man, ready to fight if the need arose, ready to do anything which God asked of him.

Abram had been living in the city of Ur, but the people there didn't worship the true God as Abram did. Abram's father, Terah, took Abram, his grandson Lot, and his daughter-in-law Sarai, Abram's wife, and left Ur. They traveled to Haran where Terah died.

It was there that God said, "Abram, I want you to leave this place and go to a land which I will show you. I will bless you and your children and your children's children, and you shall become a great nation. You shall be a blessing to all who bless you. But those who curse you, I will curse."

Abram hesitated for a moment—leave everything he knew and set out on a journey with no idea where it would end? But he loved God and believed God's promises. So preparations for the journey were made. Sarai was ready to go with him. So was Lot, his nephew.

Soon a long procession of family, servants, goats, and sheep set out with Abram leading the way. Nobody knew where they were going. They all followed Abram and Abram went where God told him.

Each night they camped and each day they moved on again. When they had traveled as far as Shechem in

Canaan, where the Canaanites lived, God said, "Abram, this is the land I will one day give to your children."

So far Abram and Sarai had no children even though Abram was seventy-five years old. But still Abram believed God's promises, and he stopped and built an altar to the Lord.

There was a famine in the land, so Abram traveled on toward Egypt. But he was worried.

"Sarai," he said, "I've heard about these Egyptians. When they see how beautiful you are, they'll want to make you Pharaoh's wife. He's their ruler and they'll want to please him. They'll have me killed. Instead, let's tell them you're my sister. Then I'll be treated well, because they'll think I'm just your brother and not your husband."

Sarai agreed to the plan. It wasn't quite a lie. She was Abram's half-sister. When they reached Egypt,

things happened as Abram had thought. Pharaoh took Sarai to live in the palace and sent Abram, whom he thought was Sarai's brother, many rich gifts.

But God was not pleased with the deceit. He made Pharaoh and all his household very ill. It didn't take Pharaoh long to realize the cause of the illness, and he sent for Abram.

"What have you done to me?" cried Pharaoh. "Why did you tell me Sarai was your sister? I might have done something very wrong. Here, she's your wife. Take her and go!"

Thankful to escape so lightly, Abram obeyed. Pharaoh gave orders that Abram, Sarai, and Lot were to leave the country at once, but he allowed Abram to keep all the gifts he had given him.

So as the long caravan set out again, Abram was a rich man.

Lot Is Captured

Abram and his nephew Lot now owned many sheep and cattle. There were nightly fights between their herdsmen over who would use the well first, for drawing enough water for all the animals to drink took many hours. It was also hard to find enough food for so many people and animals. The quarreling and the fighting grew, and Abram knew something must be done.

"Lot," Abram said, "you and I shouldn't quarrel. There's no need. Let's separate. You choose which way you want to go, and I'll go the other way."

Lot was amazed, not by the plan, which he could see was a good one, but that Abram, the leader, should give him first choice. Lot looked around. He saw the rich, green grass of the plain with the River Jordan flowing through it. There would be no problem there with grazing or water.

Quickly Lot said, "I choose the plain." Lot took his people and his animals and went to live near the town of Sodom, although the people living there were known to be very wicked.

Abram and his people stayed in Canaan, and God was pleased with Abram. God said to Abram as they stood on the high mountain, "Look in every direction. Everything that you can see I will give to you and your children and their children. You may walk through this whole land, for I am giving it to you and to your offspring, who shall be too many to be counted."

So Abram built an altar of thanksgiving to God at Hebron and settled there.

Some time later the king of Sodom, the king of its twin town, Gomorrah, and three other kings of the plain of Jordan were attacked by four neighboring kings. The kings of the plain lost the battle. Lot and his family were captured along with many other prisoners.

Somehow a messenger managed to reach Abram with the news. Abram didn't hesitate. Gathering his men, he set off. Lot was a member of the family, and he must be rescued.

When Abram and his men finally caught up with the enemy, he could see that they were heavily outnumbered. Abram planned a surprise attack under the cover of darkness. Dividing his men into groups, he sent each group to its own place so that the enemy armies were surrounded.

Tensely the men waited until night. Then at a signal, they rushed the camp, attacking from all sides. In the darkness and confusion, the enemy was badly defeated. They fled in fear, leaving behind all their possessions and their captives. Lot and his family were saved, and Abram was declared a hero.

Returning in triumph, Abram saw Melchizedek, the king of Salem and a priest of God Most High, coming out to meet them. This was a very great honor. Melchizedek brought out bread and wine, and he blessed Abram. Then Abram gave Melchizedek one tenth of all the riches.

Awhile later the king of Sodom offered to share the remaining riches with Abram, but Abram refused. He wanted nothing from Sodom because of the wickedness of the people who lived there. After giving a portion to his men, Abram returned the remaining riches to the king of Sodom.

Once more God was pleased with Abram.

After these things God appeared to Abram, who was ninety-nine, and said, "I will make my covenant with you. I will bless you and you will be the father of many nations. Your name shall no longer be Abram, but you shall be called Abraham. Your wife's name shall be Sarah, and I will bless her also. And she shall be a mother of many nations."

Escape from Sodom

Abraham pleaded with God, who was planning to destroy the cities of Sodom and Gomorrah because of the wickedness of the people who lived there. "If you find only ten good people in Sodom, will you spare it?" begged Abraham at last, looking down on the city from where he stood on the hillside.

"For only ten good people, I will spare the city," God promised. And he sent two angels as messengers to inspect Sodom.

The angels looked like ordinary men. It was evening as they entered Sodom, but Lot, who had been sitting by the gate, noticed them. Knowing they were new to the town, he invited them to his home for food and a place to stay as was the custom.

"No, thank you. We'll sleep in the open square," said the messengers.

This distressed Lot. "No, no, come and stay at my house and be comfortable," he urged.

So in the end, the messengers went with him. Lot sent for water to bathe their feet and had a meal prepared for the visitors. They were still up when the men of Sodom came banging on the door of Lot's house.

"Bring out your visitors," shouted the men. "We want to amuse ourselves with them."

Lot began to tremble, because he knew the men meant evil. He went out to them, shutting the door behind him, and tried to calm the men of Sodom.

"Please, my friends, don't harm these men," he said. "They are my guests and under my protection. Leave them in peace."

"Let us by!" yelled the mob. And to one another they said, "Lot moves here as a foreigner, then he tries to tell us what's right and what's wrong." They shouted, "It will be worse for you than it is for them before we've finished."

They charged forward. But the angels in the house had been listening. Quickly they opened the door, grabbed Lot, pulled him inside, and slammed the door in the faces of the mob just in time.

Then the angels blinded the men who were at the doorway so that they couldn't see where the door was.

As the men wandered around outside, bewildered and afraid, the messengers spoke urgently to Lot. "You must escape! This town must be destroyed. Is there anyone else here who belongs to your family? You must all run for your lives."

"My sons-in-law," responded Lot. He rushed out to warn them. But they only laughed at him, so Lot had to leave.

"Hurry!" called the messengers as Lot came back alone.

Still Lot stood hesitating. Then one messenger grabbed the hands of Lot and his wife while the other seized the hands of Lot's two daughters, hurrying them out of town. Light was dawning.

"Run for the mountains and don't stop," the messengers ordered, preparing to leave Lot and his family.

"Not the mountains!" gasped Lot. "We'll never reach them in time. Let us take shelter in Zoar."

Zoar was a small town not far away.

"Very well," agreed the messengers. "God will spare Zoar. But make haste. And remember, don't look back."

Shaking and exhausted, Lot and his daughters reached Zoar as the sun was fully risen. Then God rained down sulphur and fire on Sodom and Gomorrah. The towns were totally destroyed.

Lot and his daughters were safe. But in spite of the warning, Lot's wife had stopped and looked back. And as she stood there gazing, she was turned into a pillar of salt.

Early the next morning, Abraham went back to the place where he had pleaded with God. He looked toward the place where Sodom and Gomorrah had been. But all he could see was thick smoke billowing up from the plain.

Then Abraham knew that God had destroyed the towns. But God had remembered Abraham, and for his sake God had saved Abraham's nephew Lot.

Abraham's Son, Isaac

Some months after Sodom was destroyed, Abraham was sitting in the doorway of his tent trying to keep out of the hot midday sun.

When he looked up, Abraham saw three men standing close-by. Amazed that anyone should be out walking in the heat of the day, he hurried to greet them.

"Come and rest in the shade of the trees!" he said. "Let my servants bring cool water to bathe your feet, while I have a meal prepared."

The men accepted the invitation. Then Abraham rushed around organizing everything. His servants hurried to prepare food. Sarah, Abraham's wife, baked fresh bread.

Presently, the men sat under the trees enjoying the meal. Sarah could overhear the conversation. "Where is your wife?" asked the men.

"She is in the tent," Abraham answered. By now, he was beginning to realize that these were no ordinary visitors.

One of the visitors said, "Before the year passes and I come again, Sarah will have a son."

A son, at her age. Sarah laughed aloud. She and Abraham were old, and Sarah had given up hope of having any children.

But in due time, God kept the promise he had made to Abraham many years before, and Sarah did have a son. Abraham named him Isaac or "Laughter."

Abraham and Sarah loved the boy very much. Indeed, as the child grew,

God decided to test Abraham's obedience to God.

"Abraham," said God, "take your son to the mountains, to a place which I shall show you, and there offer him up as a sacrifice."

Sacrifice his son? Kill his beloved son—the son he and Sarah had wanted for so long? Abraham could hardly believe his ears. He wanted to cry out, "No! No!"

Yet Abraham had loved and obeyed God all his life. He would this time too; he must obey God's command.

Early the next morning, Abraham rose. With a heavy heart, he prepared his donkey for the journey, loading it with enough wood to make a fire for the burnt offering. Then he called to Isaac and two of his servants. "We are going to the mountains to make a sacrifice," he said.

Isaac was excited as he set out beside his father.

After three days Abraham saw they were near the place which God had told him about.

"Stay here with the donkey," he ordered the servants. "My son and I will go over there to worship God."

He forced himself to unload the wood and gave it to Isaac to carry. He carried the fire and the knife.

At first Isaac walked happily beside his father. Then he asked, "Father, you have the knife and I have the wood. But where is the lamb we will offer?"

Abraham was very shaken, but somehow he managed to answer,

"God will provide the lamb."

They walked on together until they reached the place God had told Abraham about. Slowly, heavily, Abraham built an altar. Then he arranged the wood. Now there were no more preparations to make. He could put the moment off no longer.

With eyes full of tears, he took Isaac, bound him with rope, and laid him on the altar. Abraham took the knife, ready to kill his son.

But just as his hand was raised to strike, an angel of the Lord called from heaven. "Stop! Don't harm the boy, for now I know you truly love and trust God. You were ready to offer God your beloved son."

Isaac was safe. Trembling with relief, Abraham freed the lad. A ram was caught by the horns in a nearby thorn bush, so Abraham offered the ram as a thanksgiving to God. He named that place The-Lord-Will-Provide.

Together he and Isaac went back to the waiting servants and home.

Genesis 24:1-67

Rebecca

Abraham was very, very old now. He wanted to see his son Isaac happily married before he died. So he sent for his most trusted servant.

"Promise me you will go to Mesopotamia, where I was born, and choose a wife for Isaac from among my own people," Abraham said.

This was a big responsibility. The servant was worried. "Suppose I choose a woman who won't come back with me?" he asked. "Shall I take Isaac there?"

"Oh no," Abraham said quickly. "That's the last thing you must do. God made a covenant, an agreement, with me that this land shall be given to my children and to their children. I don't want Isaac to go and live in Mesopotamia. If she won't come back with you, you will be freed from your promise."

So the servant made a solemn promise. The next day he set out. He took a few more servants and ten camels with him, for he had a plan.

It was beginning to get dark as he came to the city in Mesopotamia where Abraham's brother Nahor lived. Just outside the city was a well. Here the servant stopped to wait for a while. He knew the women of the town would come to draw water every evening. This was what he needed if his plan was to work.

He prayed to God, "Please help me choose well. I will say to one of the girls, 'Will you give me a drink of water?' If she answers, 'Yes, and I'll give your camels a drink also,' I'll

know she's the one you've chosen to be Isaac's wife."

The servant had hardly finished his prayer when the young girl Rebecca came walking along the path to the well. She was very beautiful.

The servant's heartbeat quickened. Was this the right girl? He watched as she drew water. Then he stammered, "Ah, ah, will you give me a drink of water?"

"Of course," she said and smiled. Rebecca offered her pitcher to him. He drank, his heart still pounding. Would she say anything more?

"I'll give your camels a drink as well," she said. She drew water from the well until all the camels were satisfied. Now the servant knew this was the girl God had chosen. But there was still a doubt. Would she leave her home and family to marry a stranger?

The servant took out some gold to show he could pay for lodgings.

"Whose daughter are you?" he asked. "Is there room in your father's house for myself and the others to stay the night?"

"My father's name is Bethuel, son of Nahor," she replied. "We have plenty of room for you to stay with us."

Bethuel, son of Nahor—the servant felt joy rising within him. God had brought him to the family of Abraham's brother.

Rebecca ran to tell her family what had happened at the well. Her brother Laban came down to speak to the servant. When Laban saw the gold the

32

man was holding, he warmly invited the servant to lodge with them. The camels were fed and bedded down, and a good meal was prepared for the men. But before the servant could eat, he knew he must speak.

He told them the whole story, explaining about Isaac. "And now," he finished, "if Rebecca will not come with me, please tell me." He waited for the answer, trembling a little.

Laban and Bethuel did not hesitate. "This is God's will," they said. "We will give permission for Rebecca to marry Isaac."

What a relief! The servant praised God. Then he brought out many rich gifts which he gave to Rebecca and to her mother and brother. They had a splendid meal, and the servant was happy.

In the morning, he and his men were ready to leave. But Rebecca's mother and brother pleaded, "Please let her stay with us for just a few more days."

"Don't stop me," said the servant. "God has made my search successful, and I must get back to my master."

Then they called Rebecca. "Will you go with this man?" they asked.

Bravely Rebecca replied, "Yes, I will."

So Rebecca and her servants with Abraham's servant and his men set out riding on the camels.

All this time Isaac had been waiting, wondering what sort of wife the servant would bring back for him. One evening as he went out in the field

to pray, he saw the camel train approaching.

Rebecca looked across the field and saw Isaac. She slipped down from her camel. "Who is that?" she asked.

"My master's son," replied the servant.

As Isaac came running, Rebecca veiled her face, as was the custom. The servant told Isaac all that had happened.

Isaac took Rebecca into his mother's tent. She had died a very old lady, and Isaac had been very sad. But now Isaac and Rebecca were married. They loved one another and Isaac was comforted.

Isaac's Twin Sons

After a while Isaac and Rebecca had twin sons, Esau and Jacob. The two boys were completely different from each other. As they grew up, Esau was always out in the wild. He became a skillful hunter. Jacob preferred to stay around the tents and devote himself to the family business. Esau soon became their father's favorite; Jacob became their mother's favorite.

One day when Esau came in from hunting, Jacob was cooking a good-smelling soup.

"I'm starving," declared Esau. "Give me some of your soup."

"Only if you'll give me your birthright in exchange," bargained Jacob. Esau had been born first and was considered the elder son. With the death of their father, Esau would inherit everything. This was his birthright.

"If I starve to death now, what good is this birthright?" asked Esau.

"Promise me," Jacob insisted.

Esau wasn't bothered about what might happen at some time in the future. He was hungry and the soup smelled good. "I promise," he said carelessly.

Jacob, very well satisfied, gave his brother soup and bread.

As soon as Esau had enough to eat, he went out again.

Many years later, after Isaac had become old and blind, he called to Esau, his favorite son. "My son, go hunting and bring back some game to make me my favorite dishes. Then bring them to me yourself so I can eat and give you my blessing before I die."

Rebecca overheard this. She watched Esau set out, then she hurried to Jacob. "Quickly! Go to our flock and get two of the best kids of the goats. I will cook your father's favorite dishes. Then you take them to him, pretending to be Esau. He will bless you instead of Esau."

"It won't work," said Jacob. "Esau's skin is rough and hairy. Mine is smooth. Even though my father is blind, he will know me when he touches me. He'll curse me, not bless me."

"The curse will be on me, not you," Rebecca reassured him. "Go quickly and get the kids before Esau comes back."

So Jacob obeyed his mother. He brought back two of the best kids which she then made into his father's favorite dishes. Next she put Esau's best clothes on Jacob, covering his hands and neck with the skins of the goats.

"Now go to your father," she said and put the plate of meat and some bread into his hands.

Jacob hesitated no longer. He went to his father. "Who's there?" called Isaac.

Jacob took a deep breath. "It is your firstborn son, Esau," Jacob answered. "Sit up and eat the food I have brought, then give me your blessing."

Isaac was puzzled. "How did you manage to find the animal so quickly?" he asked.

Jacob thought fast. "God helped me. He brought it to me."

Isaac was still puzzled. "Come close. Let me touch you," he said.

Jacob's heart thumped. He went closer to his father, and he stood still as the old man reached out and felt his hands and neck.

"The voice is Jacob's voice," said Isaac, "yet the hands are those of Esau. Are you truly my son Esau?"

"Yes, I am," Jacob said.

So Isaac ate the meal. Then he said,

"Kiss me, my son."

Jacob obeyed. Isaac could smell Esau's clothes. So he gave Jacob the blessing which should have been given to the firstborn son.

"May God make you prosper. Let people serve you and let nations bow down to you. Be lord over your brothers, and let them bow down to you. Cursed be everyone who curses you, and blessed be everyone who blesses you."

Jacob left his father's tent. Hardly had he gone when Esau came back from hunting. He also had made his father's favorite foods and took them to him. "My father," he said, "eat this food so that you may bless me."

"What?" cried Isaac. Shaking, he sat up. "Who are you?" he asked.

"I'm Esau, your firstborn son," Esau answered in surprise.

Isaac could hardly speak. "Then who came to me just now? Whom have I blessed? And he shall be blessed, for the blessing cannot be taken away."

Esau realized what had happened. "Bless me too," he cried.

"Your brother has taken the blessing," said Isaac in distress.

Esau was angry. "He took my birthright, and now he's stolen my blessing. Haven't you even one blessing left for me?"

"I've put him over you and all his brothers," Isaac groaned. "I've asked God to make him prosper. What is there left?"

Esau wept. "Haven't you more than one blessing to give?"

"You will prosper and serve your brother," Isaac answered. "But later you will free yourself from him."

Now Esau hated Jacob and determined to kill him as soon as Isaac died.

When Rebecca heard this, she was afraid for Jacob. "Go and stay with my brother, Laban," she said. "As soon as Esau forgets what has happened between the two of you, I'll send a messenger. Then you can come home."

Jacob, who was quite frightened, prepared to leave. But before he left, Isaac called for Jacob to further bless him and charge him.

"My son, do not marry a woman from Canaan. Marry one of the daughters of Laban. And may God bless you so that you will inherit the land, as he promised to Abraham."

Comforted a little, Jacob set out.

Genesis 28:10-20

Jacob's Dream

All alone, Jacob started out on his journey from Beersheba to Haran where his uncle, Laban, lived. Jacob hurried along, afraid his brother Esau would come after him to kill him.

As it began to grow dark, Jacob knew he would have to rest. He found a stone which he could use as a pillow, lay down, pulled his thick cloak around him, and then fell asleep, exhausted.

Jacob had a dream. In his dream he saw a ladder reaching from the ground nearby right up into heaven. Angels were going up and down the ladder, and the Lord God himself stood at the top.

God spoke to Jacob. "I am the God of Abraham and of Isaac. The land on which you lie I will give to you and to your children and to your children's children. And they shall spread to the west and to the east, to the north and to the south. Through you and your family, all the people of the earth will be blessed. And behold, I am with you and will keep you in all places to which you go, and I will bring you again to this land. For I will not leave you until I have done everything I have promised."

Jacob awoke. He looked around. The land was quiet in the starlight, but Jacob was afraid.

"Surely this is God's house and the gate of heaven, and I didn't know," he said.

As soon as it was light, he took the stone he had used as a pillow and stood it up on one end to make a pillar.

He poured oil over the stone and called the place Bethel. Then he made a promise.

"If God is with me to guard me and keep me and bring me safely back to my father's house," Jacob said, "then the Lord God will be my God. And of all that God gives to me, I will surely give a tenth to him."

Genesis 29:1-30; 30:22-43; 31:1-21

Jacob Works for Laban

Jacob traveled on and at last neared the end of his journey. He came to a well which had a huge stone over its mouth. Sheep were lying nearby with shepherds guarding them. Jacob spoke to the shepherds. "My friends, from where do you come?"

"From Haran," they answered.

Jacob's heart beat quickly. "Do you know Laban, son of Nahor?" he asked.

"Of course," they answered, staring at him.

"Is everything all right with him?" asked Jacob.

"Yes," they said. "And look, there's his daughter Rachel. She's bringing his sheep for water."

Jacob looked at Rachel as she came down the path. She was very beautiful. He hurried to move the heavy stone which covered the well. Then he drew the water for Laban's sheep while Rachel watched, puzzled but grateful.

When the sheep were satisfied, Jacob greeted Rachel with a kiss. His eyes filled with tears as he explained who he was. Full of excitement, Rachel ran to tell her father. Laban came hurrying out to welcome Jacob and bring him back home.

Jacob explained all that had happened to him. Laban listened and when the story was finished, Laban agreed that Jacob could stay in spite of what had happened. He was still a member of the family and would always have a place with Laban.

The next day Jacob began to work for Laban. After a month Laban said, "It's not right you should work for nothing even if I am your uncle. What would you like your wages to be?"

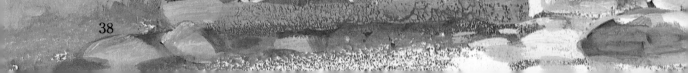

By now Jacob loved Rachel very much. So he said, "I will gladly work for you for seven years without pay if at the end of that time, I can marry Rachel, your youngest daughter."

Laban had two daughters. Leah, his oldest, had delicate eyes, but Rachel was more beautiful. Normally the eldest was given in marriage first. But Laban said, "It is better that you should marry her than a stranger."

Jacob worked hard for seven years, at which time Laban arranged a wedding, as promised. But in the evening, when it was time for the bride to go to her husband, Laban brought Leah to Jacob's tent, not Rachel.

In the morning, when Jacob discovered he had been tricked, he was furious. Laban said, "It's not our custom for a younger daughter to marry before the eldest. If you will work another seven years, I will give you Rachel to marry now." At that time men often had more than one wife, so both sisters could be married to Jacob.

So Jacob worked another seven years. But he always loved Rachel more than Leah.

Jacob had several children by Leah and their two maidservants, but Rachel was unhappy because she had none. She prayed to God, and at last a baby boy was born to her. They called the boy Joseph, and he was Jacob's favorite son.

Jacob had now stayed with Laban for twenty years and had grown rich. Laban's sons grew jealous of him, and Jacob could see that even Laban was not as friendly as he had once been.

God spoke to Jacob. "Go back to your own land. I will be with you."

Jacob was afraid. Would his uncle allow him to go? Secretly, out in the fields where no one could overhear, Jacob told Rachel and Leah what God had said.

"You must obey God," they replied.

So Jacob waited until Laban was away shearing the sheep. Then he collected all his family, his servants, his cattle, his sheep, and his possessions and fled. Unknown to Jacob, Rachel had stolen her father's household idols.

When Laban discovered that Jacob had gone, he was furious. He set out with the men of his family in pursuit. For seven days Laban chased Jacob. Finally he caught sight of Jacob's tents on the mountain.

God spoke to Laban, "Be careful what you say to Jacob."

Still angry, Laban pitched his tents near Jacob's camp; then he rushed off to find him. Trembling, Jacob faced his uncle.

"Why did you leave without giving me a chance to say good-bye to my

daughters?'' Laban roared. ''I haven't been able to kiss my grandchildren farewell. I could kill you, but God has told me to be careful what I say to you.''

Jacob felt a little better.

But Laban was shouting again. ''Why did you steal my idols, my gods?''

Jacob was truly innocent. ''I haven't stolen them,'' he said. ''If anyone here did steal them, that person shall die. Search the camp.''

Laban searched Jacob's tent and the servants' tents without finding anything. Then he came to Rachel's tent. Instead of coming to greet her father, Rachel sat on the cushions which had been on her camel. ''Please don't be angry if I don't get up,'' she said. ''I can't rise, because I don't feel well.''

Laban searched her tent. He found nothing.

Jacob protested angrily. ''When have I ever done you any wrong? I worked hard for you for twenty years!

I worked in the heat and in the bitter cold! And sometimes I didn't even stop to sleep. You kept changing my wages. You wouldn't have let me bring my own things now if you hadn't been afraid of my God.''

Laban was equally angry. ''All that you have is really mine,'' he retorted. ''But I can't take anything away from you for the sake of my daughters and their children. We'd better make a covenant, an agreement.''

So they set up a stone for a pillar and agreed that Laban would not cross to the land on Jacob's side and that Jacob would not cross to the land on Laban's side. Then Jacob made a sacrifice to God.

The men shared a meal together, and in the morning Laban and his relatives left for home.

And Laban never discovered that his household idols were, indeed, in Jacob's camp. Rachel had brought them with her and had hidden them by sitting on them throughout the search.

Genesis 32:3-32; 33:1-11

Jacob and Esau Meet

Jacob was safe from Laban. Now he began to worry about meeting his brother Esau. The last time they had been together, Esau had threatened to kill him.

Jacob decided to send messengers on ahead to tell Esau that he was returning and hoped for friendship between them.

The messengers set out. Soon they came hurrying back. "Esau is coming to meet you with four hundred men," they reported.

Four hundred men! Jacob was terrified. He thought Esau must still be angry and planning to attack him.

Quickly Jacob divided his camp into two groups. "If Esau attacks one group, at least the other will have a chance to escape," he said. Then he cried to God, "O God, I beg you to save us from my brother, Esau. I'm afraid he will kill everyone here, even my children. And you did promise my children should live and have children of their own."

That night Jacob worried. He collected 220 sheep, 220 goats, 30 camels and their young, 50 head of cattle, and 30 donkeys to use as a peace offering to his brother. He put each group of animals separately into the care of his servants. Each group was to be driven separately to his brother as a gift. To the first servant he said, "Tell Esau, 'These are your servant Jacob's. Take these as a present from him.' Tell him I am coming behind you."

Jacob sent the next servant with the same message, and so on, until all

were on their way.

By the time Esau has received all my gifts, he may no longer be angry, Jacob thought anxiously.

He sent his two wives, two maidservants, and eleven sons to the other side of a brook.

Now it was dark and Jacob was alone with his fear. Suddenly, a stranger came and wrestled with him. All night they struggled, but Jacob would not give in.

As morning dawned, the stranger said, "Your name shall no longer be Jacob. You shall be called Israel because you have struggled with God and with men and have overcome. Now let me go."

Exhausted, Jacob obeyed. "Tell me your name," he gasped.

But the stranger replied, "Why do you ask my name?" and blessed Jacob.

Then Jacob called that place Penuel, and he declared, "I believe I have fought with God face to face and yet lived."

Now the sun rose high. Jacob looked up. He saw the sight he had been dreading—Esau was coming.

Hastily Jacob went to his wives and children. He put the two maidservants and their children in the front. Then he put Leah and her children behind, and Rachel and Joseph stood in the rear. Jacob took the lead, moving toward his twin brother.

When Jacob neared Esau, he stopped and bowed low seven times, unsure what his brother's response would be.

But Esau ran to meet Jacob, throwing his arms around him and kissing him. They both wept. It was good to be together again.

Esau looked over Jacob's shoulder. ''Who are all those people?'' he demanded.

Jacob turned around. Proudly he replied, ''Those are the children God has graciously given to me, your servant.''

''And what do you mean by sending me all these sheep and cattle?'' Esau asked. ''I have enough, my brother. Keep what is yours.''

''Please accept my gifts,'' said Jacob. So Esau did. And from then on, the two brothers were friends.

Joseph the Dreamer

Joseph, the son of Jacob and Rachel, had ten older half brothers, and none of them liked him. The family was living in Canaan now, and Joseph was old enough to help his brothers in the work of caring for the animals and cultivating the land. But Joseph's brothers knew he was their father's favorite, and they were jealous.

Jacob made Joseph a coat of many colors, which the boy loved and wore all the time. His brothers wore rough tunics, and they hated Joseph with his fine coat.

If his brothers slacked over their work, Joseph reported it to his father. Then his brothers hated him all the more.

One night Joseph dreamed a dream which he told to his brothers. "We were all in the fields, binding up the sheaves of grain. And my sheaf stood up straight while all of yours bowed down to it."

His brothers were furious. "Do you think we shall ever bow down to you?" they said.

Then Joseph had another dream. This time he told it to his brothers and his father.

"In my dream the sun, the moon, and eleven stars bowed down to me," he said.

Even his father was not very pleased, "Shall I, your mother, and your brothers really bow down to you?" he asked. But Jacob did not forget the dream.

One day Jacob said to Joseph, "Your brothers have been away a very long time with the flocks. I want you to go and see if anything's wrong. They'll be near Shechem."

So Joseph set out. He reached Shechem safely, but there was no sign of his brothers or the animals.

As Joseph stood wondering what to do, a man spoke to him. "Are you looking for someone?"

"Yes," said Joseph, "my brothers."

"I heard them say they were going to Dothan," said the man.

"Thank you," Joseph replied and went on to Dothan.

His brothers were at Dothan tending the flocks.

Before Joseph reached them, they looked up and saw him coming.

"Here's our chance! We can get rid of the dreamer forever," said one.

"Let's kill him and throw him into this pit," said another.

"We'll say a wild animal must have killed him in the desert," added another.

One of the brothers, Reuben, didn't want to harm Joseph, but he knew it was no use trying to dissuade his brothers while they were in this mood. He thought quickly. "If we kill him, it will mean we have shed his blood. Let's just throw him into the pit and leave him," he suggested. "Joseph will never be able to climb out. He will die there."

"All right," the others agreed. Secretly Reuben planned to rescue Joseph while the others weren't there.

Joseph came up to his brothers and greeted them. But immediately they seized him, tore off his coat of many colors, and threw him into the pit. Then they sat down to enjoy a meal. The delicious smell floated down to Joseph. Bewildered and afraid, Joseph prayed to God for comfort and help.

Judah, another of the brothers, looked over toward the road. He saw a camel caravan approaching. The camels were loaded with spices to sell in Egypt. Now Reuben was not with them at this moment.

"Hey!" Judah exclaimed. "If our brother dies here, we gain nothing. Let's sell him as a slave to these Midianite traders. That way we will not have laid a hand on him. He is, after all, our brother and our flesh. We shall be rid of him, and we'll have some money in exchange."

The others agreed. Roughly they hauled Joseph out of the pit. For one moment Joseph thought his brothers had tired of their tormenting and were freeing him, but the next minute he realized what was happening. He was young, strong, and good-looking. The Midianites bought Joseph gladly, paying twenty pieces of silver for him.

The traders bound Joseph with rope and continued on their journey. Joseph's brothers returned to their flocks.

Meanwhile, Reuben had come back. He stole over to the pit and found it empty. Reuben tore his clothes in grief.

"The boy isn't here! What am I going to do?" he cried. His brothers told the story to Reuben. There was nothing he could do to help Joseph then.

The brothers dipped Joseph's torn coat into the blood of one of their goats. They took the coat back to their father, saying they had found it on the path.

Jacob cried out, "My son has been torn into pieces by wild animals!" He wept and no one could comfort him.

Genesis 39:1-23; 40:1-23; 41:1

Joseph, Potiphar, and Prison

Now Joseph was alone, friendless in a foreign land. He was sold as a slave to Potiphar, who was captain of the guard and one of Pharaoh's officers. But God had not forgotten Joseph.

Potiphar lived in a large, splendid house. At first Joseph was given all the heaviest work to do. But he worked willingly and well. Potiphar soon realized that Joseph could be trusted, and after a while Joseph was allowed to move about freely and was made chief servant of the household.

Just as Joseph's life was becoming easier, Potiphar's wife noticed him. She desired him and asked him to lie with her.

Joseph refused. "My master trusts me," he said. "It would be wicked of me to do as you ask, for you are his wife." As Joseph ran from her, she grabbed his garment.

Potiphar's wife was furious. She went to Potiphar, seeking revenge. "Your slave tried to force himself on me!" she said, holding up Joseph's garment. "When I screamed for help,

he fled, leaving this behind him!"

When he heard this, Potiphar was angry. He refused to give Joseph a chance to explain and had him thrown into prison.

But God was still with Joseph. Even in prison Joseph's quiet strength and clear mind were soon recognized. Before long, the warden put Joseph in charge of the other prisoners.

When he had been in prison for a while, two of Pharaoh's servants, the

47

chief butler and the chief baker, angered Pharaoh. They were put in the same prison as Joseph, and they were in his charge.

One morning he found them both looking very worried. "Is something wrong?" he asked.

"We both had strange dreams last night," they answered. "There's no one here to explain what they mean."

"Don't interpretations belong to God? Tell me your dreams, and God will help me to interpret them," said Joseph.

The chief butler spoke first. "In my dream I saw a vine with three branches. It grew buds which blossomed and ripened into grapes. I took some of the grapes and squeezed their juice into Pharaoh's cup. Then I took the cup and gave it to Pharaoh."

Joseph said, "The three branches stand for three days. Before three days are over, Pharaoh will send for you and return you to your position as chief butler. You will serve him every night, just as you used to do. When you stand in front of Pharaoh, please tell him about me. Tell him I have done nothing wrong."

The butler promised he would, for he was very pleased.

The chief baker heard the good interpretation given for the butler's dream, and he hurried to tell his own dream. "There were three baskets resting on my head, one on top of the other. The top basket was full of all kinds of baked goods that I had baked for Pharaoh. But birds were flying down and eating from the top basket."

Then Joseph spoke sadly. "The

three baskets also stand for three days. Within three days Pharaoh will send for you. But he will hang you from a tree, and when you are dead, the birds will eat your flesh."

The baker was terrified. One day passed. Then another came and went. The third day was Pharaoh's birthday, and he had a feast. He sent for the chief butler and the chief baker. He returned the butler to his old position, just as Joseph had said. And also as Joseph had said, he hanged the baker from a tree.

The butler, safely out of prison himself, forgot all about Joseph until one night when Pharaoh himself had a dream.

Pharaoh Dreams

Pharaoh sent for all his wise men. He was worried. "I have had two dreams," he said. "In the first I was standing by the River Nile when seven fat cows came out of the water and began to graze on the riverbank. As I watched, seven thin cows followed them out of the water, and the thin cows ate the fat cows."

Pharaoh shivered. Then he went on. "In my second dream, I saw seven good ears of corn growing on one stalk. Then seven thin ears of corn sprouted on the stalk and swallowed up the good ears. What do these dreams mean?"

The wise men talked together, trying to interpret the dreams, but none of them could do it. They grew very anxious because Pharaoh would be angry with them. He might even imprison them.

Then the chief butler recalled something Joseph did when they were in prison together. He hurried to Pharaoh. "Sir, when I was in prison, I had a dream. The chief baker also had a dream. A young man was there who told us what our dreams meant."

"Bring him to me at once!" ordered Pharaoh.

A messenger ran to the prison. Joseph was brought up from the dungeons. He was told to shave and put on clean clothes.

"Pharaoh has sent for you," the warden explained.

Hardly able to believe it, Joseph found himself in the palace, standing in front of Pharaoh.

Pharaoh said, "I have heard that you can interpret dreams."

"I cannot do it," Joseph replied steadily. "But my God will tell me what your dreams mean."

"Very well," said Pharaoh. Once more he told his dreams.

Joseph listened, then he said, "The two dreams have the same meaning. God has shown you what he plans to do. The seven fat cows and the seven good ears of corn mean that Egypt will have seven years when the harvests are good. But the seven thin cows and the seven thin ears of corn mean that the good years will be followed by seven years of famine."

Pharaoh was shaken. Seven years of famine! What would happen to Egypt?

"The dream was repeated because God has established that it will happen." Joseph went on, "God has shown you this so that the people need not starve. You must find a good, trustworthy man and put him in charge of all Egypt to see that your orders are carried out. You should command that during the seven good years, one fifth of all the grain is stored in barns. When the seven years of famine come, there will be enough food stored to keep the people alive. But even then the food must be distributed with care."

Pharaoh began to smile. "This is a good plan. Since it is through you that God has spoken and since in all Egypt I know of no one wiser than you, you shall be in charge. Everyone shall obey you, and only I shall be greater than you."

Then Pharaoh took his own ring and put it on Joseph's finger.

Joseph's time of hardship was over. He now wore fine clothes and a gold chain around his neck. He rode in a chariot. Men ran before it to clear the way. Everyone recognized Joseph and bowed to him.

During the seven years of good harvests, Joseph traveled throughout Egypt, making sure that a fifth of the grain was properly stored.

When the first years of famine came, the people cried to Pharaoh, "We are starving!"

But Pharaoh replied, "Do as Joseph commands, and you will all be fed."

Joseph ordered that the grain stores should be opened up. People from miles around came to Egypt to buy grain, for there was famine everywhere.

Grain for Joseph's Brothers

There was famine in Canaan. Jacob called his sons together and said to them, "Why are you sitting about here, letting us starve? There is grain in Egypt. Go and buy some."

So Joseph's ten older brothers set out. Jacob wouldn't allow Benjamin, the youngest, to go for fear harm would come to him.

The journey was long. At last weary, travel stained, and hungry, Joseph's brothers arrived in Egypt. They came to Joseph and bowed low in front of him, begging that they might buy grain.

Joseph could hardly believe it. He recognized them at once. Here were the brothers who had sold him as a slave, the brothers whom he had dreamed would one day bow down to him.

But Joseph's brothers completely failed to realize that this handsome, powerful young man dressed in fine clothes was their younger brother. Before them was the brother they had once hated.

Joseph didn't mean to give himself away just yet. He spoke to them in Egyptian through an interpreter.

"You haven't really come for food. You are spies! You have come to see what the situation is like here in Egypt," Joseph accused roughly.

"No, no," his brothers replied fearfully. "We have only come to buy food. We are ten of twelve sons from the same father. One brother is at home and much younger. The other brother is no more. If we do not get

grain, our family will starve."

When Joseph heard that his father and younger brother were still alive, he longed to see them. He especially wanted to see Benjamin, but how could it be managed?

"You are spies," Joseph insisted. "I won't believe anything you say unless you show me this younger brother. You must go back home and bring him to Egypt, and one of you shall be imprisoned here until you all return."

He had them all put in prison for three days.

On the third day, Joseph went to his brothers to see what their decision was. He found them greatly distressed. They spoke to one another,

55

unaware that he understood what they were saying.

"This is our punishment for showing Joseph no mercy," said the brothers. "Our father has lost one son. He will never let Benjamin come back to Egypt with us."

Then Reuben said, "I told you not to sin against our brother. We are getting what we deserve."

Joseph had to hide his tears, but he spoke to them as harshly as before. One of the brothers, Simeon, was left behind as a hostage until the others returned.

With heavy hearts the others set out, their donkeys loaded with grain. Secretly, Joseph had ordered that their money should be returned. Each man's money was hidden in his sack of grain.

On the first night of the journey back, the nine brothers stopped to rest. One of them opened his sack of grain and discovered his money hidden inside. He was amazed. The others were equally puzzled.

When they reached home, the others also found their money in their sacks. They were uneasy. And they had to tell their father that Simeon had been left behind in Egypt because the young ruler there wanted to see Benjamin. It was all very strange.

Jacob would not even consider letting Benjamin go. "I've lost Joseph. I've lost Simeon. And now you want to take Benjamin from me," he cried.

Reuben vowed he would bring Benjamin back safely. But Jacob would not listen.

The grain from Egypt lasted for a while; then starvation faced them once more. There was no way out. If they didn't take Benjamin to Egypt, he would die here in Canaan. They would all die.

Jacob finally allowed Benjamin to leave.

Joseph was sure his brothers would return. When at last he saw them and saw that Benjamin was with them, he was so overjoyed that he wept secretly.

But still he did not tell them who he was. "Bring those men to my house," he ordered his servants. "Bring Simeon also. We shall have a feast."

When the brothers found themselves being taken to Joseph's house, they were afraid. They began to explain that they didn't steal the money the first time, and they brought double payment this time. They brought gifts as well. They also brought their younger brother, just as they'd been ordered.

Joseph answered them kindly, tell-

ing them not to worry. They all sat down to a splendid meal, and Benjamin was offered far more food than anyone else.

After the meal, the sacks were loaded with grain. Joyfully, the brothers set off on the journey back to Canaan.

But Joseph had again ordered that their money be returned to them and had also commanded that a valuable silver cup be hidden in Benjamin's sack.

Joseph gave his brothers time to leave the town. Then he sent his steward after them, saying his cup had been stolen and their sacks must be searched.

The brothers allowed the search, sure of their innocence. To their horror the cup was discovered, and Benjamin was ordered to return.

His brothers would not let him go back alone. In deep distress they all returned. Bowing low before Joseph, they tried to explain.

Joseph said everything could be settled quite simply. Benjamin was to remain as a slave. The others were free to go.

This was too much. How could they bear to go back to Jacob and tell him that Benjamin was lost to him? Judah came forward. Humbly and desperately he pleaded with Joseph, confessing the way they had once ill-treated a younger brother. He described their father's grief at the loss of his son.

As Joseph listened, tears filled his eyes. ''Leave us!'' he ordered his servants.

Then he wept openly. ''Don't be afraid,'' he said. ''I am Joseph, the brother you sold. But I am not angry. Don't be angry with yourselves. God has been with me and sent me here so that your lives might be saved.''

At first the brothers couldn't take it in. When they began to understand, they were overjoyed. Now there was no need to feel guilty about Joseph. He was safe and they were forgiven.

''Now,'' said Joseph, ''go back to Canaan and tell my father I am alive. Tell him there will be five more years of famine, and bring him here to live with me.''

Jacob Goes to Egypt

Pharaoh had heard that Joseph's brothers were in Egypt. He sent for Joseph. "I'm glad your brothers have come," he said. "Let them go back to Canaan with plenty of grain. But also send enough carts to bring the whole family here, where they can live in plenty. It doesn't matter if they can't bring all their possessions. The best of everything in Egypt will be theirs."

Gladly Joseph carried out Pharaoh's orders, and his brothers set out again. Their donkeys were again loaded with grain, and each brother had new clothes, money in his pocket, and gifts for Jacob. Benjamin was given more money than the others and five sets of new clothes. Following the brothers was the long line of carts that Pharaoh had ordered to be sent.

The long, slow journey seemed to take forever, but at last they reached home. Eagerly they hurried to tell their father the good news.

Jacob was a very old man now and could hardly take it in. His son Joseph was not dead? The brothers explained again and, as proof, showed Jacob the carts which were to take the whole family back to Egypt.

Then Jacob believed. "It is enough!" he cried joyfully. "I will go to Egypt. And I shall see my son again before I die."

So everyone prepared for the journey, and presently they set out. Jacob was placed carefully in the first cart. Behind him came the brothers, their wives, and their children. Then came the servants, the camels, the donkeys,

the sheep, the oxen, and some household things. It was a huge procession.

Back in Egypt, Joseph had been watching and waiting impatiently. When he heard that his brothers had reached Goshen, he could wait no longer. He ordered his chariot and hurried to meet them.

At last Jacob's arms were around his son once more. At last Joseph could hug his father and weep with joy and relief.

Joseph took his father and five of his brothers and presented them to Pharaoh. Pharaoh welcomed them kindly and told Joseph to settle them in the fertile land of Goshen. Any of the men who were especially skilled could be put in charge of Pharaoh's own cattle. Jacob blessed Pharaoh in gratitude.

For some years Jacob lived happily in Egypt. But presently the time came when everyone knew he must soon die. Joseph took his two sons, Manasseh and Ephraim, to be blessed by Jacob. Manasseh was the elder, but Jacob gave Ephraim a special blessing.

''Both of them will become great,'' Jacob said, ''but Ephraim will be the greater.''

Then Jacob said to Joseph, ''I am

going to die. But God will be with you." And he asked that his other sons come to him.

When they were all present, Jacob spoke his last words. "Do not bury me in this strange land. Bury me with my fathers, next to Abraham and Sarah, Isaac and Rebecca, and Leah."

Then he lay back and died.

Joseph wept bitterly. When the proper time of mourning was over, he went to Pharaoh's court and asked that he might be allowed to go to Canaan to bury his father.

Pharaoh gave his permission, and the long, sad procession set out. All of Pharaoh's officials went with Joseph, as well as every member of Jacob's family. Only the children were left behind.

At last they reached the cave near Mamre which Abraham had bought as a burial place so long ago. And there Joseph and his brothers buried Jacob as he had asked.

Then they returned to Egypt. But Joseph's brothers were afraid. Now that Jacob was dead, would Joseph take vengeance on them for having sold him as a slave?

They sent a message to Joseph. "This is what our father, Jacob, said. He said we were to tell you that he asked you to forgive us for the wrong we did you."

Joseph wept when he received their message.

Then his brothers came themselves and knelt in front of him. "We are your slaves," they said, trembling.

"Don't be afraid," Joseph said. "It's all right. You plotted evil against me, but God used your evil for good. Because of your action, many lives have been saved during this famine. Don't worry. I will still take care of you and your children."

Joseph and all of his family remained in the land of Goshen in Egypt and were known as the Israelites.

Joseph lived long enough to see his grandchildren and his great-grandchildren. When he was very old, Joseph said to them, "Remember, God one day will bring you out of this land into the land which he has promised. The land he promised to Abraham, to Isaac, and to Jacob."

The Baby in the Bulrushes

Years passed. Joseph had died as had the Pharaoh who had been so kind to the Israelites.

Now the Pharaoh who ruled in his place became afraid.

"There are so many of these Israelites," he complained. "It seems there are more of them than there are of us. If there is a war, they might join with our enemies and fight against us. We must make them our slaves; they must work hard. Then they'll have no will of their own nor any strength for a battle."

So life became hard for the Israelites. Cruel taskmasters were put over them. They were forced to work in the fields making bricks. They built the cities of Pithom and Raamses.

But Pharaoh's plan didn't work. The more the Israelites were beaten and ill-treated, the more they grew in strength and in numbers. Pharaoh cried, "We must stop their numbers from increasing."

He ordered that every baby boy born to the Israelites should be drowned in the river. Girls would be allowed to live. They would grow up to be slaves.

The Israelites were greatly distressed. One family could not bear to follow Pharaoh's orders. Somehow the new baby must be saved.

While he was an infant, he slept most of the time, and it was easy to hide him inside the house. But as he grew, he slept less, and his cries became louder.

His mother, Jochebed, watched and worried. At last she thought of a plan.

She asked God to help her.

She went down to the River Nile and picked some of the bulrushes which grew there. Back at home, she dried the rushes in the sun; then she wove them into a basket-cradle with a lid. She covered the outside of the basket with pitch, so that it was waterproof and would float. Next she made the inside soft and cozy with blankets.

Then came the hard part. Jochebed picked up the sleeping baby, kissed him lovingly, and laid him in the basket.

Jochebed's daughter, Miriam, had been watching all this. Now she saw her mother cover the basket with the lid, pick up the basket, and beckon Miriam to follow her.

Secretly they crept down to the river. Carefully Jochebed placed the basket in the water among the reeds. Miriam held her breath. With the weight of a baby in it, would the basket sink?

It floated perfectly, rocking gently and soothing the baby inside. Miriam's eyes filled with tears. They would have to leave him now and go home.

But no!

"Hide nearby and watch," Jochebed told Miriam. Jochebed knew that every day the Pharaoh's daughter came to this part of the river to bathe. The baby would be found, and he was very beautiful.

Jochebed prayed again to God and hoped against hope.

With fast-beating heart, Miriam crouched among the bulrushes, watching and waiting.

Presently she heard voices. Peeping out, she saw Pharaoh's daughter coming with her maids. Would the baby be discovered? Would Pharaoh's daughter have him drowned? Miriam clasped her hands tightly together.

Pharaoh's daughter saw the basket-cradle. "Bring that to me!" she commanded. One of her maids obeyed. Miriam watched and felt as if she could hardly breathe.

As Pharaoh's daughter opened the lid, the baby cried.

"This is one of the Israelite babies," said Pharaoh's daughter with sorrow in her eyes.

Suddenly Miriam knew what to do. Scrambling to her feet, she ran forward. "Please, shall I find a nurse to look after the baby for you?" she gasped.

Pharaoh's daughter was surprised at Miriam's sudden appearance, but she didn't hesitate. "Yes, go," she said.

Eagerly Miriam rushed away and brought back her mother.

"Take care of this baby," Pharaoh's daughter ordered Jochebed. "I will pay you."

The baby's life was saved, and Jochebed was allowed to look after him for pay. Her heart was full of joy and thanksgiving. It was better than she had ever hoped.

Gladly she and Miriam took the baby home. They cared for him openly, for no one could now say he should be drowned.

As he grew, Jochebed taught him about God and told him stories of Abraham, Isaac, and Jacob.

When he was old enough, Jochebed took him to Pharaoh's palace to live. Pharaoh's daughter named him Moses and treated him as if he were her own son.

Moses in the Land of Midian

Moses lived in the splendid palace of the Pharaoh, but he never forgot that he was an Israelite. As he grew up, he hated to see his own people ill-treated, forced to toil as slaves.

One day as he walked through the fields, he saw an Egyptian taskmaster cruelly beating an Israelite slave. Furious, Moses glanced around. There was no one else nearby.

Moses struck the Egyptian, hitting him so hard the man died. Breathing heavily, Moses looked around again. Still no one was near except the Israelite he had helped.

Quickly Moses buried the taskmaster's body in the sand. Then he hurried on, thinking his deed would remain a secret.

The next day he saw two slaves fighting each other. "Stop that!" he shouted. "Why are you hitting one of your own countrymen?"

The men paused. One of them answered rudely, "Who made you a judge over us? Are you going to kill me like you killed that Egyptian?"

Moses was horrified. The slave must have told them. "Everyone knows what I did," he thought in panic. "Someone is sure to report it to Pharaoh."

Pharaoh did indeed hear of it. He ordered that Moses be killed.

But Moses escaped, fleeing to the land of Midian. There, lonely and tired, he sat down by a well to rest.

Seven daughters of Jethro, the priest of a nearby village, came to the well to get water for their sheep. Moses idly watched. Some shepherds came along, all men. Roughly they told the girls to get out of the way until their sheep had been given a drink.

It wasn't fair. Angrily Moses sprang up. He made the men wait and helped the girls, drawing water for them himself until all their sheep were satisfied. The girls were amazed and delighted.

When they reached home, their father said, "How is it you're back so early today? Were the men not so rough?"

"They were the same as usual," answered the girls. "But there was someone else by the well, a man dressed like an Egyptian. He made them wait. He even drew water for our sheep."

"Where is he now?" cried Jethro. "Surely you didn't leave him alone by the well? Go and invite him here for a meal."

So Moses came to Jethro's home. The two men got along well, and Moses was happy to stay with the family.

After a while Jethro gave Moses his daughter Zipporah for a wife. Moses and Zipporah were happy. They had a baby boy, and Moses became a shepherd.

But his people, the Israelites, were still in Egypt.

God had not forgotten them. He remembered the covenant he had made with Abraham, Isaac, and Jacob.

Moses and the Burning Bush

Moses now lived in the wide, silent desert, caring for the sheep of his father-in-law, Jethro. One day while searching for pastures where the flock could graze, Moses came to Mount Horeb.

There he saw a most extraordinary thing.

On the mountainside a bush was on fire. Flames were shooting up, yet the bush did not burn. Cautiously, Moses moved closer to have a better look. He jumped back as he heard a voice speaking to him. The voice was coming from the burning bush.

"Moses, do not come any closer," the voice commanded. "Take off your shoes, for this is holy ground. I am God, the God of Abraham and Isaac and Jacob."

Moses shook with fear. Quickly he slipped off his sandals.

God spoke again. "I have seen how my people suffer in Egypt, and I am going to free them. I have chosen you to be their leader, to bring them out of that land."

It took Moses a moment or two to take in the words. Then he cried, "Me? But I'm nobody special. No one will take any notice of what I say."

"I will be with you," said God.

"But the people will want to know your name. What shall I say?" asked Moses.

"*I Am who I Am.* Tell the people the one who is called *I Am* has sent you."

Moses swallowed hard. "Suppose they still don't believe me?"

"What is that in your hand?" asked God.

"My rod," Moses replied.

"Throw it to the ground," commanded God.

Puzzled, Moses obeyed. Instantly the rod turned into a writhing snake.

"Aah!" cried Moses as he ran from it.

"Pick it up," commanded God. "By the tail."

Moses stopped. Pick it up by the tail—that wasn't the way to pick up a snake, if you were foolish enough to try it at all. Pick it up by the tail—it could whip around and strike you.

Yet that was what God had commanded.

With all the courage he had, Moses forced himself to go over to the snake, bend down, reach out, and grab it by the tail.

Then the snake turned back into a rod in his hand.

God said, "Now put your hand inside your garment."

Moses obeyed. When he brought his hand out, it was white with the dreaded disease leprosy.

"Now put it back again," God ordered.

This time when Moses brought his hand out, the leprosy was gone.

"These are two miraculous signs by which you can prove I have spoken to you," said God. "If they still will not believe, here is a third sign. Take some water from the River Nile and pour it onto the ground. It will turn into blood."

Moses stood there in front of the burning bush and imagined himself in Egypt, speaking to the leaders of his own people and speaking to the Pharaoh.

"Lord," he pleaded, "I am not good at talking to people."

"Who makes men's mouths so that they are able to speak at all?" replied God. "I will help you."

Moses was still unsure. "Please send someone else," he begged.

God grew angry because Moses still didn't trust him. But he said, "Take your brother Aaron with you. He shall speak for you both. And take your rod. For you shall perform the signs. Then you shall lead my people out of Egypt."

Moses knew he must obey God and go to Egypt.

Pharaoh and the Israelite Slaves

Moses had to explain to his father-in-law, Jethro, why he suddenly wanted to leave Midian. ''Please let me go back to my own people in Egypt to see if they are still alive,'' said Moses.

This was a reason Jethro could understand. ''Go in peace,'' he said.

Moses prepared for the journey. But he was very anxious. Would there still be trouble for him in Egypt because of the man he had killed?

God reassured him. ''All the men who wanted to kill you are dead.''

So that problem was solved. But there still remained the enormous task of leading the Israelites out of Egypt.

Still anxious, Moses set out, taking his wife and sons with him. God knew how Moses was feeling and sent Aaron to meet him in the wilderness.

The two brothers greeted each other warmly, hugging and kissing, for it was years since they had last seen one another. Then Moses told Aaron of the task which God had given them to do and of the miraculous signs which Moses was to perform as proof that God was with them.

Now that Aaron was with him, Moses felt better. Together they went to the Israelites and called an assembly of the leaders. Aaron gave God's message and Moses showed them the signs.

The Israelites believed, and when they heard that God still cared for them, they worshiped him. "God has not forgotten us," they cried. "We shall soon be free."

But first Pharaoh had to agree to set his slaves free.

Moses and Aaron stood in front of Pharaoh. Aaron said, "The God of Israel says, 'Let my people go so that they can hold a feast in the wilderness and make sacrifices to me there.'"

Moses and Aaron nervously waited for Pharaoh's answer.

Pharaoh replied angrily. "Who is this God of Israel? I don't know him. Why should I do as he says? I will not let Israel go. You're keeping them from their work. They already outnumber the Egyptians. Now you want them to stop work."

Pharaoh gave orders that the Israelites should be made to work harder than ever. "Don't give them the straw to make bricks, as you have been doing," he commanded the taskmasters. "Let them find their own straw. But they must still make just as many bricks as before. Keep them busy. Then they'll have neither the time nor the energy to listen to these stories of feast days and sacrifices."

The taskmasters obeyed Pharaoh. Now the Israelites had to search for straw, which took time. The slaves simply weren't able to make the same number of bricks as before, no matter how hard they toiled in the hot sun. As a result the taskmasters beat them cruelly.

The leaders of the Israelites went to Pharaoh. "Why do you treat us so harshly?" they cried.

"Because you are getting lazy," Pharaoh answered. "All this talk of sacrificing to your God. It's just an excuse. Get busy with your brick-making."

The Israelite leaders could see there was no mercy to be had from Pharaoh. As they left the palace, they met Moses and Aaron, who had been waiting anxiously outside.

"God will judge you," the leaders shouted angrily. "You have made things much worse for us. Now we'll either die from overwork or be beaten to death."

Moses prayed to God. "Why did you send me here? Since I came, Pharaoh is treating the people worse than before, and you're not doing anything to save them."

God replied, "You'll see what I will do to Pharaoh. Because of my strong hand, he will let the people go. For I am the God of Abraham and Isaac and Jacob. I promised them I would give the land of Canaan to the Israelites. Go and tell the people that I will keep my promise."

Moses tried to give the people God's message, but they were suffering so much they wouldn't listen.

Then God said to Moses, "I will perform signs and miracles. The Egyptians shall know that I am God. Go back to Pharaoh and there do as I tell you."

The Plagues of Egypt

Once again Moses and Aaron were standing in front of Pharaoh.

"If I am to believe you bring a message from your God, show me a sign," said Pharaoh.

This is exactly what God had predicted Pharaoh would say. Aaron was prepared. He threw down his rod. Immediately the staff turned into a snake.

Pharaoh was not going to be so easily impressed. He sent for his magicians. They threw down their rods and magically turned them into snakes.

But Aaron's rod swallowed all the others.

Even then Pharaoh wouldn't listen to Moses and Aaron. Discouraged and disappointed, they left the palace.

God spoke to Moses. "Pharaoh is very stubborn. This is what you must do. In the morning Pharaoh will go down to the River Nile. Wait for him on the bank, holding the rod which turned into a snake. As he comes near, say, 'The Lord has sent me to tell you to let the Israelites go and worship in the desert. I will strike the waters of the Nile with my rod, and the river will turn into blood. This is how you will know he is God.' "

Moses listened, swallowing hard. God spoke again. "Then tell Aaron to hold out his rod, and all the rivers,

canals, and ponds of Egypt shall turn into blood.''

Moses and Aaron obeyed God, and it happened exactly as God had said. Pharaoh came down to the river. The water turned into blood. The fish in the river died. The water smelled terrible all across Egypt, and no one could drink it.

Stubbornly Pharaoh sent for his magicians. They also turned water into blood by magic.

''There you are,'' said Pharaoh, and he went back to his palace.

The Egyptian people had to dig for water along the banks of the river.

After a week went by and the waters were clearing, God said to Moses, ''Go again to Pharaoh and give him my message. Tell him if he still refuses to let my people go, I will send a plague of frogs.''

Moses and Aaron went to Pharaoh. Faithfully they repeated God's message. But Pharaoh was unmoved.

Aaron held out his rod, and up from the River Nile came hundreds and thousands of frogs. They hopped into the palace, into the bedroom, and onto Pharaoh's bed. They were everywhere: in all the houses, in the ovens, in the feeding troughs. Wherever the people stepped, there were frogs.

At first Pharaoh pretended he was untroubled. He sent for his magicians. They made even more frogs appear.

''You see?'' said Pharaoh. But

really he couldn't stand the frogs hopping out unexpectedly, frogs getting squashed underfoot, frogs croaking.

He sent for Moses and Aaron. "My people are unhappy," he said. "Ask your God to take these frogs away. Then I will let your people go to offer sacrifices in the wilderness."

Moses didn't obey immediately. "You may fix the time when I shall pray to God," he said. "And so that you will know it is God's work, when I pray, all the frogs will die except those in the river."

Pharaoh was still pretending to be unmoved. "Pray tomorrow," he said, as if there were no hurry.

Then Moses and Aaron left the palace. The next day Moses prayed to God, and the frogs died exactly as Moses had said. There were piles and piles of dead frogs. The whole land smelled of dead frogs.

Yet as soon as the frogs were gone, Pharaoh changed his mind and would not let the Israelites go.

God said to Moses and Aaron, "Strike the dust of the ground with your rod, and all through Egypt the dust shall turn into gnats."

Moses and Aaron obeyed, and gnats sprang up everywhere. They zoomed around, biting both people and animals until all the Egyptians were scratching themselves.

Pharaoh knew at once who was responsible. He sent for his magicians. But try as they might, the magicians could not make gnats appear.

"The gnats are a sign from God," they trembled. Yet still Pharaoh would not let the slaves go.

God spoke again to Moses. "Get up early tomorrow morning. Once more speak to Pharaoh as he goes to the river. Tell him if he will not let my people go, the houses of the Egyptians will be full of flies which I shall send. But so that he will know I am God, there shall be no flies in the land of Goshen where the Israelites live."

And so it happened. Pharaoh would not let the people go, and on the following day, swarms of flies filled his palace. All the land of Egypt was ruined by flies; there were flies on the food, flies in the drinking water, flies everywhere. But in the land of Goshen, there were no flies.

Pharaoh sent for Moses and Aaron. "You may sacrifice to the Lord your God," he cried. "But do it here, not in the wilderness."

Moses was feeling bolder now. "No. That wouldn't be right," he answered. "Your people would be offended. They would throw stones at us. We must make a three-day journey into the wilderness to offer our sacrifices. This is what the Lord God commands."

The flies buzzed and zoomed around Pharaoh's head. "Oh, very well," he snapped. "You may go into the wilderness, but not far. Now pray to your God to take these flies away."

"As soon as I leave the palace, I will pray for you," Moses replied warily. "Tomorrow the flies will go, but the Pharaoh must keep his part of the bargain."

"Of course," said Pharaoh.

Moses left the palace and prayed to God.

The next day not one fly remained in Egypt. But as soon as Pharaoh realized there were no more flies, he refused to let the Israelites go.

Once more God sent Moses to warn Pharaoh. God would send a cattle disease so that all the Egyptian livestock would die. But the animals of the Israelites would be untouched. Once more Pharaoh refused to listen, and once more God did as he had said.

Still Pharaoh would not let the Israelites go.

Then God told Moses and Aaron to take handfuls of soot from the fire and throw the soot into the air in front of Pharaoh. When Moses and Aaron obeyed, boils broke out on all the people of Egypt. The magicians suffered badly from the boils. Yet still Pharaoh would not let the Israelites go.

Then God sent Moses with another message for Pharaoh. Moses spoke. "So that you may know his power, the Lord God will send a great storm. The people and the animals of Egypt should all get under cover, or they will be killed."

By now some of the Egyptians believed God would do as he said. These people hurried to get their families and animals indoors.

But some people took no notice. They stayed out in the open as usual.

The storm came with mighty crashes of thunder and fiery bolts of lightning accompanied by hail. It was the worst storm Egypt had ever known. Every living thing out in the open was killed. Yet in Goshen there was no storm at all.

Pharaoh sent urgently for Moses and Aaron. As the lightning flashed and the thunder rolled, Pharaoh cried, "I know I've done wrong. Pray

to your God. No more storms like this, please. You and your people can go at once."

Moses was still wary. "When I am outside the city, I will pray to God. The storms will stop so that you may know God's power. But I can see you still do not really believe in him."

Moses left the palace. Once outside the city, he prayed as he had promised. Immediately the rain, thunder, and lightning stopped. There was calm.

But when Pharaoh realized the storm was over, he would not let the people go.

Moses was desperate, but God comforted him. "Do not get too upset. I am performing these miracles so that you will be able to tell your children's children how I treated the Egyptians. Then they will know I am indeed Lord. Now go to Pharaoh again. Warn him that if he does not let my people go, I will send a plague of locusts."

So once more Moses and Aaron stood in front of Pharaoh, giving him God's message. The leaders of the

Egyptians were afraid. "How much more must we put up with?" they cried. "Let the people go and worship their God. Don't you see that Egypt is being ruined?"

Pharaoh asked warily, "Who will go and worship your God in the wilderness?"

"Every one of us," replied Moses.

"No!" cried Pharaoh angrily. "Only the men may go." And he had Moses and Aaron thrown out of the palace.

God sent the locusts. The ground was black with them. They ate every leaf and every fruit in all the land of Egypt.

Once more Pharaoh begged Moses and Aaron to have the plague removed. Once more God removed it. But still Pharaoh would not let the Israelites go.

Then God sent darkness over the land of Egypt for three whole days. Only the Israelites had daylight.

In fear, Pharaoh sent for Moses. "Go!" he cried. "Every one of you."

"We must also take our animals," said Moses.

"No!" stormed Pharaoh. "Get out of my palace. If I ever see you again, you shall die."

"Very well," retorted Moses. "I will never come to this palace again."

Now God prepared to bring the worst plague of all on Egypt.

The Passover

God said to Moses, "After this plague Pharaoh will not only let you go, he will throw you out of Egypt altogether. But you must first give him warning of what I mean to do."

So, in spite of the way in which the two had parted, Moses once more stood in front of Pharaoh.

"This is the message from the Lord God of Israel," said Moses. "At midnight all the firstborn children in every family in Egypt shall die. The firstborn animals also shall die. But none of the Israelites shall die in this way. You shall see that God treats the Egyptians differently from the Israelites."

Pharaoh listened to the dreadful news, but still he would not let the people go.

Moses called together all the leaders of the Israelites. There was a message from God for them also. "You must kill a lamb, a young male that is without blemish. Dip a bunch of herbs into the lamb's blood, and mark your doorposts with it, both sides and at the top. No one must go outside before morning. You shall roast the lamb and eat it with unleavened bread and bitter herbs. And even as you eat, you shall be ready to leave quickly. You must have your shoes on your feet and your staffs in your hands.

"The Lord God will pass through the land of Egypt and strike down all the firstborn. But when he sees the blood on your doorposts, he will pass over. Death will not come to your household. You shall remember the passover every year as a covenant between you and God forever. You shall tell your children and your children's children how the Lord God saved all our families."

The people worshiped God. Then they went away to carry out God's instructions.

At midnight every firstborn child in Egypt died, from Pharaoh's own child to the child of the lowliest prisoner in jail. There was a great cry from every Egyptian household. Pharaoh sent for Moses and Aaron.

That morning before dawn, Moses and Aaron hurried to the palace.

"Go!" Pharaoh commanded them. "Every one of you can go—even your flocks and herds. Get out from among my people. Go and worship your God."

The frightened Egyptian people also urged the Israelites to leave. "If you don't, we will all be dead!" they cried.

Hastily the Israelites gathered up their belongings. They had been making bread, but they didn't even wait for the dough to rise before they set out.

So the huge host of men, women, and children, with their flocks, their herds, and as many possessions as they could carry, came safely out of Egypt. They were free.

But their rejoicing did not last long.

Exodus 13:17-22; 14:5-31; 15:1

The Red Sea

Traveling day and night, the Israelites reached the edge of the wilderness. There was no time to be lost, for the Egyptians might come after them. God led the way in a pillar of cloud by day and a pillar of fire by night. He led them toward the Red Sea by the desert road.

Back in Egypt Pharaoh and his people realized the Israelites really had gone. Now there were no slaves to do the work.

"Why did we let them leave?" the people cried.

"We shall get them back," Pharaoh declared. He chose six hundred chariots, the best in all Egypt, and he set out after the Israelites with his horses and his men.

The Egyptian army traveled much faster than the Israelites, who had young children and animals with them. The Israelites had almost reached the Red Sea when they looked up and saw the sight they had been dreading. The Egyptians were coming.

"Weren't there any graves in Egypt?" the people cried to Moses in fear. "Why did you bring us out here to die? Why didn't you leave us alone? It was better to be slaves in Egypt than to die in the wilderness."

"Don't be afraid," said Moses, trying to calm the people. "The Lord God will fight for you if you will only let him."

Then Moses prayed urgently to God.

God answered, "Why are you talking to me? Tell the people to keep moving forward."

How could they move forward? The sea was in the way!

God was still speaking. "Stretch out your rod over the waters. The sea will divide, and the Israelites will walk across on dry land. The Egyptians will try to follow. Then you and they shall see my power."

Now the pillar of cloud moved from in front of the Israelites to behind them. It came between the Israelites and the Egyptians, bringing darkness to the Egyptian side so that they set up camp for the night. But the cloud brought light to the Israelites on the other side.

Moses told his people to keep moving. Then he stretched out his rod over the sea as God had commanded. The Israelites watched in awe. The waters were dividing.

They started to cross fearfully at first, then more boldly. All night long the procession of people and animals walked and stumbled across the dry bed of the sea with high walls of water on either side of them.

When the Egyptians realized the Israelites were escaping, they quickly harnessed their horses. With speed they raced their chariots across the ground onto the seabed. They were catching up.

God saw the Egyptians gaining on his people and made the wheels fall off the chariots. As the Egyptians struggled in the sand, they gasped, "Let's get away from the Israelites. Their God is fighting for them." But they were stuck fast on the seabed, and the last of the Israelites was safely across.

Then God said to Moses, "Stretch out your rod again so that the seas will come together."

In excitement and fear, Moses obeyed. As he held up his rod, the seas came crashing down. The Egyptian army turned in panic, trying to get back to land. But it was useless. Every single one of the Egyptians was drowned; yet every single one of the Israelites was saved, completely unharmed.

Then the Israelites knew their God was great. They believed in him and in Moses, and they sang and danced in triumph and praise.

But once again, their happiness did not last.

Exodus 15:22-27; 16; 17:1-7

In the Wilderness

The great crowd of Israelites with their animals and possessions were traveling through the wilderness, hoping to reach the land which God had promised them. But they were becoming desperate.

For three days they had found no water. Their mouths were dry; their throats parched. They longed for a drink of cool, clear water. At last they came to a place called Marah.

"Look!" they cried. "There is water here." They rushed to drink at the pools, but soon they were spitting out the water. In rage and disappointment, they shouted at Moses. "The water is bitter. It tastes horrible. No one could drink that. What are we to drink?"

Moses prayed to God. God told him to throw a certain piece of wood into the water. Moses obeyed and the bitter water became sweet and good. Gratefully the Israelites drank their fill.

God made a covenant with them. "If you keep my laws, I will not send to you any of the plagues which I sent to the Egyptians."

The Israelites traveled on. They came to Elim where there were twelve springs of water and seventy palm trees. There in the shade, they camped to rest.

Soon they moved on. And once more they complained to Moses. "We're hungry. Why didn't you leave us in Egypt? At least we had food there. Why did you bring us out into this desert to starve?''

Then God said to Moses, ''I will rain food from heaven for them. They must collect it fresh each morning, and they must collect only enough for one day. I shall test them to see if they are ready to obey my laws. On the sixth day, they may gather enough bread for two days.''

Moses and Aaron gave the good news to the people. ''This very evening you will know that the God who brought you out of Egypt can be trusted. And in the morning you will see how glorious he is.''

They explained the rules about collecting the food. ''And remember,'' Moses finished, ''when you grumbled, you weren't grumbling at me, but at God.''

The day seemed long as the Israelites waited to see what sign God would send them.

Just before dusk flocks of small brown birds, quail, came flying low across the ground. The quail landed in the camp. There were so many that the ground was covered with them. They were very good to eat. Rejoicing, the people collected them. From all over the camp came the smell of roasting. That night the people ate a good meal.

In the morning when the dew had dried up, the ground was covered with tiny white flakes.

''What is it?'' asked the Israelites fearfully. They'd never seen anything like it before.

''This is the food God has sent,'' Moses explained. ''Collect it as he commanded.''

Most of the people obeyed, but

some were lazy. "If we collect enough for two days, we won't need to get up early tomorrow," they whispered. So they gathered twice as much as they needed.

But no matter how much they gathered, each ended up with the same amount. Some still tried to save a portion of their food for the next day. But by the next morning, maggots were in the food, and it smelled terrible.

Moses was angry. "You know the rules God made," he said.

Then the people kept the rules. But on the sixth day, Moses reminded the people, "God has said there won't be any food from heaven tomorrow. Gather twice as much, and cook all that you collect today. Then set aside some for tomorrow."

Again most people obeyed. Yet even after all their experience with God, some people went out on the seventh morning looking for bread.

God was angry. He spoke to Moses. "How long will this disobedience go on? I sent food for six days so that on the seventh day everyone may rest from work. No one is to go out on the seventh day."

At last all the Israelites did as they were told. Every evening they ate meat, and in the morning they ate the bread food, called manna. It was delicious, thin and crisp with a flavor of honey. God told Moses and Aaron to put some of it into a jar to show the future Israelites.

So the Israelites did not starve in the wilderness, but when they came to Rephidim, once more they could not find water.

They shouted at Moses, "Why did you bring us out of Egypt to make us die of thirst in this place?"

Moses lost patience. "Why are you blaming me? I have told you. It is really God you're blaming."

Moses said to God, "What am I to do with them? They look angry enough to kill me."

"Walk on in front," said God. "Take some of the leaders with you and carry your rod, the same rod which you had in Egypt. I will meet you by the rock at Horeb. Strike the rock with your rod, and water will flow from it. Then the people may drink."

Moses obeyed. Soon the Israelites were drinking clear, cool water. Would they never stop doubting God and his presence with them?

Exodus 17:8-15

The Battle with the Amalekites

The Israelites were camping at Rephidim when suddenly they were attacked by a fierce tribe, the Amalekites.

After a short skirmish, the Israelites had to prepare for a long battle the next day. Moses wondered what would be best to do. He was old now and no warrior. They needed someone young and strong, a skilled fighter to lead the Israelites in the battle.

After more thought he sent for Joshua, son of Nun. "Joshua," he said, "choose whichever men you want and lead them against the Amalekites tomorrow."

Joshua's face lit up. This was a great honor. And yet he couldn't quite help thinking that the Amalekites were strong and well-trained.

Moses explained the whole plan. "I will go up to the top of the hill and stand there holding up the rod which God has blessed so much in the past. From the hilltop I shall have a good view of the battle. I know God will help you."

Joshua nodded. He went away and carefully picked the best fighters.

In the morning he marched them out, ready to face the enemy.

Moses climbed to the hilltop, taking with him his brother Aaron and a man called Hur. As the Amalekites made the first charge, Moses lifted the rod, holding it high as he had promised.

From their viewpoint the three men could see that the battle was going this way and that. Whenever Moses's arm ached and he lowered the rod, the Amalekites began to win. Whenever Moses held the rod high, Joshua's men gained control.

Aaron and Hur realized what was happening. They found a large stone and brought it for Moses to sit on. Now they could hold up his arms for him with no strain on their own. Moses was able to keep the rod lifted high, and by evening the Amalekites were defeated.

God said to Moses, "Write this whole story down and have it read publicly in Joshua's presence."

Moses obeyed and he built a special altar to God on the hillside, calling the altar The-Lord-Is-My-Banner.

Exodus 19; 20; 21; 22; 23:1-19; 24:2-8

The Ten Commandments

The Israelites left Rephidim and went into the Sinai desert. They camped at the foot of Mount Sinai, and Moses climbed up to the top to speak to God.

God said, ''I am going to make a very special covenant with the Israelites. If you obey my words, you will be my special people, my chosen nation.''

Moses excitedly hurried back down the mountain to give the people God's great message.

''Whatever God commands, we will obey, '' the people promised eagerly.

God was pleased. ''On the third day, I will come down to Mount Sinai in a cloud,'' he told Moses. ''The people will see the cloud and know that I am with you. They will trust you. Tell them they must prepare themselves, and you must bless them. During the next two days, they must wash their clothes so that everything is very clean. Also tell them they must not set foot on the mountain, for anyone who even touches it will die. Not until the trumpet sounds may they go up the mountain.''

So Moses blessed the people, and they washed their clothes and were very clean. Then they waited expectantly for the third day to come. On the morning of the third day, thunder rolled and lightning flashed over the mountain. A thick cloud covered the top of it, and a trumpet sounded loudly. The Israelites shook with fear.

Moses led the people to the foot of the mountain. There they all waited.

Then the mountain trembled and the trumpet sounded even louder than before. The mountain was covered with billowing smoke, and God called to Moses.

Moses climbed the mountain and went into the cloud.

God gave Moses the Ten Commandments, saying, ''I am the Lord your God who brought you out of the land of Egypt. You must have no gods other than me. You must not worship statues, pictures of images, or anything which you have made yourselves. If you do not obey this law, I will punish not only you, but your children and your children's children.

''You must not use the Lord your God's name carelessly or without good reason.

''Remember the Sabbath day and keep it holy. On six days you may work, but on the seventh day, you and all your family must rest. Remember, the Lord made the world in six days, but on the seventh day, the Lord rested. The Lord blessed the seventh day and made it holy.

"Treat your father and your mother with honor and respect.

"Murder no one.

"Do not sleep with another man's wife or another woman's husband.

"Do not steal.

"Do not tell lies or give false evidence against anyone.

"Do not desire for anything which belongs to someone else."

Down below, the people saw the storm and the smoke. They moved back. From a distance they called to Moses in fear, "You speak to us. We will listen. But don't let God himself speak to us, or we shall die."

"Don't be afraid," Moses comforted them. "God only wants you to do right."

Again Moses went into the cloud where God was, and God gave him more rules for the Israelites to keep.

There were commandments, or rules, about all aspects of life. Commandments were given about the rights of individuals, treatment of property, and standards of conduct. God revealed to Moses how his people were to act and what the punishment would be for doing wrong.

God gave many more rules to Moses, and Moses came down to the people and told them.

"We will obey," the people promised again. Then Moses wrote down all that God had said and built an altar at the foot of the mountain. And he set up twelve pillars. The pillars stood for the twelve tribes of Israel.

Moses made a sacrifice to God. Then he read the laws to the people and said, "The Lord has made a covenant with you according to all that is written here."

The Ark of the Covenant

God said to Moses, "Come up to the mountaintop. I will give you tablets of stone on which I have written the commandments."

Moses called to Joshua to come with him. He told the Israelite leaders to wait at the foot of the mountain. "While we are gone, Aaron and Hur will be in charge," he said.

Then Moses and Joshua climbed Mount Sinai. Cloud and fire covered the top of the mountain. For six days Joshua and Moses waited in the cloud. At last God called to Moses. But before God gave Moses the tablets of stone, there was something else which needed to be said.

The Israelites were to build an ark, or chest, and a tabernacle, or place of worship. God told Moses exactly what offerings could be made by every Israelite who wanted to contribute: expensive gifts of gold, silver, or bronze and gifts of goat skins or olive oil, which the poorer people could afford. There were to be gifts of acacia wood; of blue, purple, or scarlet yarn; fine linen; and many other things.

The Ark was to be made of acacia wood. It was to be about forty-five inches long and about twenty-seven inches wide and twenty-seven inches high. It was to be covered with gold inside and out. Four rings were to be made and fastened to its four corners. Two rings would be on one side, two on the other. Poles made of acacia wood and covered with gold were to be slipped through the rings. The poles were never to be taken out of the rings so that the Ark could always be lifted up and carried.

The written laws were to be kept in the Ark, which would be known as the Ark of the Covenant.

God gave more details on the Ark and its support table.

God described exactly how the Ark would be kept in the Tabernacle. He said the Tabernacle was to have a curtain hanging in it that would divide the Holy Place from the Most Holy Place. The Ark would be kept in the Most Holy Place.

Then God described what the priests of the Tabernacle should wear. He had even chosen the men who should make all these things.

When God had finished speaking, he gave Moses the two tablets of stone. But Moses had been on the mountain for forty days and forty nights, and the Israelites were growing tired of waiting for him to come down.

The Golden Calf

At the foot of the mountain, the Israelites waited and waited.

They saw the clouds covering the mountaintop. They heard thunder and saw lightning. But still Moses had not returned.

The people spoke to Aaron. "You will have to make us a god to go in front of us. Who knows what's happened to Moses, our leader who brought us out of Egypt. It seems he will never come back."

All those years in Egypt and in the wilderness, it had been Moses who talked with God. It had been Moses who then told Aaron what God wanted them to do. Without his brother, Aaron felt lost.

Perhaps Moses had fallen on the mountain. Perhaps he had been killed. The people were restless. They might become violent. Aaron remembered there had been times when even Moses had been afraid for his life because of the people's discontent.

Forgetting that when the people had been unhappy, Moses had always prayed to God for help, Aaron made a decision on his own.

"All right. Bring me all your gold earrings and necklaces," he said.

When they obeyed, Aaron melted down the gold over a hot fire. Then he made it into the shape of a calf.

"There is our god," shouted the people. "That's the god who brought us out of Egypt."

When Aaron heard what they were saying, he was afraid. Quickly he built an altar in front of the calf. "Tomorrow we will make a sacrifice to the Lord God," he said.

The next morning the people got up early and made burnt offerings. Afterward they held great feasts of eating and drinking, and they worshiped the calf.

Up on the mountain, God spoke to Moses. "Go down at once! The people have made themselves an idol. They are kneeling in front of it. They are saying it brought them out of

Moses moved quickly down the mountainside, carrying the two tablets of stone.

Joshua was waiting anxiously for him on the slope. "Listen," Joshua said. "There is war in the camp."

"That is not the sound of war," Moses answered grimly. "It is the sound of singing and dancing."

He hurried far enough down the mountain to see the camp. Then he saw the golden calf.

Moses was furious. He threw down the tablets of stone, and they shattered into pieces at the foot of the mountain.

Then he rushed into the camp, seized the golden calf, and hurled it into the fire. When it was melted, he ground it into powder and scattered the powder into water. He then forced the terrified Israelites to drink it.

Moses turned to Aaron and said, "Why did you do it?"

"They told me to," Aaron said, trembling. "They thought you were probably dead. I asked them for their jewelry, and when they gave it to me, I threw it into the fire. This golden calf came out."

Moses could see that Aaron simply wasn't able to control the people. This was why God had chosen Moses, not Aaron, to lead the people.

In bringing order to the camp, three thousand men died.

With mixed feelings, Moses climbed the mountain once more. Again he pleaded with God to forgive the people. For forty days more, Moses stayed on the mountaintop.

When he came down from the mountaintop with two new stone tablets, the Israelites were waiting for him. They saw that his face was shining. He had seen God's glory.

Egypt. I shall destroy them all and only you will be saved."

Moses was deeply distressed. He pleaded with God, trying to think of a reason why God should not destroy the Israelites. "Please don't be so angry with them. Don't let the Egyptians say, 'Their God took them out of Egypt so that he could destroy them in the wilderness.' Remember all the promises you made to Abraham, to Isaac, and to Jacob—that their children would number more than anyone could count and would reach the promised land."

God listened to Moses and decided to let the Israelites live.

Departing from Sinai

The Israelites had promised once more that they would obey God. Now it was time to leave Sinai and move on toward the promised land. This time the Ark of the Covenant was carried in front of them, and the cloud of the Lord was over them. Whenever the Ark of the Covenant was lifted up, Moses said, "Rise up, Lord, and let thine enemies be scattered." And when it rested, he said, "Return, Lord, to the many thousands of Israel."

So the Israelites journeyed on and, as usual, began to grumble. "Can't we have more meat to eat? We remember all the fish we had in Egypt, and it was free. And we had melons, cucumbers, leeks, onions, and garlic. Now we never have anything but this manna. Day after day after day. We can't eat any more of it. Not one more mouthful."

God grew angry and Moses spoke to him resentfully. "Why did you make me leader of these people? They're not my children. Where can I get meat for them? It's all too much for me. I wish you'd let me die right now."

God had sympathy for Moses. "You're doing too much," he said. "Too many people are bringing you their disputes to settle."

Moses sighed. He did indeed feel tired.

91

"Bring me seventy of the leaders of the people," said God. "I will speak with them about the task of leading the Israelites, and I will put some of your spirit on them." And then he said grimly, "The people shall have meat. Not for one or two days, but for a whole month, until they become sick of it. This will happen because they have not trusted me."

"How?" responded Moses. "There are six hundred thousand men here. Even if we kill every animal we have with us, there won't be enough meat for every day for an entire month."

"Has my arm been shortened?" God demanded. "You shall see whether or not what I say will happen."

And God made a wind blow from the sea, bringing on it hundreds and thousands of quail. For two days and a night, the people gathered up the birds to cook and eat them. But the meat made the people ill, and many of them died.

For a while there was no more grumbling about manna.

The journey continued. Moses's sister Miriam and his brother Aaron began to feel jealous of Moses as he led the way. "Hasn't God spoken through us?" they demanded. "Why does he talk only to Moses?"

Moses had often wondered the same thing. He'd never thought he was anyone special.

But God was very angry with Miriam and Aaron. "I speak only through Moses because he is the only one I can trust. I can speak clearly to him. How dare you speak against him?"

And God made Miriam ill with leprosy and commanded that she be put outside the camp for seven days.

Moses begged God to heal her; and after the seven days, she was quite well again.

As soon as Miriam was back in the camp, the Israelites moved on again, still traveling toward their promised land.

Would they ever reach it?

Twelve Spies Explore Canaan

God spoke exciting words to Moses. "Choose twelve men, one from each of the twelve tribes of Israel. They are to go on a secret mission to explore the land of Canaan, the land I have promised to give you."

At last the Israelites were nearing the promised land.

The twelve men would need to be brave, strong, and skillful if they were not to be discovered by the Canaanites. Moses picked them carefully, and Joshua was among them.

Moses told them exactly what they needed to know about Canaan and its people, if the Israelites were to try an attack. His final instruction was, "Try to bring back some fruit."

The twelve men set out. The rest of the Israelites waited as patiently as they could in their camp at Kadesh. For forty days they waited. Then they saw the men returning.

By then every one of the Israelites knew which men had left the camp, where they had gone, and why. Eagerly the people crowded around, shouting, "Tell us! What's Canaan like?"

The twelve men gave a full report on their successful mission.

"It's a very rich land with good harvests. Look what we brought back: grapes, figs, and pomegranates. It's a land which flows with milk and honey. But . . ."

The Israelites, who had been getting ready to celebrate, stopped to hear more.

93

"The cities are large and well-defended," one of the spies said. "And the people are huge, like giants. We felt like grasshoppers beside them."

The Israelites all began to talk at once.

Caleb, another of the spies, silenced them. "Listen. Although the cities are strong and the people are powerful, we should certainly make our attack. With God on our side, we can fight and win."

But the other spies said, "No! We could never win a battle against the Canaanites." And they spoke so discouragingly among the people that the Israelites were not even willing to try.

The people shouted angrily at Moses and Aaron. "It would have been better if we'd died in Egypt. Why did God bring us here to die in a battle and have our wives and children captured?"

Then everyone wept. Some said, "Let's find another leader, one who will take us back to Egypt."

Joshua stepped forward to stand beside Caleb. The two men tore their clothes as a sign that what they had heard was blasphemy against God. Joshua tried to reason with the people.

"The land of Canaan is well worth fighting for," he said. "Do not disobey God. Don't be afraid. We will beat those Canaanites. They have no protection which can match the power of our God."

But the Israelites were too agitated to listen. Some of them picked up stones. Seeing this, many others joined in, ready to throw stones at Caleb and Joshua.

God could not let the dispute go any farther. In a cloud of glory, he appeared at the Tabernacle so that all the Israelites could see his majesty. He spoke to Moses. "How long will these people refuse to trust me in spite of all they have seen me do? I will destroy them all."

Moses pleaded, "If you kill them here, the Egyptians will say you were not able to bring your people into the promised land. I know you are slow to anger and full of love. You forgive sin and disobedience."

Once more God listened to Moses, "Very well. I will forgive them, and they shall live. But not one of the people who were in Egypt shall ever reach the promised land; only their children shall do so. Now turn back into the wilderness. You shall live there for forty years—one year for each of the forty days the spies were in the land of Canaan. Of all the men here, only Joshua and Caleb shall reach the promised land."

The Israelites were bitterly sorry for the way they had behaved. Some of them even made an attack on Canaan without God's help, but the attack failed. They were thoroughly defeated.

For forty long years, the Israelites wandered in the desert wilderness.

Moses Dies

"I'm too old now to lead you," Moses told the Israelites. "And God has said I shall never reach the promised land. You must have a new leader."

Moses called Joshua, son of Nun, to come forward. In front of everyone, Moses spoke to him. "Joshua, be brave and strong, for you must now be the leader. God will go in front of you and be with you. He will never leave you and never forsake you. You must not be afraid. You must never lose heart."

Joshua listened intently. God himself made a promise to Joshua. "You will bring the Israelites into the land which I have promised them. I myself will be with you."

For the last time, Moses wrote down the laws which God had given to the Israelites, and the book was placed in the Ark of the Covenant. Then Moses wrote a song as God told him to. It told the story of the past and reminded everyone of the power of God. Moses taught the song to the Israelites so that they would always remember their history.

Now Moses knew he was near death. But before he died, God told him to climb Mount Nebo to look across the Jordan River to Canaan spread out below.

"That is the land which I promised to Abraham, to Isaac, and to Jacob," God said. "I wanted you to see it before you go to your forefathers."

Moses died there on Mount Nebo, and the Lord buried him. There would never be another man like Moses.

But Joshua was the Israelites' new leader, full of strength and wisdom. Moses had blessed him, and the people listened to him.

Joshua told them it was time to prepare to enter the promised land.

Joshua Sends Out Spies

Joshua sent two men on a secret mission. "Find out how strong the city of Jericho is," he ordered.

They entered Jericho quite openly, pretending to be ordinary visitors to the town. Once inside they looked for somewhere to lodge overnight. The two spies found their way to the house of Rahab. On the way they noted Jericho's strong walls and well-guarded towers.

"It's more of a fortress than a town," they said to one another gloomily.

Rahab let them in. But they had been recognized.

A messenger rushed to the king of Jericho. "Some Israelites are here, spying in the city!" he panted. "They are in Rahab's house."

The king, angry and fearful, sent men to capture the spies. It was already dark as the king's men reached Rahab's house. They banged on her front door, shouting, "Bring out the Israelites! We know you have spies in there."

We are trapped! thought the Israelites desperately.

But to their amazement, Rahab was beckoning to them. Her face was pale with fear, but swiftly and silently she led them up to the roof and hid them under stalks of flax which she had laid out earlier that day to dry in the sun.

She left the spies there and hurried down to open the door for the king's soldiers.

"It's true that some men did come," she said, "but they left at dusk because they knew the town gates would soon be shut. I don't know which way they went, but if you hurry, you can surely catch them."

"They'll have gone toward Jordan," yelled the king's men and set off in pursuit.

Up on the roof, the Israelites heard the noise and shouting fade into the distance. They lay still in their hiding place, and presently Rahab crept up to them.

"They've gone," she whispered. "They'll be outside the gates by now. I will tell you why I saved you. We've all heard that your God has given you this land of Canaan. We're afraid of you because we know how powerful your God is. We heard how he dried up the Red Sea so that you could cross safely. Now I beg you, when you attack the city, please don't harm me, my family, or our possessions. Remember, I have saved your lives."

The men looked at one another in the starlight.

"We will see that you are all saved," they promised, "on one condition—

you must not say one word about us to the king.''

''Not one word,'' Rahab agreed.

Her house was built on the town wall. She let down a rope from the outside window so that the spies could slide down it and get away.

''Go and hide in the mountains for three days,'' she advised in a low voice. ''The search will be over by then.''

And they said, ''We shall keep our promise to you. When the Israelites come, you must tie a piece of scarlet cord in this window. Bring your whole family into your house. As long as none of you go outside, you will not be harmed.''

''I will do it,'' she said.

As soon as they had gone, Rahab found a piece of scarlet cord and tied it at the window, taking no chance of being unprepared.

The spies reached the mountains and hid for three days, until the king's men had given up and gone back to the city.

Then the two spies made their way back to Joshua and gave their report. ''God has given us the city. All the people of Jericho are terrified of us.''

Gratefully Joshua asked God just how the Israelites should occupy the city.

Jericho Falls

Every gate into the city of Jericho was tightly closed and bolted. The people who lived in the city were terrified. They knew the Israelites were about to begin the attack.

But Joshua was not sure how to go about it. The Israelites were not trained fighters as were the men of Jericho, and the walls of Jericho were very thick and well-fortified.

Then God spoke to Joshua. "I will deliver Jericho, its king, and all its fighting men into your hands. This is what you must do." And God gave Joshua specific instructions.

Joshua listened with growing amazement. This was indeed a new way to attack a city. But he trusted God, so he gave the orders to the people. And whatever they thought, the people obeyed.

Every day for six days, they marched around the city of Jericho. The warriors went first. Next came the Ark of the Covenant, carried by the priests. Seven more priests blowing trumpets of rams' horns walked in front of the Ark. Then the rest of the people followed.

"You must be silent, not giving your battle cry until I tell you," Joshua warned the people. So the only sounds were the rams' horns and the tramp, tramp, tramp of marching feet, echoing eerily through the city of Jericho.

On the seventh day, the Israelites got up at dawn and started their march around Jericho. But on this day, they circled Jericho seven times. The seventh time, the Israelites completely encircled the city, the priests blew loudly on the trumpets, and Joshua yelled, "Shout, for the Lord has given you the city!"

Then the people shouted their battle cry, and the walls of Jericho fell down.

The hordes of Israelites swarmed into the city, destroying everyone and everything in it, except the silver and gold and other valuables which Joshua had ordered put into the treasury of the Lord. Joshua forbade the Israelites to keep the gods, or idols, of the people of Jericho so the camp of Israel would not be cursed.

Joshua said to the two spies, "Go quickly to the house of Rahab. Bring her and her family safely out of the city. They can stay with us in our camp."

So Rahab's family was saved, as the men had promised. But the rest of Jericho burned to the ground.

And the Israelites knew that God was with Joshua, as he had been with Moses.

Joshua Conquers Canaan

Jericho had fallen, but the rest of the land of Canaan wasn't yet conquered. Joshua had to decide on the next step in his campaign. He knew that the hard years in the wilderness had made the Israelites stronger. He could see that without memories of the easier life in Egypt, these people had the spirit of adventure. This is what God needed in people who were to work with him. Joshua was sure the Israelites were ready to fight.

But he did not know that one man, Achan, had disobeyed orders. In the ground under his tent, Achan had buried a bar of gold, some silver, and a beautiful cloak which he had stolen from the treasures of Jericho.

Joshua sent men to spy in the city of Ai. "It will be easy," they said when they came back. "You'll only need two or three thousand men. There are hardly any people in Ai."

So Joshua sent three thousand men, and they were defeated soundly. They ran from the city with the men of Ai chasing after them.

Joshua could hardly believe it. He threw himself down on the ground in front of the Ark.

"Lord, why did you bring us to this side of the River Jordan? Everyone will hear about this defeat. They will band together and attack us. We shall all be destroyed. Then who will be left to honor your name?"

God answered, "What are you doing, flat on your face? Stand up. One of the Israelites has stolen. The people have lied. The covenant between us is broken. That is why your men were defeated. I was not with you. And I shall not be with you until the man who has stolen is punished. This property devoted to heathen gods must be removed."

Then God told Joshua how to reveal the identity of the guilty man.

Joshua called the Israelites together. Grimly he told them what had happened and why they had been defeated. Achan listened, quivering with fear. Joshua went on speaking. The people were to prepare themselves, for tomorrow God would speak. The man who had stolen would be found out.

All night Achan worried. In the morning Joshua called for the twelve tribes of Israel to come forward, one by one. With God's help he picked out the tribe of Judah. Achan was one of the tribe of Judah.

From the tribe of Judah, Joshua picked out the clan of the Zerahites. Achan belonged to that clan. He watched Joshua coming closer and closer.

From the clan of the Zerahites, Joshua picked out the family of Zimri. Achan was part of that family.

By now Achan was helpless with fear. Sternly Joshua started to question each man in Zimri's family. God had guided Joshua to the right man. Achan was discovered.

"Tell the truth before God," Joshua ordered.

Achan confessed. His secret hoard was dug up, and he was put to death.

Joshua was upset. But God said to him, "Do not be afraid or discouraged. Attack Ai once more. This time I will be with you, and you will triumph."

So Joshua planned carefully and gave orders to his army. Most of them were to hide near Ai while he took a small group of men to make an attack.

As Joshua attacked, all the men of Ai came rushing out, expecting to chase the Israelites away as they had done before. But even as Joshua's army turned and ran, the rest of his army was entering the city, which had been left defenseless.

When the men of Ai stopped to glance back, they saw smoke rising from the city. They realized that they had been tricked and that Joshua's army was burning down the city. They raced back to save the city, but it was no use. Joshua's group now turned and chased them. They were caught between the two parts of Joshua's army, and the men of Ai were defeated. Joshua's plan had worked perfectly.

Joshua built an altar to God and offered a sacrifice of thanksgiving. Then he read the Laws of Moses to the Israelites. The whole nation worshiped God, and God once again blessed them.

Joshua had many more adventures, and in the end he overcame the whole of the land of Canaan.

He divided the land among the twelve tribes of Israel, as God ordered, and for a while there was a rest from war.

The Israelites behaved as usual. Sometimes they remembered God, and things went well for them. But sometimes they forgot God, and disaster followed.

God Chooses Gideon

Joshua had died years before. Now many of the Israelites worshiped false gods, and God had allowed the fierce tribe of the Midianites to overcome Israel.

Gideon was a strong, young Israelite. Yet he had to hide in a winepress as he threshed the wheat that belonged to his family. He was afraid that if he threshed in the open, the Midianites would steal the wheat.

But Gideon was angry as he threshed his wheat. The Israelites were almost starving. Didn't God care? How long would this have to go on? Where was God?

Gideon was startled by a voice, "God is with you, mighty warrior."

Mighty warrior? Him? Gideon turned to look. A man was sitting nearby, watching him. Was the man making fun of him, calling him a mighty warrior when he was hiding in fear? Did he really say God was with Gideon?

Gideon spoke harshly, "God has deserted us. He has simply handed us over to the Midianites."

The man replied, "Go and save Israel. I am sending you."

Then Gideon realized this was no ordinary man. It was an angel with a message from the Lord. And what a message! Save Israel?

"Me?" asked Gideon. "How can I save Israel? My clan is the weakest in all the tribe. And I'm the least important member of my family."

God spoke through the angel. "I will be with you. You will be able to defeat the Midianites as if they were just one man."

Gideon tried to understand. "If what you say is true, please give me a sign. Will you wait here a minute?" he begged.

"I will wait," promised the angel.

Gideon rushed away and came back with an offering of meat and bread.

"Put them on that rock," instructed the angel.

Trembling and wondering what would happen, Gideon obeyed.

The angel stretched out the rod he was carrying and touched the food with its tip. Flames of fire instantly sprang up. The food was burned to nothing, and the angel disappeared.

Gideon was terrified. "I have seen the face of the Angel of the Lord," he cried. And he expected to die at once.

God answered him, "Don't be afraid. You're not going to die."

That night God told Gideon how to begin the work of saving Israel. He was to destroy the altar to Baal which Gideon's father had set up in the marketplace. Then he was to build a new altar to God.

Gideon swallowed hard. His father would be very angry. And not only his father, but the townspeople would also be furious. They might even kill Gideon. Yet Gideon was ready to obey God.

He thought about it. He didn't dare destroy the altar in daylight, but it might be managed under cover of darkness.

When it was not yet light, Gideon called ten of his servants. They crept down to the marketplace. As quietly as they could, they pulled down the false altar to Baal. In its place they built an altar to God, and Gideon made a sacrifice on it as God had commanded. Then they crept home.

When the townspeople awoke the next morning, they saw what had happened. They were furious. "Who did it?" they yelled. They didn't give up their investigations until they discovered it was Gideon, son of Joash.

The townspeople turned on Joash. "Bring out your son! We shall kill him!"

Gideon quivered with fear. Would his father hand him over?

But Joash loved his son dearly. "What?" he said, thinking quickly. "Are you trying to save a god? If Baal really is a god, surely he can defend himself. Let Baal come down and kill my son."

The angry mob listened. If they acted themselves, it would seem as if they thought Baal could do nothing.

"All right," they muttered, "we'll leave it to Baal to punish him."

They waited to see what would happen. Gideon was relieved. He knew Baal had no power at all. And sure enough, he remained completely unharmed. The story soon spread.

When men from all the tribes of Israel heard that Gideon had been chosen by God to be the new leader, they came together to follow him. The sight of so many men ready to trust him almost overwhelmed Gideon. He begged God to send him another sign. God gave him two special signs. Gideon knew that the task of leader really had been given to him and that God would be with him.

He began to think about the task ahead. How could the Midianites be defeated?

Gideon and the Midianites

Gideon had decided on a battle plan. He and his thirty-two thousand men were camped by the well at Harod. The place had been wisely chosen, for the spring which rose there flowed down the hill in a stream, providing plenty of water for an army.

God spoke to Gideon. "You have too many men. If I let you overcome the Midianites with this huge army, the Israelites will say they did it by themselves without my help. Tell anyone who is afraid that they can go home."

Gideon could hardly believe what he heard. This would indeed be a strange way to speak to an army. But he obeyed. The men listened in silence. There was a pause while they looked at each other out of the corners of their eyes. Was anyone going to admit to being afraid?

First one man began to move away, then another, and another, until huge crowds of men were hurrying back toward home. Gideon watched in amazement. Twenty-two thousand men went home.

Now Gideon understood more of God's meaning. It would have been impossible to control such an enormous number of frightened men in battle. They would have been more of a hindrance than a help. Any victory would have been due to God, but no one would have believed it.

Gideon looked at the men who remained. Ten thousand men of courage would be enough.

But God said, "There are still too many." Still too many? Gideon felt anxious.

"Take the men down to the water to drink," said God. "I will show you which ones to choose."

Puzzled, Gideon ordered his men to go down to the stream. As they reached the water's edge, Gideon watched them closely. Most of the men lay on their stomachs to lap water with their tongues. Only three hundred knelt, scooping up the water in one hand.

"Those are the men to choose," said God. Then Gideon realized why. These men were alert, on guard even while they drank. The others had forgotten the enemy in their thirst.

But only three hundred? Against the entire army of the Midianites?

"With these three hundred, I will give the Midianites into your hands," God promised.

So Gideon told the other men to go back to their tents. But he was very frightened.

God understood. That night he said to Gideon, "Take your servant, Purah, and go under cover of darkness to the Midianite camp. Listen to what they are saying. You will gain courage."

It was good to be up and about rather than tossing and turning, trying to sleep. Gideon called to Purah, and together they made their way over the hills to the enemy camp.

At first sight of it in the starlight, Gideon was astounded. The valley was thick with tents. Even the camels were too many to be counted. This army was to be defeated by three hundred men?

Gideon crept down to the edge of the camp. As he sneaked up to listen outside a tent, one of the Midianites inside was telling a dream to a friend.

"I dreamed a loaf of barley bread fell on the camp, and it hit this tent so hard the tent collapsed," he said.

The other Midianite spoke in fear. "The loaf of barley bread stands for the army of Gideon, son of Joash. Their God fights for them. We shall all be destroyed."

Gideon felt a surge of joy. The Midianites were in no mood to win a battle. He praised God. Then swiftly he and Purah returned to their own camp.

"Get up!" Gideon shouted to his three hundred men. "We are attacking at once. God will give us the victory."

He divided the men into three groups. To each man he gave a trumpet and an empty jar with a torch inside it. The men looked at Gideon in amazement. Could he be serious? What kind of battle was this to be?

"Follow my lead," Gideon ordered. "We will surround the camp in the darkness. When I and my group blow our trumpets, you must blow yours and shout, 'The sword of the Lord and Gideon.' "

Tense with excitement, the small band of men crept down toward the Midianites. Splitting into three groups, they took up their positions surrounding the camp.

On the signal from Gideon, they all blew their trumpets and smashed the empty jars. Holding up the torches in their left hands, they yelled their battle cry, "The sword of the Lord and Gideon."

The shouting, the trumpets, the sound of the jars being smashed, and the light of the torches startled the

sleeping Midianites. In the darkness, noise, and confusion of the tents, each man believed the other was one of the Israelites whose attack they had been dreading. The Midianites began to kill each other. Gideon's astonished army stood firm as the escaping Midianites rushed away from the camp in all directions.

When light dawned, there were only a small number of men left to fight. Gideon's army was victorious, as God had promised.

The Israelites were delighted and wanted Gideon to rule over them.

Gideon refused. "No, God will rule over you." And as long as Gideon was alive, there was peace in the land. The Israelites worshiped the true God.

But Gideon died. And there were more wars and more leaders. The Israelites had many enemies. Among their enemies were the Philistines. Because the Israelites were again doing wrong, God allowed the Philistines to overcome them.

For forty years the Israelites suffered under the Philistines. But God was about to choose the man who would begin to free them.

Samson and Delilah

Samson was the man chosen by God to help free Israel from the Philistines.

Samson was immensely strong and had a terrible temper. He was always in trouble, either with his own people or with his enemies, the Philistines. For years the Philistines had plotted to capture him, but Samson had always escaped by using the strength given to him by God.

At last the Philistines realized that the only way they would ever catch Samson would be by trickery. So they watched and waited. One day they learned that he had fallen in love with a woman named Delilah.

"Here's our chance," said the Philistines. They promised Delilah large sums of money if she could discover what made Samson so strong.

Delilah was no true friend of Samson nor of the Israelites. She was greedy for the money, so she asked Samson about his secret.

"How could anyone possibly tie you up?" she asked, pretending to be playing. For a while Samson teased her with wrong answers. Each time, Delilah told the Philistines what he'd said. Each time, the Philistines had men hiding in the room, ready to spring out and capture Samson as soon as Delilah had tied him up. But each time, Samson easily broke the bonds before the men had shown themselves.

Delilah kept on asking, and finally Samson told her. "My strength lies in my hair, which has never been cut. If my head were shaved, my strength would leave me."

Quickly Delilah sent yet another message to the Philistines. Secretly they came, bringing her promised reward with them. Then while the Philistines hid nearby, Delilah coaxed Samson to sleep with his head in her lap. And while he slept, a man cut off all Samson's hair.

Then Delilah cried, "Samson, wake up! The Philistines are upon you!"

Samson jumped to his feet, thinking his strength would save him yet again. But his strength was gone. Then Samson realized that his head had been shaved.

109

The Philistines blinded him, put him in chains, and took him to the prison. There they set him to heavy work at the grinding mill. Dejected and humbled, Samson struggled with the task.

But while he was in prison, his hair started to grow again.

Some time later, the Philistines held a celebration. It was partly in honor of their god Dagon and partly because they had captured Samson. In the middle of the feast, they called for Samson to be brought, so that they could taunt him.

In shuffled the once proud Samson, totally blind, a boy leading him by the hand. Amid the jeers of the crowd, Samson was forced to perform for them. But he managed to whisper to the boy, ''Put me near the pillars that hold up this building so that I can lean on them.''

The boy did so. Samson could tell that the temple building was crowded with people. More than three thousand men and women were present. Most were on the roof watching Samson. Samson prayed, ''God, give me my strength just once more.''

He reached toward the two main pillars which held up the temple. He put his right hand on one pillar, and he put his left hand on the other. Then Samson said to God, ''Let me die with the Philistines.''

With a mighty effort, he pushed the pillars apart. Down crashed the building, killing the rulers and many others. Samson died in the middle of his enemies.

Naomi, Ruth, and Boaz

At the time when the judges were ruling in Israel, there was a famine in the land. Elimelech, who had been born in Bethlehem, took his wife Naomi and his two sons, Mahlon and Chilion, to live in the country of Moab. Elimelech died there, leaving Naomi a widow.

Her sons married two Moabite women, Orpah and Ruth. Later Mahlon and Chilion also died.

When the famine was over, Naomi wanted to return to her own people. So she and her daughters-in-law set out on the journey back to Bethlehem.

Before they had gone far, Naomi stopped. If she took Ruth and Orpah to Bethlehem, they would be far from their own people. Naomi knew how lonely that felt, so she said, "You must each go back to the home of your mother. You've been very good to me, and I hope you'll soon find new husbands in your own land."

The girls looked lovingly at Naomi. "No!" they cried. "We'll come with you."

But in those days a woman without a family to protect her would have a very hard life. Naomi spoke as firmly as she could through her tears. "I'm never going to have any more sons who would be your husbands. Besides, they would be too young for you. You must go back."

They were all crying now. Weeping bitterly, Orpah kissed Naomi goodbye and started off toward home. But Ruth clung to her mother-in-law.

"Don't ask me to leave you," she sobbed, "nor to return from following after you. For wherever you go, I will go. Where you live, I will live. Your people shall be my people and your God, my God. Wherever you die, I will die and there be buried. Nothing but death shall separate us."

Then Naomi hugged and kissed Ruth, and the two of them went on together.

At last they reached Bethlehem. The people who had known the family years before stared at them. "Is it really you, Naomi?" they asked, hardly recognizing her.

"Don't call me Naomi," she answered. "Call me Mara, 'bitter,' because my husband and sons are dead."

Ruth tried to comfort her mother-in-law. They both felt very lonely. But Naomi did have some relatives in Bethlehem. One of them was a man named Boaz, who owned some fields nearby.

It was the time of the barley harvest. Ruth said, "We must have food. Let me go out to the fields and pick up the grain which the harvesters leave behind on the ground. Then we will be able to make bread and eat."

"Very well. Go," said Naomi.

So with the other people who were too poor to get grain any other way, Ruth went to the fields to glean.

She unknowingly chose to work in

the field which belonged to Boaz. It was hard work. Gleaners had to bend low to see the grain, and it could take all day in the hot sun to fill even a small sack. By evening the gleaners' backs were aching painfully, and their eyes could hardly see.

When Ruth had been working for some hours, Boaz came by. He called a greeting to the harvesters. Then he noticed Ruth.

"Who is that girl?" he asked his foreman.

"Her name is Ruth," the man answered. "She came back from Moab with Naomi, your relative. Early this morning she asked if she could glean here. She has hardly stopped to rest all day."

Boaz called to Ruth to come to him. Nervously she approached. Would he send her away?

"Don't go to any other fields. Stay in mine," said Boaz. "And if you are thirsty, drink from my water jars. I'll tell the men not to bother you."

Ruth was very grateful. "Why are you being so kind?" she asked. "I'm a foreigner here."

"I've heard how good you are to Naomi," Boaz answered. "May God bless you because of it. Come and share our meal with us."

Thankfully Ruth obeyed. She had been feeling very hungry. But as soon as she had eaten enough, she went back to work.

Boaz watched her for a moment. Then he said to his men, "Let her take as much grain as she wants. Drop some for her to pick up."

Ruth gleaned all day. In the evening she threshed the grain she had gathered and took the barley home to Naomi.

Naomi was amazed. "However did you get this much?" she asked. "Where did you glean?"

"In the field belonging to Boaz," Ruth replied.

"He is one of our close relatives," Naomi answered thoughtfully.

In those days if a man died, it was usual for his brother or closest relative to marry the widow. He would take responsibility for her and for the dead man's land.

Naomi instructed Ruth to make her need for a husband known to Boaz. He was not Ruth's closest relative, but he wanted to marry her. Before he could do that, he had to settle things with the man who was her closest relative.

Boaz went to the city gate to speak to the man. "Do you want to buy the piece of land which belonged to Elimelech?" he asked. "It is your right as closest relative. If you don't want it, I'll buy it."

"Well, yes, I do want it," said the man. Boaz had expected this. "If you buy the land, the law is that you must also marry Ruth so that the field stays in Elimelech's family," he said.

The man thought again. "Then I won't buy it," he said. "It would get in the way of the rights of my own children."

So in front of witnesses, Boaz bought the land. Now he was not only free to marry Ruth, it was the law that he should.

Boaz and Ruth were married. They had a son called Obed. In time Obed had a son called Jesse. And Jesse had a son called David. David was to become king of Israel, a great man.

But first, there were many more years while the judges ruled Israel—years during which the boy Samuel was born.

1 Samuel 1:1-28; 2:18-21; 3

Samuel in the Temple

There were two Israelite women, Hannah and Peninnah, who were both married to the same man, Elkanah. (It was the custom in those days for a man to have more than one wife.) Peninnah had lots of children, but Hannah had none.

Every year Elkanah and his whole family went to the Temple at Shiloh. There they worshiped God and made a sacrifice to him. Elkanah always gave portions of the meat to Peninnah and her children, but he gave twice as large a portion to Hannah because he loved her very much, knowing how she felt about having no children.

Peninnah also knew, and every year she made things much worse for Hannah by teasing her cruelly.

"What's wrong?" Elkanah asked tenderly. "Am I not worth more to you than ten children?"

But Hannah wept and refused food. Later when she went to the Temple, she prayed desperately to God. "Lord, if you will only let me have a baby son, I promise I will give him back to you. He shall serve you all his life."

Eli the priest noticed her. When he heard her story, he spoke kindly. "Peace be to you. May the Lord God give you what you ask."

Hannah felt better. She even felt hungry enough to eat some food.

The family returned home to Ramah, and before too long Hannah did indeed have a baby boy. She was overjoyed and named him Samuel. She loved him very much, but she hadn't forgotten her promise to God.

That year when Elkanah and the family went to Shiloh, Hannah and the baby stayed at home.

"He's too young to leave me yet," she said, cradling Samuel in her arms.

115

"Do whatever you think is best," Elkanah answered gently.

Another year went by. Hannah watched her baby growing bigger. Soon he was able to walk, able to run, beginning to talk. Sometimes her heart ached, but she never faltered in her resolve.

Finally when the child had been weaned, Hannah knew it was time to complete her promise. That year when it was the time for sacrifice, Hannah and Samuel went to the Temple at Shiloh with the others.

Elkanah made the sacrifice. Then with a pounding heart, Hannah carried her tiny boy over to where Eli the priest stood. Elkanah was beside her, but it was Hannah who spoke.

"Do you remember me?" she asked Eli. "I'm the woman who prayed so hard for a child. This is the boy God gave to us. Now I give him back to God."

So Hannah left Samuel with Eli the priest to grow up in the Temple, and she and Elkanah returned to Ramah.

At first they missed Samuel very much, but they saw him every year when they made their visit to Shiloh. Hannah always took new clothes for him, and Eli always blessed Hannah and Elkanah, asking God to send them more children. Before long Hannah had three more boys and two girls, so she was happy.

Eli was very glad to have Samuel. His own two sons were wicked and no comfort to him.

As Samuel grew up, he listened as Eli taught him about God, and he helped more and more in the work of the Temple.

One night the boy was lying on his bed in the Temple near the Ark of the Covenant when he heard a voice call his name.

"Samuel."

Samuel had been almost asleep. Now he quickly awoke. He sat up. Who had spoken? In the dim light of the lamp which was always kept burning, he looked around.

There was no one to be seen. It must have been Eli calling him. Eli was old now and almost blind. Maybe something was wrong. Samuel sprang up and ran to Eli's bedside. "Here I am," he panted. "You called me."

Eli was puzzled. "I didn't call you," he said. "Go back to bed."

Perhaps he had been dreaming. Samuel went back and lay down.

"Samuel."

The voice called again. Samuel scrambled to his feet and ran in to Eli. "Here I am. You did call me," he said.

"No," said Eli, still not properly awake. "I didn't call you. Go and lie down."

Slowly Samuel made his way back and lay down. He was wide awake. He lay there in the near darkness, and the voice called again.

"Samuel."

Samuel got up slowly. Slowly he went to Eli. Taking a deep breath, he said, "Here I am. You did call me."

Now Eli was fully awake too. He realized what was happening. God himself was calling Samuel.

"Go and lie down," Eli said gently.

"And if you hear the voice again, say, 'Speak, Lord. Your servant is listening.' "

Once more Samuel lay down in the Temple near the Ark of the Covenant.

Half excited and half afraid, he waited. Again God spoke.

"Samuel."

Samuel found his voice. "Speak, Lord. Your servant is listening," he said.

Then God gave Samuel a message for Eli. It was such a sad message that as Samuel listened, he wanted to cry. He didn't go rushing in to tell Eli. He lay still.

In the morning he got up and started work, trying to keep out of Eli's way. But Eli called him over. "Samuel, my son, what did God say to you?"

Then Eli saw the look on the boy's face. "Don't be afraid to tell me," he said gently.

So Samuel repeated the message. Eli's family was to be punished because of the wickedness of Eli's two sons.

"God knows best," Eli answered quietly. "Let him do whatever seems right to him."

As Samuel grew older, all the Israelites knew that God was with him, and they listened to his words.

But before long the punishment of Eli's family and the Israelites was to begin.

The Philistines and the Ark of the Covenant

The Israelites were again fighting with the Philistines, but this time, because of the wickedness of the Israelites, God allowed the Philistines to overcome them.

"Let us take the Ark of the Covenant into battle with us," cried the leaders of the Israelites when their defeated army came straggling back. "The Ark will give us victory."

So some men went to Shiloh to get the Ark, and Eli's two sons were among the priests who came back with it.

When the weary Israelites saw the Ark of the Covenant being carried into their camp, they gave a great shout of gladness.

Over in their own camp, the Philistines heard it. "What's going on over there?" they wondered. A defeated army did not usually shout in triumph.

The Philistines sent spies out. Later the spies came back saying, "A god has come into the camp of the Israelites."

Then the Philistines were even more afraid. They said, "We must fight harder or the Israelites will make us their slaves."

So the Philistines attacked with all their might. Thousands of Israelites were killed, including Eli's sons. Worst yet, the Ark of the Covenant was captured by the Philistine army.

A messenger ran from the battlefield to Shiloh. His clothes were torn and dust was on his head. As soon as the townspeople saw him, they guessed the battle was lost. When they heard the whole truth, there was a tremendous commotion from the heartbroken Israelites.

Eli was completely blind now. He had been sitting anxiously on a seat by the side of the road, waiting for news of his sons. When he heard the cries of the people, he asked desperately, "What is it? What's happening?"

The messenger hurried over to the old man. "I've just come from the battlefield," he said.

"And?" Eli asked.

The messenger swallowed hard. "Israel was defeated. Your sons are dead. And the Ark of the Covenant has been captured."

With the news of the Ark, Eli fell back off his seat and died of a broken neck.

The triumphant Philistines had carried the Ark into the temple of their god Dagon in Ashdod. But when they came back in the morning, Dagon had fallen flat on his face in front of the Ark.

The Philistines stood him up again. But the next morning not only was Dagon lying flat on the ground, but his head and his hands were broken off as well. The people of Ashdod became afflicted by tumors, and they begged their rulers to take the Ark away.

The Ark was moved to Gath. The people of Gath became ill. They were terrified and sent the Ark to Ekron. But when the people of Ekron saw it being brought into the city, they called out, ''Don't bring it here or we shall all die! Send it back to the Israelites.''

The frightened Philistines asked their priests how they should return the Ark.

''You must send it with an offering to show you are sorry,'' the priests replied. So the Philistines placed the Ark in a cart, with images of golden rats and golden tumors in a chest beside it. They harnessed to the cart two milk cows that had never been yoked and set if off along the road toward Beth Shemesh where the Israelites were.

The people of Beth Shemesh were harvesting in their fields. When they saw the driverless cart coming down the road, they realized the Ark of the Covenant was inside. As they watched, spellbound, the cart stopped beside the field of Joshua. The Israelites ran to it and lifted out the Ark with great rejoicing.

When the watching Philistines saw that the Ark was safely back, they returned to Ekron, breathing sighs of relief.

The Israelites sacrificed the two milk cows to God. When Samuel heard the news of the Ark's return, he said, ''If you are really ready to serve the Lord God, destroy all your false gods.''

The Israelites obeyed. Before long the Philistine army again attacked. But now God was on the side of the Israelites. The Philistines were soundly defeated.

For many years there was peace in the country, but then the Israelites grew restless.

The Israelites Demand a King

Samuel was growing old. He was too old to go on ruling over the Israelites, so he appointed his two sons in his place. But his sons were unjust and took bribes.

The people complained. ''We want a king to rule over us,'' they declared. Samuel was distressed. He prayed to God about it.

''Tell them,'' said God, ''if they do have a king, he will treat them harshly. They will cry to me for help, and I will not listen to their cries.''

Samuel gave God's message to the people, but they paid no attention. ''We want a king,'' they repeated stubbornly. ''Besides, if we have a king, we shall be like all the other nations.''

Samuel told God what the people said.

''Very well,'' said God. ''We shall give them a king.''

Saul Becomes King

Saul was a young Israelite of the tribe of Benjamin. One day his father, Kish, said to Saul, "Our donkeys have strayed. Take one of the servants and go look for them."

Saul obeyed. He and the servant walked many miles, searching for the animals without success. After three days Saul said wearily, "Let's go back or my father will be more worried about us than he is about the donkeys."

"Wait," said the servant. "I've heard of a holy man who lives in a town near here. Let's see if he can advise us which way to go."

"All right," said Saul. So they set off to find Samuel, the holy man.

Only the day before, God had said to Samuel, "The man whom you must anoint as king of Israel will come to you tomorrow. He will be from the tribe of Benjamin."

Now Samuel stood at the gateway of the town. As soon as he caught sight of Saul coming toward him, God said to Samuel, "This is the man."

Saul unsuspectingly walked straight up to Samuel. "Will you tell me how to get to the house of the holy man?" he asked.

Samuel answered quietly, "I am the man for whom you are looking. Come and have a meal with me. Don't worry any more about the donkeys that were lost three days ago. They have been found."

While Saul still gazed at him in astonishment, Samuel said, "You are the man the people of Israel have been wanting."

"What?" responded Saul. "But I come from the smallest tribe in Israel. And my family is of no importance even in our small tribe."

"Come," said Samuel. Saul and his servant went with Samuel. They shared a meal with about thirty people, and Samuel ordered that Saul be given a special portion of meat. Afterward Samuel took Saul up to the roof of his house. They sat in the cool light of the stars and talked. When Saul grew sleepy, Samuel gave him a bed on the roof.

The next morning Saul awoke refreshed. Then he and his servant set out for home. At the edge of town, the servant was sent on ahead while Samuel quietly anointed Saul's head with oil in the ceremony that was to be used to anoint Israel's kings throughout the years. Samuel told Saul signs by which Saul could know he really was the man chosen by God to be king of Israel.

Saul set off along the road with his thoughts whirling. By the time he reached home, God had spoken to him through several signs. Saul's behavior was so different that his family wondered what had happened to him. But Saul did not yet tell them of his encounter with Samuel.

Then Samuel called the Israelites together. "You wanted a king," Samuel said. "Now God will show you who it is to be."

One by one, all the tribes of Israel came forward, but Samuel sent each tribe back until the tribe of Benjamin approached him. After choosing the tribe of Benjamin, Samuel saw each family in the tribe and chose the family of Kish. Finally, Saul was chosen, but he was nowhere to be found.

The people asked God, "Where is Saul?"

"He's hiding among your possessions," answered God.

Then the people ran and found Saul, and they brought him out. As Saul stood in front of them, he was unsure whether to be proud or embarrassed, because he was much taller than anyone else there.

"See the man whom God has chosen," announced Samuel. "There is no one like him."

"Long live the king," shouted the Israelites.

Then Samuel explained to the people exactly what the powers of a king were and what rules should be kept. Then he wrote everything down, so that there might be no misunderstandings.

So Saul became king and began his rule over the Israelites. Samuel warned the people, "Remember what great things God has done for you. Love and serve God faithfully, for if you keep doing wrong, you and your king will be overcome by your enemies."

David, Jesse's Son

At first Saul ruled well and kept God's laws. He had a son, Jonathan, whom he loved dearly.

But after some years, Saul grew proud. He began to do as he wanted and then made excuses to Samuel.

"Your kingdom won't last," Samuel warned him sadly, "because you keep disobeying God."

Finally God said to Samuel, "How much more time are you going to waste being sad about Saul? I no longer want him to be king. Go to Bethlehem to the house of a man called Jesse. I've chosen one of his sons to be the next king. You must go and anoint the boy."

"If Saul discovers why I've gone, he'll kill me," protested Samuel.

God said, "Go to Bethlehem, but take a calf with you. Tell the people there that you have come to make a sacrifice."

Samuel loved and trusted God, so he took the calf as God had commanded. When he reached Bethlehem, the elders of the city came out to meet him with fear on their faces.

"Why have you come?" they asked nervously.

"I have come in peace," Samuel reassured them. "I'm going to offer a sacrifice to God here."

Then he sent a message to Jesse, asking him to bring his sons to the sacrifice.

Jesse and seven of his sons hurried to wash themselves and put on clean clothes, as was the custom before making a sacrifice. Then they came to Samuel.

One at a time, Jesse ordered his sons to stand in front of the holy man. When Samuel saw Eliab, the eldest, he thought this must be the one, for Eliab was very handsome.

"No," said God. "You are looking only at the outside of a person. I look at his heart. What a person believes, how he feels, and the way he acts are more important than the way he looks. I have not chosen Eliab."

The next son stood in front of Samuel, and the next, until all seven had stood there. But still God made no sign.

Samuel was puzzled. Then he had an idea. "Have you any more sons?" he asked.

Jesse stared at Samuel in surprise.

"Only David," he replied. "He's the youngest. He's out looking after the sheep."

"Send for him," Samuel ordered.

Soon David arrived, flushed and panting. He was handsome and his eyes were full of courage.

"This is the one," God said to Samuel. "Anoint his head with oil."

Samuel obeyed. David's father and brothers watched in amazement. Did this mean David was to be a follower of Samuel?

Samuel did not explain. David went back to tending the sheep. But from that day, the Spirit of the Lord was with him.

Soon God's plan for David began to take shape.

David Meets Saul

The Spirit of the Lord was no longer with Saul. Instead, he felt tormented, utterly sad, and hopeless. At times he felt angry and violent.

Saul's servants noticed that music could soothe him and would often cure him for a while.

"Sir," they said, "why not appoint a musician to your court? Then he could play for you whenever the distressing spirit comes upon you."

"Find me a musician," Saul ordered. "But he must play well."

Then one of his servants answered, "Sir, I know of a musician. He sings his own songs and plays the harp. He plays extremely well. He is a brave young man who would make a very good warrior. He is a son of Jesse of Bethlehem, and the Spirit of the Lord is with him."

"Send for him," commanded Saul.

Messengers rushed to Bethlehem. "King Saul wants to see your son David," they told Jesse. Jesse was puzzled by this new interest in his youngest son.

Once more David was called in from tending the sheep. Hurriedly he was told the news, and almost before he could take it in, David found himself being hustled into clean clothes for the journey. Jesse rushed about to find some gifts David could take to the king.

Soon David set off with the messengers and the gifts: a donkey loaded with bread, a skinful of wine, and a young goat.

"Where's your harp?" asked the messenger. "Don't forget that."

"It is here," said David. He always had his harp with him.

When they arrived at the court, David was taken to the king. Saul liked the look of him at once. "You shall be one of my armorbearers," Saul announced. And he sent a messenger to Jesse asking that David be allowed to stay for a while.

After that, David lived partly with Saul's men and partly at home, caring for the sheep.

But whenever the distressing spirit came upon Saul, David was sent for. He hurried to court and played his harp until the beautiful sounds calmed Saul's tormented mind.

But trouble was coming for the Israelites.

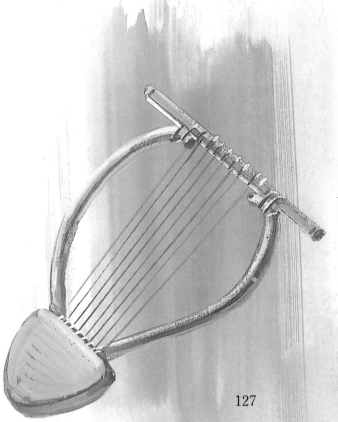

127

1 Samuel 17:1-52; 18:2

David and Goliath

The army of the Philistines marched into the land of the Israelites, intending to occupy it. King Saul gathered his army to repel the Philistines, and the two armies set up camp on either side of a valley. Neither army wished to start the battle, because whoever attacked first would be at a disadvantage, having to fight uphill. The soldiers would be an easy target for the spears and arrows which the enemy would hurl down.

It seemed as if the armies would be there forever. Then one day, out from the Philistine camp marched Goliath, an enormous man over nine feet tall. He was protected by heavy armor, and he carried a huge spear. Goliath bellowed a challenge across the valley to King Saul's army.

"If any man can defeat me single-handedly, we will be your slaves. But if I defeat him, you Israelites will be our slaves."

His voice echoed around the mountains, and instead of taking up his challenge, King Saul's men turned away in fear.

King Saul offered a reward of immense riches and marriage to his daughter to the man who would fight Goliath. But no one volunteered. Every day Goliath hurled his challenge across the valley. Every day Saul's men cowered in a silence of fear and anger.

In Saul's army were three of David's older brothers. David was looking after the sheep at home when his father, Jesse, called to him. "I want you to go and see how your brothers are doing," he said. "Bring me word from them. Take them this food and these presents."

Gladly David set out. It was a half-day's walk, but he kept going until at last he could see the tents of King Saul's army.

Just as he reached the camp, the army was ordered to go to their battle positions. Eagerly David left the gifts with the keeper of supplies and ran to find his brothers.

Before he could do more than greet them, Goliath marched out from the camp of the Philistine army and yelled his challenge.

David waited, expecting someone to spring forward in reply. Instead the Israelites turned away.

David couldn't believe his ears and eyes. "Who is this man who challenges the army of God's people?" he asked. "If no one else will fight him, I will!"

"You?" jeered his brothers. "We

know how you love to show off. You only came to watch the battle. Go home and look after the sheep.''

David flushed angrily, but he had learned self-control. He answered quietly, ''Can't I even speak?''

He talked to more of the soldiers, and some of them went to tell the king what David was saying.

Saul sent for David. Soon David stood in front of the king. David's heart beat quickly, but he spoke steadily.

''No one needs to be afraid of Goliath. I will fight him.''

''You?'' responded Saul. ''You're only a youth. He's a trained fighting man.''

''I am a shepherd,'' David answered. ''When a bear came to carry off a lamb, I killed it. Another time I had to kill a lion. God saved me from the lion and the bear, and God will save me from this Philistine.''

So King Saul said, ''Very well. Go, and the Lord be with you.'' The king put his own armor on David and gave him a sword.

Clank, clank, David tried to walk. He could hardly move. The armor was too heavy, and David had not been trained to fight with a sword. He struggled out of the armor and put on his own shepherd's tunic. Then he took his rod and his shepherd's sling, the sling from which he'd often thrown stones to drive wild animals away from the sheep. David went out to face Goliath.

A silence fell over the whole valley. David's brothers watched, hardly daring to breathe.

Calmly David walked down to the little stream which flowed through the valley. Bending down, he carefully picked out five smooth, round stones from the water's edge. Then he stood up and spoke clearly. ''I am ready,'' he said.

Goliath stepped forward and saw David. ''You're just a boy! You dare to challenge me? Am I a dog that you come to fight me with a stick? I'll cut you into pieces and give you to the birds and beasts to eat.''

David replied steadily, ''I come in the name of God. He is with me. I will kill you, Goliath, and everyone will know that the God of the Israelites is the one true God.''

Furious, Goliath moved forward to attack. But David rushed ahead and placed one of the stones in his sling. Then he whirled the sling around.

The stone flew straight as an arrow, striking Goliath's forehead with full force. Down fell the giant, flat on the ground. David ran forward, took Goliath's own sword, and cut off the giant's head.

When the Philistines saw that their champion was dead, they turned and ran. With a great shout, King Saul's army pursued them. The Philistines were defeated thoroughly and chased out of the country.

On that day King Saul took David in, and he lived with the king. For a while, David was happy in the palace, but more trouble was coming.

David and Saul

David's life had changed completely. He was treated as if he were King Saul's own son. And Saul's son Jonathan, far from being jealous, became David's greatest friend.

Whatever Saul asked David to do, David did well. Whenever David led his men in battle against the Philistines, the Israelites won. At first Saul was pleased. But soon he noticed how popular David was becoming. The Israelite women sang a song: "Saul has killed thousands in his battles, but David has killed tens of thousands."

When Saul heard those words, he fumed, "I suppose soon he'll be wanting my kingdom."

The next day the distressing spirit came upon Saul. As always, he sent for David, who played his harp in an attempt to soothe Saul. Saul sat watching the boy while dark and angry thoughts grew in his mind.

Saul remembered how everyone had praised David far more than they had praised the king. Perhaps David really might be the man God had chosen to be king in Saul's place. The thought was too much. Without warning, Saul sprang up and hurled a spear at David, meaning to pin him to the wall.

Although David was taken completely by surprise, he was too quick for Saul. David leaped to one side. Twice Saul hurled a spear. Twice David escaped by leaping aside. David stood panting and watchful, ready to dodge yet again.

But Saul realized he could never harm David that way. He would need a plan. Saul ordered David to leave.

Later Saul made David captain over a thousand soldiers, thinking that when David next led the soldiers into battle, he would be killed. But David was not killed. He fought bravely and won many honors, because God was with him. David behaved so wisely and so well that the people loved and praised him more than ever.

Saul pretended to be friendly toward David, but inwardly his hatred and fury grew. Then his daughter Michal fell in love with David.

"I can use her love as a trap," schemed Saul. He sent his servants with a message to David. "The king is pleased that his daughter loves you," said the servants. "You can marry her and become his son-in-law."

"What?" replied David. "I'm a poor man. I can't marry a princess."

Secretly delighted to hear that David had answered as expected, Saul sent another message. "The king says you may marry the princess if you will pay the price."

"What price?" asked David, puzzled. Saul knew he had no riches of his own.

"No gift is required, only you must provide proof that one hundred of the king's enemy, the Philistines, have been killed," said the servant.

"I accept," said David. Saul was overjoyed. Surely David would be killed now in trying to kill one hundred men.

But David killed not only the hundred Philistines that Saul required,

but two hundred. Inwardly raging, Saul was forced to honor his promise, and David married Saul's daughter Michal.

Saul made plan after plan to trap David, but each time David escaped unharmed, once with the help of his wife, Michal.

Saul could hide his anger no longer. He went to Jonathan and his servants. "Catch David and kill him," he ordered.

But Jonathan was David's friend and would never harm him. Slipping away from the camp, Jonathan hurried to warn David.

"My father wants to kill you. Tonight you must go into hiding. I'll speak to my father about you, and I'll warn you when he is about to move against you."

So David hid. The next morning Jonathan went to Saul and asked, "Why do you want to harm David? He has served you faithfully."

As Jonathan pleaded, Saul listened, and his anger melted away. Saul made a promise. "As surely as our God is alive, David will not be killed by me."

Gladly Jonathan ran to tell David and bring him back to Saul. For a short time, the friends were as happy as before. But soon war again broke out. David fought as bravely as ever. Again the people shouted his praises, and Saul, far from being grateful to David, felt the old hatred return.

Saul was again troubled by a dark spirit. Remembering that his music had often calmed the king, David took his harp and began to play. But this time, music did not help. Saul seized a spear and once again tried to pin David to the wall. As before, David was able to avoid Saul. Overcome with his rage, Saul drove the spear deep into the wall.

David knew he must get away.

David and Jonathan

David began running from King Saul. But the king's men chased David from place to place. After many months of running, David grew tired and weary. He needed to talk to Jonathan.

"Why is your father trying to have me killed?" he asked.

"He's not," said Jonathan. "He promised. Besides, he never does anything without telling me. Why should he hide this? It isn't true."

But David answered, "Your father knows we're friends, and he doesn't want to upset you. But I tell you there's only one step between me and death."

David was so certain that Jonathan agreed to do whatever his friend thought best.

The next day was a special festival, and David was to dine with the king. Instead, David planned to hide in a field where Jonathan practiced shooting his arrows. Jonathan, however, would dine with Saul. If the king grew very angry because David was missing, Jonathan would know for certain that Saul was still plotting David's death.

"Who will tell me what happens?" asked David, afraid to trust anyone.

"I will tell you myself," Jonathan replied. "We'll have a secret sign. I'll shoot my arrows to land near your hiding place. Then I'll send a boy to bring them back for me. If I call out to him, 'Look, the arrows are on this side of you,' you'll know everything is safe. But if I say, 'Look, the arrows are over there. They've gone beyond you,' it means you must escape quickly."

So it was arranged. While Jonathan dined with the king, Saul asked where David was. As Jonathan spoke about David, Saul's face grew purple with rage. Saul was so angry, he hurled a spear at Jonathan.

Jonathan knew that David was right. Sadly he went to the field. After shooting an arrow, he sent his assistant to retrieve it. Jonathan called out, "Look, hasn't the arrow gone beyond you? Hurry, go quickly."

David understood the secret message. Jonathan told the boy to take the arrows back to the town. David came out of hiding. He wouldn't leave without saying good-bye to his friend Jonathan.

Both friends were very sad. They knew they might never see each other again. David must go at once. Jonathan could only remind him that they would always be true friends.

As long as Saul lived, he made no

peace with David. Twice David had Saul at his mercy, yet spared his life.

Finally Saul fought his last battle with the Philistines. Jonathan and Saul's two other sons were killed in the battle, and Saul was badly wounded. Rather than allow the Philistines to kill him, Saul took his own sword and fell on it. As he was dying, he asked an Amalekite to give him the final blow.

When David heard the news, he mourned bitterly for his friend Jonathan. He was also sad about Saul. David wrote a song about it. "How the mighty are fallen! Tell it not in Gath, lest the daughters of the Philistines rejoice. Saul and Jonathan were lovely and pleasant in their lives, and in death they were not divided. They were swifter than eagles; they were stronger than lions. How the mighty are fallen in the middle of the battle! I am distressed for you, my brother Jonathan. Your love to me was wonderful. How the mighty are fallen!"

In due time David was made king of Israel in Saul's place. One of his first tasks was to capture Jerusalem from the Jebusites. He made it the capital city of Israel, and it was called "The City of David." He brought the Ark of the Covenant to Jerusalem, and there was a great feast with singing and dancing. David wanted to build a temple so that the Ark might be kept in it, but God said, "No. Not David, but one of his sons shall build the Temple in Jerusalem."

All this time David had not forgotten his friend Jonathan. "Are none of his family left alive?" David asked.

"Jonathan's son still lives," his servants answered. "He is named Mephibosheth, and he is a cripple. He cannot walk properly."

David sent for Mephibosheth and for Jonathan's sake gave back to him all the land which had belonged to Saul. Mephibosheth lived at the palace with David and was treated kindly.

After many years David was old and knew he was about to die. He sent for his son Solomon. David's voice was weak as he spoke to Solomon.

"I am going the way of all flesh on earth," said David. "You must be strong. Do as the Lord says. Walk in his ways. Lead the people of Israel to do right in his eyes. Then the Lord will keep his promises to Israel. Be wise, my son, and show yourself to be a man."

David gave a few more instructions to Solomon. Then wearily, he lay back on his pillows and fell asleep. And in his sleep, he died.

During David's long life, he wrote many songs. Some of David's songs, called psalms, are still sung today. They are contained in the Book of Psalms.

A Psalm of David

The Lord is my shepherd; I shall not want.
He makes me to lie down in green pastures;
   he leads me beside the still waters.
He restores my soul; he leads me in the paths of
   righteousness for his name's sake.
Yea, though I walk through the valley of the shadow
   of death, I will fear no evil, for you are with me;
   your rod and your staff, they comfort me.
You prepare a table before me in the presence of my
   enemies; you anoint my head with oil; my cup runs over.
Surely goodness and mercy shall follow me all the days
   of my life; and I will dwell in the house of the Lord
   forever.

1 Kings 3; 4:34; 5:4, 5

Solomon's Wisdom

After David died, Solomon became the ruler of thousands of Israelites. He felt he could never cope with it. People kept bringing problems to him which he was expected to solve. And his father, David, was not there to advise him.

Solomon tried to follow his father's instructions and keep God's laws. His people were still making sacrifices in many places of worship because there was no temple.

One day Solomon himself went to Gibeon to offer a sacrifice. That night as he lay sleeping, God came to him in a dream. "Solomon," said God, "what gift would you like to have from me?"

"Oh," said Solomon, "give me wisdom. I am so young, and I don't know how to give the right answers when people bring me their problems. I don't know how to rule your people wisely."

God was pleased. "You haven't asked to be rich or to have a long life. You haven't even asked that I give you victory over your enemies. Because you have asked for wisdom, I will give it to you. You shall be wiser than anyone ever was. No one shall ever be as wise as you again. And I will give you the honor and wealth which you did not ask for. If you keep my laws, I will give you a long life as well."

Solomon stirred in his sleep, woke up, and opened his eyes. Had it just been a dream?

In the morning Solomon went up to Jerusalem to offer a sacrifice. Then he held a great feast for all the members of his court.

Two women asked for an audience with him. One of them carried a baby in her arms.

"My Lord Solomon," pleaded the other woman, "this woman and I share a house. I had a baby. Three days later, she had a baby. During the night, her baby died because she rolled over on him in her sleep. There was no one else in the house, and I was asleep. She took my baby and put her dead baby beside me. When I woke up, I started to feed my son and saw that he was dead. I cried and cried. But when the morning light came, I looked at him, and I could see it wasn't my baby at all. She had my baby."

"No," cried the second woman, hugging the baby to her. "She's lying. Her baby died. This one is mine."

"One of you is lying," said Solomon. "The baby cannot belong to both of you. Tell me the truth."

"I am telling you the truth," they both said.

Solomon searched desperately in his mind for an answer to the problem. An idea came to him.

"Bring a sword," he ordered. There was a puzzled silence in the court. Everyone watched as a soldier came forward with a sword.

"Now," said Solomon, "the child shall be cut in half. You can each have half."

"No!" screamed the first woman. "That would kill the baby!"

But the second woman nodded. "It is fair. Neither of us should have him. Divide him in two." The soldier lifted the sword.

Sobbing, the first woman pleaded with the king. "No, no, give the baby to her. Don't kill him!"

The soldier looked at Solomon.

Solomon spoke. "Give the baby to the first woman. She is his real mother. It is obvious who truly loves the child."

Still sobbing, the woman took her baby and held him close. Because of this, all the people marveled at Solomon's wisdom.

Solomon continued to give wise judgments. In only four years as king, he became rich and powerful as God had promised. People of all nations came to listen to him and ask for help with their own problems. Each one brought gifts.

Solomon wanted to show his love for God. It was time to start building the Temple where God could be worshiped, where the Ark of the Covenant could be kept in safety and with honor.

Building the Temple

The work of building the Temple began. Solomon wanted only the most skilled craftsmen to work on it and only the finest of materials to be used. To search for these, he sent messengers to all parts of Israel and beyond.

Materials began to arrive. Sweet-smelling cedar wood from Lebanon was used for the walls and ceilings. Pine trees were sawed into planks for the floors. All the stone used was cut and shaped in the quarries, so that no sound of iron tools should disturb the peace of the Temple Courts, even

141

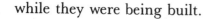

while they were being built.

The Temple was about ninety feet long, thirty feet wide, and over forty-five feet high. It was three stories high. It had an inner room, called the Holy of Holies, or Most Holy Place. In the inner room was the altar where the Ark of the Covenant would be placed.

Two cherubim were carved from olive wood and overlaid with gold. They were placed so that their wings would be outstretched over the Ark. All the walls were beautifully carved; and in the inner room, they were overlaid with gold. The altar was made from cedar wood overlaid with gold. By the time the Temple was finished, all the inside surfaces were overlaid with pure gold.

Solomon went to Tyre to see a man called Huram. Huram was especially skilled at working in bronze. Solomon gave him instructions, and Huram built two huge columns of bronze to stand at the entrance to the Temple. Each was about twenty-seven feet high and beautifully carved. The columns were given names. The one on the south side was called Jachin, which means "he (God) establishes," and the one on the north side was called Boaz, which means "in him (God) is strength."

For seven years the building of the Temple continued. At last it was finished. The Temple had been built to the glory of God, and it was very beautiful.

Solomon brought all the treasures which had belonged to King David and placed them in the Temple. Then offering sacrifices, the priests lifted up the Ark of the Covenant on its two poles and carried it to the place prepared for it in the Holy of Holies.

All the people rejoiced and were glad. But Solomon's reign was not over.

1 Kings 9:26, 27; 10

The Queen of Sheba

Solomon built a large navy with ships which sailed to many ports, and so his fame spread. News of his wisdom reached the court of the Queen of Sheba. For a while she listened to the tales told about King Solomon. Then she declared, ''Nonsense, no man could be so wise.''

''Indeed, the stories are true,'' her attendants persisted.

''I shall go and see for myself,'' announced the queen. She traveled across the desert with a great number of servants and brought many splendid gifts of gold, precious stones, and silks.

The arrival in Jerusalem of the Queen of Sheba was magnificent. Solomon, dressed in his most beautiful robes, sat on his throne awaiting her. In she swept, wearing silks and linens, splendid with pearls and rubies. A long line of slaves carrying the gifts came behind her.

The two rulers greeted each other. Then the queen began to test Solomon, asking him many questions to judge his wisdom.

But Solomon answered every one of the questions wisely. There was nothing he did not know.

Presently he led the way to his banquet hall, where a great feast had been prepared. The herbs in the food were as rare as any the Queen of Sheba had ever tasted, and perfumes as rich as those of her own court scented the air.

Then Solomon took her to the entrance of the Temple. She looked at its magnificence and cried, ''Enough, I was wrong. Everything I heard about you is true. Blessed be the Lord your God who has shown you such favor. Surely God must love Israel very much to give it a king such as you.''

She gave Solomon many gifts, and in exchange he gave her anything she asked for. It was a splendid and satisfying visit.

The Queen of Sheba and her attendants returned to their home, but Solomon's wealth continued to grow. As more people heard of the wisdom which God had given him, many came to ask him questions, each one bringing gifts. Solomon's army grew to twelve thousand horsemen and one thousand four hundred chariots. In Jerusalem he made silver as plentiful as stones.

Through the gift of wisdom, God had made Solomon a very great king. But perhaps Solomon had become too great.

144

Solomon's Reign Ends

Solomon became very proud. He did not remain loyal to God, and he began to worship false gods.

God was very angry. "For as long as you live, I will keep my promise," God said to him. "Israel shall remain one nation. But when you die, the people shall divide into two nations, and the two tribes of the south shall be at war with the ten tribes of the north."

For forty years Solomon reigned over Israel, and it did remain one nation. Then Solomon died.

Elijah, the Ravens, and the Widow

Now Israel was divided into two kingdoms. Both were ruled by wicked kings, but Ahab, who had made himself king of the ten tribes of the north, was the worst. Most of the people in Ahab's kingdom forgot about God and began to worship Baal.

But one man, Elijah, remained faithful, and God gave him a message for Ahab.

Bravely Elijah stood in front of the king. "I am the prophet of the true God," said Elijah. "And I tell you that unless I say so, there will be no rain nor dew in this country for the next few years." Then he rushed hastily from the palace before the furious Ahab could have him arrested.

"Go and hide by the brook Cherith near the River Jordan," God commanded. "I will send ravens to feed you there, and you will be able to drink from the brook."

It was not the time to stand and argue. Glancing warily from left to right, Elijah hurried to the hiding place. But he wondered how ravens could feed him. Was he to catch and kill them?

That evening as Elijah was sitting by the brook, ravens came flying toward him. They were carrying bread and meat in their beaks. The birds dropped the food and Elijah ate. Every evening and every morning for as long as Elijah hid there, the ravens came with food.

But after a while, the brook dried up because there had been no rain.

147

Now what? thought Elijah. I shall die of thirst.

But God had a plan. "Go to Zarephath. I have ordered a widow who lives there to feed you."

Elijah set off for Zarephath. Sure enough, as he reached the gates of the town, he saw a widow gathering sticks for a fire. Thirsty and hungry, Elijah spoke. "Please, will you bring me some water so that I may drink?"

The widow turned at once to bring it. Elijah called after her, "And please, will you bring me a small piece of bread?"

She paused anxiously. "Truly, I have no bread. All I have left is one handful of flour and a little oil. I'm gathering these sticks so that I can cook one last meal for myself and my son. After that, we shall starve to death."

This was a strange reply from someone who God had promised would be able to feed Elijah. Yet God could surely be trusted.

"Cook your meal," said Elijah, "but first make me a little cake. Afterward make some for yourself and your son, for the Lord God of Israel promises that your bin of flour shall not be empty, nor shall the jar of oil, until the day when he shall send rain on the land again."

The widow could hardly believe Elijah's words, but she obeyed him. And sure enough, each time she took flour from the bin, there was just as much left. So it was with the oil as well. She, Elijah, and her household had food for many days.

After Elijah had lived in the house for a while, the widow's son became ill and stopped breathing. The widow cried out to Elijah, "Did you come here to show me I had done wrong and to kill my son?"

"Give the boy to me," Elijah answered. He carried the boy up to the room where he was staying and prayed desperately. "My Lord God, have you brought evil on this woman by killing her son? Let his life return to him, I beg you." Then Elijah laid the boy on the bed. He stretched himself over the boy three times. God heard Elijah's cry for help, and the boy began to breathe.

Elijah carried him downstairs where the mother sat weeping. "He's alive," cried Elijah.

Not daring to hope, the woman raised her head. Elijah gently placed the boy in her arms. For a moment she gazed at the boy; then softly she spoke to Elijah. "Now I know you are a man of God, and the message you bring from him is the truth."

Soon Ahab was to make the same discovery.

1 Kings 18:1, 2, 19-46

Elijah and the Prophets of Baal

After three years God said to Elijah, "Go again to Ahab to give him my message."

Bravely Elijah obeyed. "God will send rain," he told Ahab. "But first you, your people, and your priests must meet me on Mount Carmel."

If Ahab wanted rain, he would have to obey God. Angrily Ahab sent orders out to all the people.

Soon a great crowd was assembled on Mount Carmel.

Elijah spoke. "How much longer will you take to make up your minds?" he cried. "You cannot have two gods. Either Baal or the Lord God of Israel is the true God. Choose!"

The people gazed at him. No one moved or spoke.

Elijah tried again. "I'm the only one here who serves the Lord. Over there stand four hundred and fifty priests of Baal. Let them choose two young bulls. They will prepare one for sacrifice. I will prepare the other. We will lay the sacrifices on two separate altars. We will light no fire under either of them. Then you pray to Baal, and I will pray to the Lord God. The god who answers with fire shall be the one true God."

The people shouted, "Yes, yes!" The priests of Baal dared not refuse the challenge.

The two bulls were killed and prepared for sacrifice. The priests of Baal stood around their altar. "O Baal, hear us. Send fire," they prayed.

Everyone waited. Nothing happened. The priests of Baal began to jump and dance around their altar, calling to Baal.

Nothing happened. At midday Elijah began to mock them. "You'd better call louder. He is a god, isn't he? Maybe he's gone on a journey. Or maybe he's asleep. You'll have to wake him up."

Furiously the priests of Baal continued their cries. They cut themselves with knives until their blood ran. They knocked down the second altar as they leaped about. But still there was no sign that Baal could hear them.

When evening came with still no sign, Elijah said to the people, "Come close." They gathered around him. He went to the altar which had been broken down and built it up using twelve stones, one for each of the tribes of Israel. Then he dug a deep trench all around the altar. He arranged the wood for the fire and placed the sacrifice on the altar. He amazed the people with his next request.

"Bring four barrels of water, and pour them over the sacrifice," he commanded.

Pour on water? thought the people in surprise. How could a fire burn if everything was soaked with water?

Yet they dared not disobey. Three times they poured the barrels of water over the sacrifice. The water ran down and filled the trench all around the altar.

When everything was thoroughly soaked, Elijah spoke to God. "Lord God of Abraham, of Isaac, and of Israel, let it be known today that you are the one true God and I am your servant, so that the people may turn from their false gods and worship you."

As he finished speaking, there was a mighty flash of flame. With a great roar, the fire burned up the sacrifice, the altar, and even the water in the trench. Nothing remained.

The people fell on their faces, cry-ing, "The Lord is God! The Lord is God!"

The priests of Baal had been spell-bound with fear. Now they tried to run.

"Don't let them get away," shouted Elijah. "With their lies they have brought great evil on you."

When all the false priests had been put to death, Elijah spoke to the people again. "Go home and eat and drink, because I can hear the sound of rain. The drought and the famine will end."

Ahab went off for a meal, but Elijah climbed to the top of the mountain. There was still no rain. He said to his servant, "Look out to sea. Are there any clouds coming?"

Six times the man looked and saw nothing. But the seventh time, the servant called down to Elijah, "There is a cloud. It's about as big as a man's hand."

"Run!" Elijah commanded. "Tell Ahab if he doesn't set off at once, his chariot will be overwhelmed by rain."

Now the sky was black with clouds. The wind began to blow. Rain pelted down. Ahab drove off in his chariot, rushing back to his palace.

Excitement filled Elijah, and power from God came to him. So he tucked his garment up into his belt and ran all the way back. He reached the palace ahead of Ahab and his chariot.

But his excitement was soon to change.

151

Jezebel and Elijah

Still shaken by the happenings on Mount Carmel, King Ahab told the story to his wife Jezebel.

Jezebel had worshiped Baal, and when she heard that Baal's priests had been killed, she sent a heated message to Elijah. ''Because you have had the priests killed, I shall kill you.''

Elijah fled. He took his servant with him as far as Beersheba. Then he went on alone a day's journey into the desert. Exhausted, he sank down under a juniper tree. ''I can't take any more,'' he groaned. ''Let me die.''

He fell asleep, miserable and worn out. A gentle touch on his shoulder awoke him. An angel stood beside him. ''Eat your meal,'' said the angel.

Meal? Elijah looked around. There beside him was newly baked bread. The bread smelled delicious. Also beside Elijah stood a jar of cool water.

Elijah ate and drank. Comforted, he slept once more.

A second time the angel prepared a meal for him. ''Eat,'' said the angel.

''You will need strength for your journey.''

Elijah obeyed. Then he traveled on until at last he reached Mount Horeb. There he took refuge in a cave.

All night Elijah slept in the cave.

In the morning God spoke to him. ''What are you doing here, Elijah?''

Didn't God know? The words burst from Elijah. ''I've done my very best working for you. The Israelites have killed all your other prophets. I'm the only one left. And now they're trying to kill me.''

''Go out and stand on the mountain before the Lord,'' said God.

Leave his hiding place? Stand alone before the Lord? Elijah trembled as he went to the front of the cave.

He heard a great and powerful wind tear past the cave. But God was not in the wind.

A rumbling earthquake shook the ground. But God was not in the earthquake.

A fire sprang up. But God was not in the fire.

After the fire and the noise, there was a silence. And in the silence, Elijah heard a still, small voice.

Then Elijah pulled his garment around him and went to the entrance of the cave.

"What are you doing here, Elijah?" the voice asked again.

Quietly Elijah repeated his earlier reply.

God said, "Go back. Your work for me is almost finished. Anoint Hazael as king of Syria. Anoint Jehu as king of Israel. And then anoint Elisha, son of Shaphat, to be my prophet after you."

Greatly heartened, Elijah set out. He found Elisha and dropped his mantle, or cloak, over Elisha's shoulders as a sign that Elisha was to follow him. So Elisha went with Elijah to become his servant. Then God gave Elijah another task.

Naboth's Vineyard and the Departure of Elijah

King Ahab wanted the vineyard next to his palace, but its owner, Naboth, refused to sell it.

When Queen Jezebel heard what had happened, she schemed with the elders of Jezreel to have Naboth declared guilty of speaking against both King Ahab and God. Naboth was stoned to death.

Ahab took possession of the vineyard, but God sent Elijah to give him terrible news. "Your blood shall be spilled where Naboth died, and Jezebel's body will be eaten by dogs at the wall of Jezreel."

The message came true. God gave Elijah more messages, and Elijah faithfully delivered them until at last he knew his work on earth was done.

"I'll never leave you," declared Elisha, his assistant.

Elijah knew the two of them must be parted. "What can I give you before I go?" he asked gently.

"Give me your spirit," Elisha said, trying to hold in his tears. "Give me

a double portion."

This gift was what a father usually gave to his oldest son.

Elijah said, "If you see that which is about to happen, then you will know God has chosen you to be his prophet. You will have what you ask."

Suddenly, a chariot and horses of fire appeared. Elijah was lifted into the sky. And Elisha did see it.

"My father!" he cried desperately. Then he picked up Elijah's mantle, or cloak, which had fallen to the ground. He put it on. Elisha knew that the spirit of Elijah was on him. He was a prophet of God, appointed to continue Elijah's work.

2 Kings 5:1-15, 19; 25:10, 11

Naaman Is Healed

Naaman was a great man, commander of the king of Syria's mighty army. But he had caught the dreaded disease leprosy, and it seemed there was no hope of a cure.

But Naaman's wife had a young slave girl who had been captured and brought from Israel.

"If only my master would go to the prophet who is in Samaria, he could be healed," the girl said earnestly.

It was worth trying. The king of Syria gave Naaman a letter to take to the king of Israel asking for help.

When the king of Israel got the letter, he was terrified. "I can't cure leprosy. Maybe the king of Syria is trying to pick a quarrel with me," he said.

Then Elisha said, "Send Naaman to me."

Naaman's horses and chariots soon arrived at the door of Elisha's house. Elisha sent out a message. "Go and immerse seven times in the River Jordan, and you will be healed."

"What?" Naaman replied, feeling insulted. "Aren't our own rivers better than the Jordan? I thought the prophet himself would come out and heal me." Then he turned to go home.

But Naaman's servants persuaded him to try doing what Elisha had told him to do.

Naaman was cured.

Humbly he went back to Elisha. "Now I know that your God is the true God, and I will worship him," he vowed.

"Go in peace," said Elisha.

After a long life of serving God, Elisha died.

Time passed. Many kings ruled in Judah. The people did not worship the true God, and hard times came upon them. Eventually Jerusalem was destroyed, and the people were taken as captives to Babylon where they were very unhappy. But God had not forgotten them. Among the Israelites taken to Babylon was the boy Daniel.

Shadrach, Meshach, and Abednego

Nebuchadnezzar, king of Babylon, chose some of the most clever and handsome children from among his captives, and he ordered that they should live in the palace as members of his household. Four of these were Daniel, Shadrach, Meshach, and Abednego.

The four boys were friends, and as they grew, they never forgot God. So when Shadrach, Meshach, and Abednego were ordered to worship the golden statue which Nebuchadnezzar had built, they refused. They worshiped God and no one else.

Nebuchadnezzar was furious. He ordered that they be securely tied up and thrown into a fiery furnace, a furnace so hot that the heat killed the men who threw them in. Yet Shadrach, Meshach, and Abednego stood unbound and unharmed in the middle of the flames.

Nebuchadnezzar was overcome with awe. "I see four men walking in the fire," he whispered, "and the fourth looks like a divine being."

He called for the three to come out of the fire, and not one hair of their heads was the least bit burned.

Nebuchadnezzar ordered that in the future no one was to speak against the God of Israel, and the three men were given important jobs in Babylon.

When Nebuchadnezzar died, his son Belshazzar became king. Belshazzar gave a great feast where something extraordinary happened.

Belshazzar's Feast

King Belshazzar's feast was a merry success. All the guests were enjoying themselves. Suddenly the king turned pale with fear. A hand was writing a message on the wall!

Terrified, the king cried, "Whoever can tell me what this message means shall become third ruler in the land."

All the wise men attempted to explain the message but failed. Then the queen remembered Daniel. He had sometimes interpreted dreams and riddles for Nebuchadnezzar.

The king sent for Daniel. Refusing all the rewards offered by Belshazzar, Daniel quietly told him the meaning of the writing on the wall. God had judged Belshazzar's deeds and found them utterly unworthy. Belshazzar's kingdom would fall and be divided among his enemies, the Medes and Persians.

Daniel's words came true. That same night the Medes attacked Babylon. Belshazzar was killed, and Babylon was conquered.

But Daniel's work for God was not over.

Daniel in the Lions' Den

King Darius, king of the mighty Medes and Persians, needed someone to be chief ruler in captured Babylon. He knew that Daniel was brave, wise, and honest and would make a good ruler.

The other rulers were furious. "We will get rid of him," they whispered jealously, and they worked out a trap to catch Daniel.

The Medes and Persians worshiped many gods, but Daniel worshiped only the God of Israel.

The nervous rulers approached the king with the first phase of their plan.

"O King, live forever," they began. "All the rulers have agreed that you should make a law saying that for thirty days no one should pray to any god or man except you. If anyone disobeys the law, he should be thrown to the lions."

King Darius was flattered. The rulers must think him a great king, if they wanted this law. Of course, he was a great king. He smiled and nodded.

The rulers hadn't finished. "This law should be written down immediately," they declared. They waited nervously for a reply.

King Darius nodded again. "Very well," he said.

The rulers watched him write, for once a law of the Medes and Persians was written down, it could never be altered.

The law was made known. As soon as Daniel heard it, he knew it was a trap set for him. He must either give up his daily prayers to God or be thrown to the lions.

With his head held high, he walked boldly down the road toward his home, knowing that his enemies were watching him. He could save his life

159

by not praying to God for thirty days. He could save it by praying secretly in his head. He could try to find a hiding place and pray there.

He walked into his house. He went upstairs to the front room where he always prayed. Boldly he opened the windows which faced toward Jerusalem, his own country so far away.

Then Daniel prayed to God for help.

His enemies in the street below saw him and knew their plan had worked. Triumphantly they rushed back to the king. Once in front of him, they controlled themselves and spoke softly.

"King Darius, live forever. Did you not make a law saying anyone who prayed to any god or man except you for these next thirty days should be thrown to the lions?"

"Yes, I did," Darius agreed.

Then they said, "Daniel, who is one of the Jews captured and brought to Babylon years ago, takes no notice of your law. He still prays to his God, three times a day."

Then King Darius saw the trap which had been laid. Greatly distressed because Daniel was a favorite of his, he tried to find a way out. All day he thought, but it was no use. He had written the law himself, and it was unchangeable.

That evening the rulers came back and reminded him that the law must be carried out. So the king consented, and Daniel was brought to the edge of the lions' den.

Below, the hungry lions paced back and forth, roaring. Trusting God, Daniel waited.

The men threw him into the den, and the king cried out, "Daniel, may the God to whom you are so faithful save you!"

Hardly able to bear it, Darius watched as a huge stone was rolled into place over the entrance to the den. The king had to seal the stone with his own ring, so that everyone would know if the stone had been moved in a rescue attempt.

Afterward King Darius made his way back to the palace. All night he was tormented by his thoughts. He could not sleep or eat. At the very first sign of dawn, he hurried back to the lions' den.

Then he stopped short. What would he see? Had his friend been torn to pieces? Fearfully, he made himself call out. "Daniel, has your God saved you?"

He waited, hardly daring to hope. Then Daniel's voice came strong and clear. "O King, live forever. I am safe. God did not let the lions harm me."

Overjoyed, King Darius shouted, "Get Daniel out!"

The men who had thrown Daniel into the den now lifted him out. Sure enough, he was completely untouched by the lions. After a joyful greeting, King Darius ordered that Daniel's accusers and their families be thrown into the lions' den.

They were thrown in, and before they even touched the floor of the den, the lions attacked them.

Then King Darius wrote for all the people in his kingdom to see, "I command that everyone should respect Daniel's God, for he is great and will last forever."

Rebuilding the Temple and Walls of Jerusalem

Many years after the destruction of Jerusalem, Cyrus, king of the Persians, issued a proclamation. God had ordered him to see that the Temple was rebuilt in Jerusalem. Cyrus was also freeing all Jews who had been captured as slaves.

With great rejoicing, thousands of Judeans, or Jews, made the long journey back to their own land.

There they began to repair the city of Jerusalem. After many months, the people started to rebuild the Temple. Throughout the reign of Cyrus, enemies tried to stop the rebuilding. When Darius became king, he ordered that the Jews should be allowed to work without harassment.

At last the Temple was finished. It was splendid. But Jerusalem still had no mighty walls to protect the city.

Nehemiah, cupbearer to the king of Persia, was troubled about this. He got permission from the king to have the walls rebuilt, and he inspired the Jewish people to persevere with the task in spite of all the difficulties put in their way by their enemies.

Finally with God's help, the work was completed. The walls stood triumphantly.

God continued to care about the people he had created and be hurt by their disobedience. Now he looked at the wicked city of Nineveh and knew he must find someone to take a message of warning to its people.

Jonah

God spoke to Jonah. "Jonah, I want you to go to the city of Nineveh and tell the people there that they are so wicked that their city is going to be destroyed."

"Me?" cried Jonah. He imagined himself giving such a message. The people would probably kill him. No, no, he couldn't go. Anyway, God was kind and merciful. Surely he'd never destroy a whole city.

"I must get away," thought Jonah. "If I stay here, God will know I'm disobeying him. I'll leave by ship."

So Jonah hurried down to the port of Joppa, and there he found a ship about to sail for Tarshish. Perfect, he thought. I'll go in the opposite direction from Nineveh.

Afraid God might stop him, Jonah paid his fare to the captain and went below. He thought he was safely out of God's sight.

Relieved after all of his worrying, Jonah lay down and went to sleep.

The ship set sail. Suddenly a great storm blew up. The crew was terrified. They all knelt and prayed to their gods, but still the ship tossed violently on the huge waves. They threw cargo overboard to lighten the ship, but things were no better.

Making his way below to check the hold, the captain discovered Jonah still sleeping soundly.

"Wake up!" The captain shook him. "We are in deadly peril. Pray to your God, and maybe he will save us."

Jonah struggled to wake himself, unsure of what was happening. The sailors had already decided Jonah must be the reason for the storm. As he clambered up onto the deck, they shouted through the noise of the wind and the waves, "Who are you? Where are you from? What is your country?"

"I'm a Hebrew," Jonah answered. "I worship the God who made the sea and the earth. I was trying to run away from God."

The crew was even more terrified. "What can we do?" they pleaded.

"Throw me overboard," said Jonah. "Then the sea will be calm."

The sailors looked at one another. Throw a man overboard? Was there no other way? "We'll row for the shore," they said. They went to their stations and heaved on the oars with all their strength, but the storm grew even worse.

Then the sailors cried out to God, "Lord, please don't blame us for killing an innocent man." They picked up Jonah and threw him into the sea.

Immediately the storm died away. The sailors were very frightened.

They offered a sacrifice to God and promised to serve him.

Meanwhile, Jonah was sinking under the water, sure he would drown. But God sent a huge fish, like a whale, which swallowed Jonah in one gulp. Coughing and gasping, Jonah tried to get his breath back. He was in total darkness. He was inside an enormous fish.

But Jonah was alive. He began to pray to God. Jonah realized how stupid he'd been to think there was any way that he could hide from God. He saw that even though he'd disobeyed God, God had saved his life. Jonah was grateful.

For three miserable, uncomfortable days, Jonah lived inside the fish. Then at God's command, the fish gave a great belch and spit Jonah onto the shore.

As he blinked in the light and took in great gulps of fresh air, God spoke to him again. "Jonah, go to Nineveh. Give the people my message."

This time Jonah couldn't get there fast enough. When he reached Nineveh, he gave the people God's message. To Jonah's surprise they believed him at once. The people took Jonah's message to the king. The king also believed and commanded that everyone in the city should pray to God for forgiveness. To show they were truly sorry for their wickedness, they took off their fine clothes and wore sackcloth. They did not eat or drink.

When God heard their prayers and saw how sorry they were, he forgave them and did not destroy Nineveh.

Jonah was furious. "I knew that's how it would be!" he declared. "I went through all this for nothing." And he went into the desert, sat down, and sulked.

God made a bushy plant grow up behind him to give him shade. But the next day while Jonah was still sitting there, God commanded a worm to attack the plant.

The plant withered and died. Jonah was sorry for it and angry that it had died so soon. The sun's rays beat down on him, and the scorching wind blew over him. He began to feel so ill that he lay down and prepared to die.

Then God spoke gently to Jonah. "You felt sorry for the plant when it died so soon. Yet you didn't plant it, and you didn't care for it. Think how much more sorry I would have been to destroy the people of Nineveh and their animals, for I made them and love them. Do you really think that I should not have let them live?"

Micah 6:8

Words from Micah

"He (God) has shown you, O Man, what is good;
and what does the Lord require of you but
to do what is just, to love mercy, and to walk
humbly with your God."

THE NEW TESTAMENT

The Angel Gabriel Visits Mary

For Mary, the day had begun just like any other. She lived in the small town of Nazareth in Galilee and was engaged to be married to Joseph, the local carpenter. Joseph was honest and kind. He was strong, yet gentle. She loved him very much.

As Mary sat thinking, she suddenly felt there was another presence in the room. She looked up to see the angel Gabriel standing close-by. He said, ''God is with you. You have found favor with him.''

Mary was terrified. What did this mean? The angel said, ''Don't be afraid, Mary. God loves you. You are going to have a baby son, and you must name him Jesus. He will be great, and he will be called the Son of the Most High. God will give him a kingdom, the throne of his forefather David. And this kingdom will never end.''

Mary tried to calm herself and to understand.

''But how can I have a son?'' she asked. ''I have not yet slept with a man.''

''The Spirit of God will come upon you, and the power of the Most High will then overshadow you,'' Gabriel answered. ''The child which shall be born will be the Son of God. Your cousin Elizabeth is also going to have a child, although she has grown old and people say it is impossible. With God nothing is impossible.''

Mary listened. All her life she had loved and trusted God. She took a deep breath. ''I will do anything that God asks of me,'' she said quietly. ''Let this happen just as you have said.''

After the angel left her, Mary sat for some time, trying to take in the tremendous news. Elizabeth—the angel had mentioned Elizabeth.

Mary quietly prepared for a journey. She would go and visit her cousin.

Luke 1:5-25, 39-79

Mary Visits Elizabeth

Elizabeth was married to a man called Zacharias (sometimes written Zechariah), a priest of the Temple. Elizabeth had often prayed for a son. Now as Mary came into the house and greeted her, Elizabeth was full of joy, for she had just felt her baby move inside her.

"How blessed am I!" she said. "The mother of the Son of God has come to see me. And you, Mary, are blessed indeed."

Mary could see it was true that Elizabeth was going to have a child. Her cousin's words helped Mary accept what was happening. The two women hugged each other.

Elizabeth said, "Let me tell you about my baby. Zacharias was in the Temple one day when the angel Gabriel came and told him I would have a baby son, whom we must call John. Our son is going to be special, Mary. When he grows up, he will tell the people to be ready because their Savior, the Messiah, is coming."

170

Mary listened quietly as Elizabeth continued to speak. "Zacharias wouldn't believe what the angel told him because we're both so old. So the angel made Zacharias speechless. He can't say a word. When he wants something, he has to make signs or write on a tablet. This is how I found out what happened with the angel in the Temple."

Mary said softly, "My soul praises the Lord God, and my spirit rejoices in him. He has done great things for me, and holy is his name."

Mary stayed on with Elizabeth for about three months before returning to Nazareth. Soon afterward Elizabeth's baby was born. Her friends and relatives thought she would name him Zacharias, after his father.

"No!" Elizabeth insisted. "He is to be called John."

"But why?" asked her relatives. "No one else in our family is called John."

They made signs to Zacharias about the name, sure he would agree with them. Zacharias pointed to his writing tablet. They watched eagerly as he wrote.

When he held up the tablet, the people were astonished. Zacharias had written, "His name is John."

Suddenly Zacharias found that he could speak again. He joyfully began to praise God. Soon everyone in Judea had heard the story and wondered about it.

"What will the baby be when he grows up?" they asked themselves. "Surely God is with this child."

But Mary's baby was yet to be born.

Joseph and Mary

When Joseph heard that Mary was expecting a child, he was puzzled and distressed. He loved her too much to hurt her, but the proper thing for him to do was to break the engagement. In those days the only way to do this was divorce, either publicly or by a private decree. Joseph decided to do it secretly.

But God sent an angel to Joseph in a dream. "Joseph, son of David," said the angel, "do not be afraid to take Mary to your house as your wife. The Holy Spirit has come upon her, and she will have a son. You must name him Jesus, which means 'Savior,' because he will save the people from their sins."

Joseph was reassured, and he and Mary began to make preparations for the baby. One day, as the time of birth was drawing near, Joseph came home with bad news.

Caesar Augustus, the Roman ruler, wanted to know exactly how many people were living under Rome's command; so everyone was ordered to go and be counted in the place from which their families came. Wives were to go with their husbands.

Since Joseph's family was from Bethlehem in Judea, Mary and Joseph had a long trip ahead. It was more than one hundred miles from Nazareth to Bethlehem.

No Room

There was no way to avoid the journey. Joseph and Mary packed into bundles everything they thought they would need for their trip. Mary even packed some soft swaddling cloths for the baby. Then with Mary riding on a donkey, she and Joseph set out for Bethlehem.

The road was long and hard. There were many other people making the same journey. With sinking hearts Mary and Joseph soon realized that the small town of Bethlehem would be full to overflowing. Where would they find lodging?

Because they had to travel slowly, they arrived in Bethlehem long after most of the other travelers had settled in. Joseph led the donkey through the narrow, bustling streets to an inn. Mary watched as Joseph knocked on the door. Sounds of laughter and talking came from within. Joseph and Mary could smell food being prepared. But they were outside, tired, hungry, and friendless in a strange place.

Joseph knocked again. The door was thrown open. The innkeeper stood there. "No room, no room," he said and started to close the door.

"Please," Joseph's voice stopped him. "Is there nowhere we can rest?"

The innkeeper paused. This time he looked past Joseph at Mary. He felt very sorry for her.

"The inn is full," he said. "But there is room in the stable. The lady would at least be sheltered there, if you don't mind being with the animals."

"Anywhere," said Mary gratefully. She knew the baby would be born very soon.

And so it was that God's son was born in a stable in Bethlehem. Mary wrapped him in soft, warm swaddling cloths and laid him tenderly on the sweet-smelling hay in the manger.

Then Mary and Joseph tried to rest. But soon the baby was to have his first visitors.

The Visit of the Shepherds

On the hills around Bethlehem, shepherds kept their sheep. The work could be exciting and dangerous. Not only did the shepherds have to lead their flocks along steep, narrow paths to the patches of grazing land, they had to be constantly aware of wild animals which might attack the flocks.

Even at night the shepherds stayed with the sheep, wrapping themselves up in their garments and sleeping fitfully in the open air by the campfire.

On the night Jesus was born in Bethlehem, the shepherds were out on the hillside as usual. It was a clear, quiet night. The only light came from the stars and the dull glow of the fire. The only sounds were the soft bleating of the sheep and the restless movement of the lambs.

Then all at once, a bright, glorious light began to fill the sky, surrounding the sleeping shepherds with its brilliance.

The brightness woke the shepherds. They were terrified to see the night sky as bright as day. What sort of light is this? they wondered. What is happening?

They covered their faces in fear. There was no place to hide. Then they heard the beautiful voice of an angel of the Lord.

"Do not be afraid. I have good news for you and all people. For unto you is born this day in the city of David a Savior who is Christ the Lord. And this will be a sign to you. You will find the baby wrapped in swaddling cloths, lying in a manger."

Then the amazed shepherds saw the whole sky filled with a multitude of angels saying, "Glory to God in the highest, and on earth peace and goodwill toward men."

The light faded and the voices of the angels died away. Once more there was starlight and silence.

The shepherds tried to take in what they'd seen and heard. The city of David meant Bethlehem. Was it true that in little Bethlehem that night a baby was born—a baby who was the Christ, the Savior?

The shepherds said to one another, "Let's go to Bethlehem at once and see the baby!" Leaving their sheep, the shepherds raced along the paths, stumbling in the darkness and stubbing their toes without concern. They only wanted to see if this news was true.

When they reached Bethlehem, they paused, catching their breath. Which way now? Bethlehem seemed to be silent, asleep. In the town there were many mangers, or animal feeding boxes. Everyone who owned a donkey would have a manger for it.

The shepherds began to walk along the streets, looking for signs that someone was awake. They came to the inn. There from the stable, a dim light was shining.

The shepherds stood still, looking at one another and hardly daring to hope. Then trembling, they looked inside.

In the manger, wrapped in warm cloths exactly as the angel had said, lay baby Jesus with Mary and Joseph watching over him. Quietly the shepherds knelt to worship.

They told Mary and Joseph about the message of the angels. As dawn broke, the shepherds returned to their flocks on the hillside, and they joyously told the good news to everyone they met.

Mary remembered all these things that had happened and thought deeply about them.

When the time came, Joseph and Mary prepared to take baby Jesus to be presented in the Temple in Jerusalem as God commanded in the laws written down by Moses.

Simeon and Anna in the Temple

In Jerusalem there lived a man named Simeon. Simeon was old, but God had promised him he would not die until he had seen the Messiah, the Savior for whom the Jewish people were waiting. So Simeon waited and prayed. At last God said to him, "Go to the Temple today, Simeon. Today you will find the Messiah there."

Trembling with excitement, Simeon made his way to the Temple as fast as he could. He looked around at the people in the crowd. Which one was the Messiah?

When Mary and Joseph carried the baby Jesus into the Temple, Simeon knew.

The old man tottered up to Mary. "Please, may I hold him?" he asked. Simeon's face was filled with excitement and love as Mary handed the baby to him.

Simeon praised God. "You have kept your promise, Lord. Now let your servant depart in peace, for I have seen your salvation with my own eyes, the salvation which is for everyone. The light which shines here shall shine for all nations, and it will bring glory to the people of Israel."

Mary and Joseph listened in amazement. Simeon blessed them and said to Mary, "This child will alter the lives of many. But some people will speak against him, and your own soul will be pierced with sorrow."

Gently he handed the baby back to her. A very old lady named Anna who never left the Temple came up to them at that moment.

"This is the Messiah!" she proclaimed. She thanked God and told the people around her that the Savior had come.

Mary and Joseph carried out the ceremony of presenting the baby to God, which the Law demanded. And they made their offering of two turtledoves as a thanksgiving, for they couldn't afford the lamb and the dove which richer people would offer.

While Jesus was still a baby, there were other surprises to come. This young child was to receive very special visitors.

178

The Wise Men and the Flight into Egypt

King Herod sat in his palace in Jerusalem, knowing nothing of the angels, the shepherds, or the extraordinary things which had been happening to Mary and Joseph. Then one day wise men from far away to the east asked for an audience with Herod.

Politely the wise men bowed low, but their words filled Herod with horror. ''Where is the new baby king?'' the wise men asked. ''As we studied the sky, we saw his star rise in the east, and we have come to worship him.''

A new baby king to replace him. Herod went pale with rage and fear. He ordered his chief priests and lawyers to search in their books. ''Discover where this new king is to be born!'' he commanded.

They soon returned with the answer, ''In Bethlehem of Judea.''

Herod took the wise men to one side. ''Go to Bethlehem,'' he said. ''Search carefully for the child. When you've found him, come back and tell me where the child is. I want to worship him too.''

Unaware of Herod's true feelings, the wise men left the palace. They looked up and saw the star, the same star they had seen in the east. It went ahead of them, leading them to the

179

place where Jesus lay. There it stopped and there the wise men found Mary, Joseph, and Jesus.

Mary and Joseph watched in astonishment as these splendid travelers from foreign lands knelt and worshiped the child. They watched as the wise men searched among their treasures and presented him with rich gifts of gold, frankincense, and myrrh. Gold was a present given to kings. Frankincense was burned on the altar of the Lord. And myrrh was used to help preserve the bodies of people when they died. Mary shuddered. Why were these wise men giving her baby myrrh?

It was late now. As the wise men rested for the night, God sent them a dream.

"Do not go back to King Herod. He means to harm the child. Go home another way."

So in the morning, the wise men departed and obeyed God's instruction to keep away from Herod.

Joseph also had a dream. An angel appeared to him and said, "Get up. Take the boy and his mother and escape into Egypt. Stay there until I tell you it is safe to return, for Herod means to kill the child."

Joseph woke with a start. It took him a moment to realize what had happened. Then he hastily got up, stumbling in the darkness.

"Mary!" he whispered urgently. "Wake up! We must take the child and leave at once." And he told Mary about his dream.

Soon the donkey was saddled, their few possessions were bundled up, and the sleepy boy was wrapped warmly.

They set out in the starlight, hurrying along the streets of Bethlehem with only the clip-clop of the donkey's hooves breaking the silence. Would they escape?

Matthew 2:16-23; Luke 2:41-52

The Boy Jesus

God's warning had come in time. Joseph, Mary, and Jesus reached Egypt in safety. But when Herod discovered he had been outwitted by the wise men, he was furious. In rage and fear, he ordered that every boy two years old or younger who lived in or near Bethlehem was to be killed.

There was great weeping and mourning in Bethlehem, but Herod was soon satisfied that no baby king existed to threaten his throne.

Meanwhile in Egypt, Jesus was alive and unharmed. He grew bigger and stronger as Mary and Joseph watched over, loved, and taught him.

At last King Herod died, and an angel again appeared to Joseph in a dream. It was now safe to leave Egypt.

So Mary, Joseph, and Jesus went to Nazareth in Galilee. There they lived in a small house like all their neighbors, and Joseph took up his work as a carpenter again.

When Jesus was old enough, he went to school in Nazareth. He learned to write by drawing letters in the sand with his finger. He learned how to read from the scrolls. And he asked a lot of questions.

On the Sabbath he went to the synagogue with Joseph. Mary went as well, but she sat with the other women, as was the custom.

As Jesus grew older, he listened very carefully to all he heard in the synagogue. And he had more questions to ask.

Every year Joseph and Mary went to the Temple in Jerusalem for the Feast of the Passover, the time when Jews remembered their escape from Egypt during the days of Moses. When Jesus was twelve years old, he went with them to Jerusalem, as was also the custom.

181

There were many other people on the road. Some were from Nazareth and some were not, but all were going in the same direction. Jesus thought it was exciting to be going so far to see Jerusalem, about which he had heard so much.

But the most exciting and wonderful part of the trip was going into the Temple itself, taking part in the special ceremonies, and listening to the wisdom of the scribes and teachers there.

When the festival was over, Joseph and Mary set out for home. They were with a large group of people from Nazareth. As usual, the women and children walked in one part of the group, and the men and older boys in another. So neither Joseph nor Mary worried because Jesus wasn't beside them. Each thought he was with the other one.

All day they traveled, and when darkness began to fall, the people began to set up camp for the night. It was then that Joseph and Mary realized that Jesus had not been with either of them.

Slightly irritated, Joseph and Mary inquired among their friends and relatives. Then they became more and more anxious because no one had seen Jesus since they left Jerusalem.

Joseph and Mary tried to think. Could Jesus have come to some harm along the road? It was unlikely. Wild animals and robbers wouldn't attack a crowd of people. That was one reason why groups traveled together. Jesus wouldn't have wandered off alone. Even if he had, someone would have seen him go.

No, there was only one answer. Jesus must still be in Jerusalem. He had somehow been left behind.

Deeply distressed, Mary and Joseph hurried back to the city. It was still full of people, and they wondered where to begin their search.

For three days Mary and Joseph scoured Jerusalem. At last, almost without hope, they entered the Temple. What twelve-year-old boy would want to spend time there?

Mary and Joseph stopped in amazement. There was Jesus, sitting among the wise men of Jerusalem. He was talking to them and asking them questions. The men were astonished at the kind of questions he asked and the amount he understood.

After a moment Mary moved forward. "Son, why have you behaved like this? We've been searching everywhere for you!"

Jesus was surprised. "Why were you searching? I thought you would know I was here in my Father's house."

Joseph and Mary looked at him, unable to understand. "Come home with us now," they said.

Jesus obeyed immediately.

They went back to Nazareth and life went on as usual. But Mary remembered all that had happened and often thought about it as she watched her son grow into manhood.

Jesus knew he must soon leave home and start on the task for which he had come.

His cousin John had already begun.

John the Baptist

John, son of Elizabeth and Zacharias, grew up seeing much of life in the Temple in Jerusalem where his father was a priest.

But John felt that the Temple, with all its rules and regulations, wasn't the place for him. So as soon as he was old enough, he left.

He went into the desert to live by himself, and there God spoke to him. John believed God's words. The Messiah, the Savior, was coming soon, and it was John's task to tell everyone. John was to prepare the people to listen to the Messiah when he did come.

Matthew 3:1-17; Mark 1:1-11; Luke 3:1-22; John 1:29-34

The Baptism of Jesus

While still in the desert, John started to preach to the people.

"Prepare, for the Kingdom of Heaven is to come soon. Confess to the wrong things you have done. Show that you are sorry by living a better life. Come and be baptized."

"Baptized" meant being "washed" —being dipped in the water as a sign that the wrong things in a person's life were being washed away, and he was ready for the new life to begin. It was because he baptized people that John was given the name "John the Baptist."

184

Soon people in the towns were talking about John.

"He wears clothes made from camel hair with a leather belt around his waist. He lives in the desert all the time and eats locusts and wild honey. You should see his hair! He's preaching a new message."

The more they heard, the more curious they grew. And soon crowds of people were going to see John.

speaking to him, and he cried out, "Look! Here is the one I've been telling you about. He is the one who will take away the sins of the world!"

Quietly Jesus came up to John. Almost overcome by the realization of who Jesus was, John said, "No, this is not the way it should be. You should baptize me. You are much greater than I am."

Jesus answered softly, "This is the way God wishes it to be."

So Jesus and John went together

They went because they were curious, but they stayed to listen. Many of them believed John's message, and John baptized those people in the River Jordan.

Some people wondered if John was the Savior, the Messiah for whom the Jews had long been waiting. John told them he was not.

"I baptize you with water," he said, "but someone is coming who is much more powerful than I am. I'm not fit even to untie his sandals. He will baptize you with fire and with the Holy Spirit."

Jesus heard about his cousin John's preaching and came from Galilee to the River Jordan to be baptized.

When John saw Jesus, he felt God

into the River Jordan, and John baptized Jesus.

Jesus's baptism was different from everyone else's because he had done no wrong which needed to be washed away. As he came back onto the bank, the sky was opened and the Spirit of God came down to him in the shape of a dove.

God's voice was heard. "This is my beloved son, in whom I am well-pleased."

Then Jesus was full of the Holy Spirit. And he knew he must go into the wilderness for a while to be by himself and to prepare for the work which he had come to earth to do. But it was not easy for him in the wilderness.

Jesus in the Wilderness

For forty days and forty nights, Jesus stayed in the wilderness. He spent a lot of time thinking deeply about the power which God had given him and about how he should use it. He ate nothing in all that time.

At the end of forty days, Satan tempted him. "Look at these stones. If you are really the Son of God, you could turn these stones into bread."

Jesus was very hungry. But he knew his power had not been given to him to use for himself.

"Man shall not live by bread alone, but also by the word of God," he answered from Scripture.

Satan, although he had lost this time, tried again. He took Jesus to the highest ledge of the Temple in Jerusalem. "If you are really the Son of God," whispered Satan, "throw yourself off this ledge." Satan then spoke some words from Scripture himself. "It is written, 'God will order his angels to take care of you. In their hands they will hold you up and not let you even bruise your foot on a stone.' "

Jesus knew that if he did throw himself down from this height without harm, people might flock to him to become his followers. But they would follow him for the wrong reason—because they would think him to be some sort of magician, not because they had heard and understood his true message from God.

Jesus refused to impress the crowd in this way. He answered, "But it is also written, 'Do not tempt the Lord your God.' "

Satan was defeated again, but he would not give up yet. He led Jesus to a very high place.

"Look," he whispered. "You can see all the kingdoms of the world from here. I will give you authority over all the world and all the splendor of the world if you worship me."

But Jesus answered, "Go away, Satan! It is written, 'You shall worship the Lord your God, and him only shall you serve.' "

Satan gave up for the moment, waiting for another opportunity.

Angels came to Jesus and took care of him.

Then Jesus went back to Galilee, and all through the countryside, people began to tell one another about him and the things he said and did.

They wanted to see and hear more.

Matthew 9:9-13; 10:1-4; Luke 4:16-30; 5:1-11; 27-32; Hosea 6:6

Jesus's Disciples

Except in his own village of Nazareth, the people of Galilee crowded around Jesus to listen to him wherever he went.

One day four fishermen, Simon, Andrew, James, and John, were at the shore of the Sea of Galilee. They were gloomily cleaning their nets while their empty boats bobbed on the water behind them. They went out fishing at night because that was usually the best time to catch fish. But last night they'd caught nothing.

Now as they worked on the nets, they heard a commotion. Looking up, they saw Jesus coming. A crowd of people was following him, pushing and jostling each other as they tried to get close to him. The fishermen watched anxiously. Was someone going to get hurt?

Jesus had noticed the boats at the water's edge.

"Simon," he said, "may I borrow your boat?"

Simon jumped to his feet. Jesus was asking him for help. Gladly he agreed. Jesus stepped into the boat. The people on shore watched. Was Jesus trying to get away from them?

Jesus asked Simon to row a short distance out from shore. Then he sat down and began to speak to the people.

Now everyone could see and hear. The crowd settled down to listen. The four fishermen listened too.

When Jesus had finished teaching the people, he looked at Simon.

188

"Sail out to the deep water, and there let down your nets," he said.

Simon hesitated. "Master, we've been fishing all night, and we haven't caught a thing. The fish don't seem to be here, but I'll do as you say."

Andrew, Simon's brother, waded out and climbed into the boat as well. They sailed over to the place Jesus had pointed out. Not knowing whether to be hopeful or not, they let down the nets.

From their own boat, James and John watched.

Suddenly there was a great tugging on the nets. Simon and Andrew began to haul in the nets. They were so full of fish that the nets began to break.

"Help!" Simon called to James and John, who quickly rowed over. Now they were all desperately trying to get the fish on board, more fish than they had ever seen before. There were so many fish that both boats came close to sinking under the weight of them.

Simon was suddenly afraid. "Master," he said, "I'm not good enough for you to be with me. Please go."

But Jesus answered, "Don't be afraid, Simon. From now on you will catch men, not fish."

Simon understood that Jesus meant for him to help in the work of telling men about God's message.

As quickly as they could, Simon, Andrew, James, and John landed their boats safely on the shore. Then they left everything and followed Jesus to become his special helpers, his disciples.

Jesus needed more disciples. He saw Matthew, a tax collector, sitting at his table collecting taxes.

To Matthew's amazement, Jesus stopped to speak to him. Jesus was a Jew, and most Jews hated the tax collectors. Not only did the tax collectors cheat by taking more money than was due, they worked for the Romans, who had occupied the country and now ruled it.

But Jesus said, "Follow me." Matthew was amazed. Jesus wanted him? He could hardly believe it. Matthew gladly jumped up, leaving everything behind as the others had done. Then he had an idea.

"Jesus," he said, hardly daring to speak the words. "Jesus, would you come to a party at my house if I invite other tax collectors?"

He held his breath, sure that Jesus would refuse. But Jesus smiled. "I will come," he said.

Matthew raced away to make the preparations, and soon a huge party was going on at his house.

Some of the Pharisees, Jews who were very strict in the way they kept the laws of Moses, saw the party. They were shocked because they thought there was only one right way to behave—their way. They said to the disciples, "How can your leader possibly eat with people like that—tax collectors and people who don't keep the law? Why does he do it?"

Jesus overheard them. "People who are well don't need a doctor," he said. "I came to give God's message to everyone, not just to talk to respectable people. Go and read the Scriptures where it says God wants kindness to be shown. He wants more than just the sacrifice of animals; God wants mercy."

The Pharisees thought they were the ones who knew the Scriptures. Insulted, they moved away.

Jesus chose other disciples, until finally he had an inner group of twelve: Simon Peter, Andrew, James, John, Philip, Nathaniel (or Bartholomew), Matthew, Thomas, James (son of Alphaeus), Thaddaeus, Simon the Zealot, and Judas Iscariot.

Some of his disciples were with him at a wedding party which turned out to be very special.

The Wedding at Cana

There was a wedding at Cana in Galilee. Jesus's mother, Mary, was one of the guests, and Jesus and his disciples had also been invited. The party was going splendidly with laughing and talking and eating and drinking. Then Mary came over to Jesus. She whispered anxiously to him. "Jesus, the wine is all gone! There's none left!"

The host and hostess would be very ashamed because they had run out of wine. They would remember it with shame every time they remembered the wedding.

Jesus spoke gently. "Why are you telling me? It isn't yet time for me to use my power."

But Mary was absolutely certain that Jesus would help his friends. The servants were standing nearby. So Mary said to them, "Do whatever Jesus tells you."

Jesus looked around. He saw six huge stone jars standing in the corner of the room. The jars would hold about twenty gallons of water each and were there so that people could wash their hands and feet as they came into the house.

"Fill those jars with fresh water," Jesus said to the servants, who had been looking at him expectantly.

They obeyed, getting water from the well and filling the jars to the brim.

"Now," said Jesus, "pour some of

it out and offer it to the chief guest.''

The servants looked at one another. Offer water to the chief guest? They looked again at Jesus and did as he said. They anxiously watched as the guest took a sip.

''Well!'' exclaimed the chief guest. ''Most people serve their best wine first and keep the worst until last. After people have already had much to drink, they hardly notice the taste. But you have kept the best wine until last.''

The water had been turned into wine, and there was plenty of it.

The host hesitated. Then he began to smile. Everyone smiled and laughed, and the party continued.

Jesus had performed his first miracle in Cana of Galilee. His disciples saw it, and they began to trust him completely.

Soon Jesus would perform other miracles.

Luke 5:17-26

The Man Who Couldn't Walk

There was a man living in Capernaum who was paralyzed so that he couldn't walk. He was very unhappy. His friends knew he was miserable because he couldn't get about and had to beg for a living. But they didn't know that the man was unhappy for other reasons as well. He knew he'd done many wrong things in his life, and it was thinking about them that made him really unhappy.

One day as he lay on his bed, four of his friends came rushing up. "Jesus is in Capernaum," they said. "He's healing sick people."

"What good is that to me?" grumbled the man. "I can't go and ask him to heal me. You know I can't walk."

"You don't have to walk," replied his friends. "All you have to do is lie still. We'll carry you to the house where Jesus is." They each grabbed a corner of his bed, and off they went.

His friends puffed and panted as they carried him down the road, and the man thought about Jesus. Would Jesus really be able to cure him? Then the man thought about the wicked things he had done. He thought of the other people who were more deserving than he was. He began to think that Jesus probably wouldn't want to have anything to do with a person like him.

They reached the street they were looking for. It was easy to tell which house Jesus was in. There was a huge crowd of people around the doorway, all trying to hear what Jesus was saying to the Pharisees and teachers inside the house.

"Excuse us," said the four friends. "Please, let us through. This man needs to be healed."

It was no use. No one would give way. The people had enough trouble getting space for themselves.

"We'll have to give up," said the man who couldn't walk. "You'd better take me back." He was very close to tears.

His four friends looked at him, then at each other. No, they wouldn't give up so easily. There must be a way.

Then they saw how it could be done. They carried the man, still on his bed, up the outside stairs and onto the flat roof of the house.

"What are you doing?" cried the man when he realized what was happening. His friends were too busy to answer. Before anyone could tell them to stop, they began lifting off some of the roof tiles. Soon they had created

an opening large enough for the bed to go through.

They looked down over the edge of their hole. They could see Jesus teaching below. He was surrounded by the Pharisees and teachers who had come from all parts of Galilee, even from Judea and Jerusalem, to listen to him.

Slowly, carefully, the four men began to lower their friend down through the hole in the roof, using ropes attached to each corner of the bed. The man clung tightly to his bed, hoping he wouldn't fall.

In the room below, Jesus stopped talking. He looked up at this extraordinary sight. The Pharisees and teachers looked up too. They were horrified. How dare anyone behave like this?

The four friends continued to lower the man into the middle of the crowd and right in front of Jesus.

Jesus looked up at the faces of the men. He could see they were certain he had the power to heal their paralyzed friend. Then he looked down at the man. And the man looked up at Jesus. Jesus could see the misery and fear in his eyes, and he understood.

"My friend," Jesus said gently, "the sins you have committed are all forgiven."

Jesus was calling him "friend," and Jesus was forgiving him for those sins that haunted him.

The Pharisees and teachers began thinking, What? He's forgiving sins? Who is this man? He speaks blasphemy! Only God can forgive sins!

Jesus knew what they were thinking. He turned to look at them. "Which is easier," he asked, "to say 'your sins are forgiven' or to say 'get up and walk'?"

They were silent.

Jesus went on. "So that you can know that I have the power to forgive sins," he turned toward the paralyzed man again, "I say to you get up, pick up your bed, and walk."

There was a hiss of whispered surprise from the watching crowd. This man hadn't walked in years, if ever. Now Jesus was telling him to pick up his bed.

But the man who lay on his bed wasn't concerned with the crowd or the Pharisees. He could feel strength flowing into him. He moved his legs. He moved the legs that had been paralyzed and helpless for so long. He sat up. He struggled to his feet and wobbled a little. "Praise God!" he yelled. His face aglow with joy, the man bent to pick up his bed. The next moment he was pushing his way through the crowd. People stepped back in awe to let him pass.

The four friends came rushing down the stairs, and they were beside themselves with joy as they greeted their friend. Still praising God, he headed home. Everyone who saw him was astonished at the change that had taken place.

"We've seen something amazing happen here today," they said to one another.

Other amazing things were to happen.

The Roman Centurion's Servant

Most Jews hated the Roman soldiers who had overcome their country and now occupied it. But in Capernaum there was one Roman soldier whom they liked and respected.

He was a centurion, in charge of a hundred men. He was a strong, good leader. He was also kind and considerate. When the Jews' synagogue became too old for them to use, he had a beautiful new one built for them. He was concerned about everyone's welfare.

The centurion also had a servant whom he valued very much. The man was a willing, faithful worker and served his master well. One day the servant was taken ill. All the usual remedies were tried, but nothing worked. The centurion could see that his servant was close to death.

The centurion had heard about Jesus, and he knew that he had healed many people, even those who were dying. But Jesus was a Jew. He probably wouldn't want to help a Roman.

Desperately the centurion wondered what to do. Then he had an idea.

The chief rulers and elders of Capernaum were his friends. Surely they would speak to Jesus for him. He went to ask them. Wanting to help the centurion, the elders went to Jesus.

"Please," they begged, "come and heal the servant of this centurion, who is a good man and has been very kind to us. He respects the fact that we are Jews. He even built a new synagogue for us."

196

"Of course I'll come," said Jesus, and they set out together.

Back at home, the centurion was feeling dreadful. How could he possibly have asked Jesus to take all the trouble of coming to the house? It was worse than going to Jesus himself.

The centurion was embarrassed at the thought. He still felt that he couldn't speak to Jesus himself, but he had to do something.

Some of his friends were nearby. Quickly he spoke to them. "Please, take a message for me."

Seeing how upset and anxious he was, his friends agreed. They listened as he told them what to say.

"Hurry!" he urged.

They hurried and met Jesus along the road.

"Lord," they said, "the centurion says please don't go to the trouble to come to his house. He feels he doesn't deserve a visit from you, and he's not a good enough person to speak to you. If you'll just say the word, he knows his servant will be healed. He's used to giving orders himself. If he tells a soldier to go, the soldier goes. Or if he says come, the soldier comes. His servants obey him as well. So he knows your word is enough."

Jesus was utterly amazed. He turned around to the crowd of people who were constantly following him. "Listen," he said to them, "I haven't found anyone else with such great faith as this, not even among the Jews."

When the centurion's friends went back to the house, they found that his servant was quite well again.

Crowds of people continued to follow Jesus about, but sometimes he felt he just had to get away.

Mark 4:30-41; 5:1, 2, 21; Luke 8:22-27

The Storm on the Sea of Galilee

Jesus had spent most of the day talking to crowds of people who had gathered to listen to him.

"How can I tell you what the Kingdom of God is like?" he asked. He thought for a moment, then said, "It's like a mustard seed—the smallest of the seeds you plant. Yet once planted, it grows and grows until it's the largest plant in the garden. It's so big that the birds can perch in its branches and be shaded from the heat of the sun."

The people listened as Jesus continued to tell them stories. Later, when the crowds were gone, Jesus would explain everything more carefully to his disciples, for they were trying desperately to understand his teaching.

By the time evening came, Jesus was weary, but the crowds still did not leave. It was no use trying to walk away from them, for they would simply follow him. Jesus had been talking to them near the shores of the Sea of Galilee. Now as he looked around, he noticed the fishing boats on the shore.

"Let's sail over to the other side," Jesus said to his disciples, who were concerned about him and wanted him to be able to rest.

"Yes," they agreed. They all climbed into a boat and immediately pushed off from the shore and set the sail.

Jesus went to one end of the boat and lay down, resting on a cushion. The waters slapped at the side of the boat. The sail flapped softly in the wind, and the boat gently rocked up

and down. As the disciples talked quietly among themselves, Jesus fell asleep.

But then a sudden storm blew up. The boat began to toss violently. The disciples struggled to get the sail down. The boat almost capsized as huge waves rose up and crashed down into it. The disciples were terrified, yet Jesus still slept.

The waves lifted the boat high, then tossed it down again. The frightened disciples could bear it no longer. They scrambled down to the end of the boat where Jesus was sleeping.

"Master! Master!" Their voices could hardly be heard above the noise of the wind and waves. They touched him on the shoulder. "Master, wake up! We're in dreadful danger. We're likely to drown. Don't you care?"

Jesus woke up. He looked at the frightened faces staring down at him. He felt the tossing of the boat in the rough waves. And he got to his feet.

The disciples clung to the sides of the boat and watched him. What was he going to do? What could anyone do in a storm like this?

Jesus stood up straight and unafraid. He said to the storm, "Peace, be still."

Immediately the wind died down. The waves calmed and the water became smooth again.

Jesus turned to look at his disciples. "Why were you afraid? Why didn't you have even a little faith?"

The disciples gazed at him in awe. They whispered to each other, "Who is this man? Even the wind and the waves do as he tells them."

The boat sailed on. Everyone landed safely on the far shore, where, as usual, people were waiting to ask Jesus to help them.

Jairus's Daughter and the Sick Woman

It was the morning after the storm, and Jesus and his disciples were sailing back across the Sea of Galilee.

They looked toward the place where they were going to land. There was a crowd of people already there, waiting for Jesus.

As Jesus stepped ashore, they surrounded him in welcome. They were pleased that they'd guessed correctly about his return. Then a man named Jairus pushed his way through the crowd. His face was white and tense with anxiety.

Jairus was an important man, a ruler of the synagogue, but now he desperately threw himself down at Jesus's feet.

"Please," Jairus cried. "Come to my house. My daughter is dying. She's only twelve years old. Please come!"

Jesus gently helped Jairus to his feet. "Of course I'll come," he said. They set out at once. Jairus wanted to run, but the crowds flocked around, hemming them in. Pushing his way through, Jairus turned to see if Jesus was following.

But Jesus had suddenly stopped. He was standing still. He asked, "Who touched me?"

The people looked at him in amazement, and his disciple Peter said, "Master, people are all around you."

"Someone touched me in a special way," Jesus insisted. "I felt power going out of me."

A trembling woman knelt at his feet. "I touched you," she confessed.

"I've been ill for twelve years, and no one could help me. I knew if I just touched the hem of your robe, I would be healed." Her face began to light up as she added, "I am healed. I know that I am!"

Jesus looked at her with great kindness. "Because you had faith in me, you have been made well," he said. "Your faith has made you whole. Go in peace and be free from your suffering."

Jairus watched anxiously. Why didn't Jesus hurry? There was no time to be lost.

But just as Jesus moved toward him, Jairus saw some men coming from his house. A chill went through Jairus as the men made their way through the crowd to him.

"Your daughter is dead," they said. "Don't trouble Jesus anymore. It's too late."

Jairus was filled with grief. But Jesus, hearing the men's words, said, "Don't be afraid. Trust me, your daughter will be healed."

Then Jesus began to walk quickly toward Jairus's house. Jairus followed, afraid to even hope, yet still trusting Jesus.

When they reached the house, a crowd of people had already gathered. Everyone was crying and wailing because the child was dead.

"Hush," said Jesus. "She isn't dead. She's only asleep."

"What?" they exclaimed and began to laugh at him. Asleep indeed, as if they couldn't tell whether or not

a person was dead. The girl had died. They were certain of that fact.

Jesus sent everyone out of the room except three of his disciples—Peter, James, and John—and the girl's mother and father. Jairus looked sadly down at his beloved daughter's face. He saw that she was dead.

Quietly Jesus went to the girl. He took hold of her hand. "Child, wake up," he said gently.

The five people watching stood transfixed, for the girl who had been dead was starting to breathe again. She stirred a little and opened her eyes. She looked up at the faces of her father and mother and at the face of Jesus.

Then she sat up.

The next moment she was standing up, perfectly well again. Still her parents gazed, too amazed to move or speak.

Jesus smiled at them. "Give her something to eat," he said.

His words were so practical that they brought everyone back to their senses. Jairus hugged his daughter while her mother rushed to get a meal ready. The girl hadn't had a good meal in a long time.

Jesus looked at the three of them with great love in his eyes. "Don't tell anyone what happened here today," he said.

Then he and his disciples left.

Feeding the Five Thousand

Jesus had sent his disciples out into the nearby villages. They were to heal the sick and tell everyone about God's kingdom while Jesus continued to teach alone.

Now the disciples had returned to report all that had happened. It had been an exciting, but very tiring experience. Jesus and the disciples wanted to rest and enjoy a meal in peace. But people kept coming to them to be healed or to talk or to listen.

At last Jesus said to the twelve, "Come with me. We'll go to a quiet place to be by ourselves."

They went down to the shore, got into a boat, and set sail for the small town of Bethsaida. But someone had seen them go. Quickly the message spread, and people from the surrounding towns ran swiftly to get to the place where they knew Jesus would soon land.

Jesus saw the people waiting for him, and he felt a great love and pity for them. They needed him so much. He couldn't bear to try to get away from them again.

After landing the boat, Jesus and the disciples climbed a short way up a hillside so the people could see and hear him better. He talked to them, telling them more about God and his kingdom. He healed the sick people and told stories to the children who were there.

The day passed. Even though it grew late in the afternoon, the crowd remained as huge as ever. The disciples began to worry. They imagined all those people trying to get home in the dark, stumbling over the rough ground with only the light of the stars to guide them. And the crowd must be very hungry, for they hadn't eaten all day. Surely Jesus hadn't noticed how late in the evening it was getting.

They went to him and said, "Master, this is a very lonely place, and it's going to be dark soon. We really believe you should tell all these people to leave now so that they can get food for themselves and find somewhere to spend the night."

Jesus looked at their anxious faces. "You give them food to eat," he said.

"What?" said Philip, one of the twelve. "It would take eight months of a man's wages to be able to buy enough bread to feed them all!"

"Find out how much food we have," said Jesus.

The disciples inquired among the people, and soon Andrew came to Jesus, leading a small boy. "This boy has five small barley loaves and two small fish," said Andrew. "That's all we've been able to find." He looked around hopelessly. "What use is this among such a large crowd?"

Jesus said, "Tell everyone to sit down in groups of hundreds and fifties."

The disciples looked at one another; then they obeyed. Soon the people were sitting on the grassy hillside. There were about five thousand men, and many more women and children.

The boy watched as Jesus took the five small barley loaves and gave thanks to God for them. Then he gave the loaves to the disciples to pass out to the people.

Next Jesus took the fish, gave thanks to God for them, and gave them to the disciples to pass out.

And there was plenty of food. Everyone could eat as much as they wanted.

When the people were so full that they couldn't eat any more, Jesus said to the disciples, "Go around and gather up any leftovers so that nothing is wasted."

The boy was amazed. The disciples were also amazed as they collected enough scraps of food to fill twelve baskets.

Jesus saw how tired the disciples were. "Return to the boat and go on ahead of me," he said. "I'll tell the people it's time for them to leave."

Gladly the weary disciples obeyed. But the people were not ready to be sent away. They were talking excitedly among themselves.

"Surely Jesus is the prophet we have been waiting for. Let's make him our king!"

Jesus knew what they were saying, but it was not God's will for him to be king. He quietly left the people and made his way alone further up into the hills. There he prayed.

Meanwhile, his disciples had gone down to the seashore.

Matthew 14:22-32; Mark 6:45-52; John 6:16-27

Jesus Walks on the Water

It was almost dark. The fishing boat lay waiting at the edge of the water. Some people stood nearby, and they saw the disciples come to the boat. They were surprised to see the disciples without Jesus.

The twelve climbed into the boat.

"Should we wait for Jesus?" one of them asked.

"No, he told us to go on without him," the others replied.

They started to row. It had become quite dark. A strong wind was blowing against them, and the sea was rough. Wearily the disciples pulled on the oars. They would have had a hard time of it even if they had been well-rested. Now the journey seemed endless. The disciples had been rowing for some time, but because of the rough waves, they had traveled only three or four miles.

By the dim light of the moon, the disciples suddenly saw a figure coming toward them, walking on the water. They did not realize it was Jesus.

The disciples froze in terror. "It's a ghost!" they cried out.

At once Jesus spoke to them. "It's me. Don't be afraid."

The disciples strained to see. Peter said, "Master, if it's really you, tell me to walk on the water toward you."

"Come," said Jesus. The disciples watched in silent awe as Peter climbed over the side of the boat and walked toward Jesus. He took a few steps in perfect safety. Then he realized what he was doing. He saw the roughness of the wind and the waves, and he was afraid. Immediately he began to sink.

"Lord, save me!" Peter cried.

Instantly Jesus reached out and caught him. "You have so little faith," he said. "Why did you doubt?"

Together they got into the boat. At that same moment, the wind ceased to blow and the sea became calm.

In the moonlight the disciples looked at Jesus. Reverently they said, "Truly you are the Son of God."

They crossed the Sea of Galilee and came safely to the other side. The next day the people who had seen the disciples leave in the boat without Jesus were confused. They said, "Jesus is over on the other shore. But he wasn't in the boat when it left here, and there was only one boat."

The Man Who Couldn't Hear

There was a man living in the territory of the Ten Towns who was deaf.

Life was hard for him. He couldn't hear the sounds of people joking and laughing. He couldn't hear music, a bird's song, or stories.

Because he couldn't hear words, he couldn't learn to speak correctly. Also he may have had something wrong with his tongue.

So he had great difficulty in making himself understood. He couldn't easily ask for what he needed or tell others what had happened to him. He couldn't share good news or be comforted when life was sad. He felt lonely and isolated, as if no one cared.

But some people did care. They heard that Jesus, who healed the sick, was nearby.

Eagerly they rushed to tell the deaf man. Out of breath from running, they found him. How would they tell him?

They stood in front of him, excitedly waving their arms about and saying, "Jesus is nearby. Jesus!"

Puzzled, the man tried to make out what they were saying. Impatiently they shouted, "Jesus! Quickly! Before he's gone!"

Still the man didn't understand. Then one of them seized his arm. "Come with us," he said and motioned for the man to follow him.

Still puzzled, but aware of their excitement, the deaf man went with them.

As usual, there was a crowd around Jesus. But they stood back to let the little group get through. Jesus looked at the eager faces of the little group and at the puzzled face of the deaf man.

"Please!" begged the people who had brought him. "This man is deaf, and he can't speak properly. If you will just touch him, he will be healed."

Jesus looked at them again and at the crowd around them. Then he gently took the bewildered deaf man by the arm and led him to one side, away from all the noise and confusion. The deaf man gazed into Jesus's face, trying desperately to understand. Jesus didn't try to speak to him. Instead, he put his fingers into the man's ears. The man nodded. He couldn't hear.

Jesus touched the man's tongue. Again the man nodded. He couldn't speak. The man knew that Jesus understood his problem. Here was someone he could trust.

Jesus looked up to heaven. He sighed. Then he said, ''Ephphatha,'' which means ''open up.''

At once the man's ears were clear. He could hear! He could hear perfectly. He could hear the voices of the crowd a little way off, the sound of the wind in the trees, the song of the birds. Joy surged through him. He tried to speak and found that he could. His tongue was working correctly.

The people who had brought the man saw his glowing face and heard him using his voice. They too were overjoyed.

Jesus smiled at them. ''Don't tell anyone,'' he said.

But they couldn't help it. They were so glad that they couldn't keep quiet about what Jesus had done. And people who had known the deaf man were utterly amazed.

''Jesus does everything so well,'' they said. ''He can even make deaf people hear and mute people speak.''

The news about Jesus spread. A group of ten sick men heard of him.

Luke 17:11-19

The Ten Lepers

Jesus was now making his way to Jerusalem through Samaria and Galilee. Ten men who suffered from the disease of leprosy learned that he was going to pass quite close to where they were living.

Leprosy was a dreaded disease because no one knew how to cure it. The disease would eat away at whichever part of the body was affected. Fingers and toes could be lost, and faces disfigured. As if the ugliness alone was not enough to bear, the lepers also had the added problem of trying to manage with only the stumps of fingers or toes. Because leprosy showed up as white patches on the skin, it was impossible to hide it for very long. Everyone was afraid of catching it, so lepers were forced to leave their homes and go outside the village to live.

They could never again kiss the people they loved or hug their children. They could never mix with their former friends. Indeed, they soon began to dread meeting anyone because of the fear on other people's faces when they saw a leper. They hated the way people would shout at them to go away.

There was no hope for them. Lepers were utterly isolated and miserable. They were forced to wear torn clothes and to let their hair grow long and untidy in order to cover the lower part of their faces. They were required by law to call out, "Unclean, unclean," if they saw anyone coming.

But these ten had heard that Jesus healed sick people. Could he heal them? Would the crowds who always followed him even let them get near enough to ask? One of the men, a Samaritan, was even more concerned because Jesus was a Jew, and for many years the Jews and the Samaritans had disliked and mistrusted each other.

But the ten lepers resolved to try to reach Jesus.

They watched and waited near the road, and sure enough, at last they saw Jesus coming. Other people were with him, as they'd expected. Not daring to attempt to get closer, the lepers called out, "Jesus, Master, help us!"

Jesus heard their voices and turned to look at them. He saw their troubled, desperate faces and called back to them, "Go and let the priests examine you."

The lepers looked at each other for a long, silent moment. Go and show themselves to a priest? They'd had to show themselves to a priest when they first caught the disease. It was the priests who decided which people did have leprosy and thus must live outside the village. People only went back to the priests if they wanted to prove they were well and didn't have leprosy after all. Yet Jesus must have seen the patches of leprosy still on them.

But the lepers trusted Jesus, so they set out to find the priests. As they walked together, their skin cleared. Excitedly they checked each other for signs of the disease. Their skin had been healed.

Then one of them, the Samaritan, came rushing joyfully back to Jesus, praising God as he came. He threw himself down at Jesus's feet. "Thank you! Oh, thank you!" he cried.

Jesus looked down at the Samaritan. Then he looked at the people who were with him. "Weren't all ten healed?" he asked. "Where are the other nine? Is this foreigner the only one ready to praise God?"

Then gently Jesus spoke to the Samaritan. "Get up and go on your way. Your faith has made you well."

The news about Jesus continued to spread rapidly among the people. And the children heard of him too.

Matthew 19:13-15; 20:17-19; Mark 10:13-16, 32, 33;
Luke 18:15-17, 31-34; Isaiah 53:7-12

Jesus and the Children

The people wanted to ask Jesus to bless their sons and daughters. And the children who were old enough to understand longed to see Jesus for themselves. But it wasn't easy to get small children safely through the crowds which usually surrounded Jesus.

One day a group of parents and children came eagerly toward Jesus as he sat and rested for a while. This could be their chance. They could reach him, talk to him, and listen to him. Excitedly the children tried to run on ahead.

But the disciples turned and saw the little group. "Why are you bothering Jesus with all these children?" the disciples asked the parents harshly. "He can't talk to you now."

The mothers and fathers stood for a moment in great disappointment. After all their efforts to get their children here, they would have to go away.

But Jesus had heard the disciples' words, and he spoke sternly. "What are you doing? Let the children come to me. Don't try to stop them. The Kingdom of Heaven belongs to such as these."

He opened his arms wide, and the children ran to him. He said to the people who were watching, "I tell you all, if you don't receive the kingdom in the same spirit as a child does, you'll never enter it."

The parents were happy and smiling now. Jesus took the children into his arms and blessed each one. The people who crowded around tried to understand what he was saying. They were to accept God's kingdom in a spirit of trust, the way a young child trusts his or her parents.

The mothers, fathers, and children happily went back to their homes. Jesus and his disciples continued on their way toward Jerusalem. He intended to be there for the Feast of the Passover. But the people who followed him were afraid.

Jesus had been walking a little way in front of his disciples. When he noticed their anxious faces, he called them to one side. He knew exactly what was troubling them. The chief priests and the Pharisees had often been angry over the things Jesus said and did. They made up their minds he wasn't the Son of God, the Messiah. They decided he was just an ordinary man. The priests and Pharisees were afraid that the people would try to make Jesus their king,

that there would be trouble with the Romans, and that the priests and Pharisees themselves would suffer. So they were waiting for a chance to kill Jesus. And the disciples thought that if Jesus went to Jerusalem, he would be walking into a trap.

"Listen," Jesus tried to explain. "We are going to Jerusalem. The Son of Man will be handed over to the chief priests and the teachers of the law. He will be condemned to death by them. They will hand him over to the Roman soldiers, who will mock him, torture him, and crucify him. This must happen, just as the prophets foretold. But three days after his death, the Son of Man will rise to life again."

The disciples listened, but they couldn't understand what he was talking about. They only knew that Jesus was quite set in his purpose. They loved him, and if he went to Jerusalem, so would they.

First they had to pass through Jericho, and as usual, someone was waiting eagerly for Jesus to come by.

Mark 10:46-52; Luke 18:35-43

Bartimaeus

In Jericho there lived a man named Bartimaeus, who was blind.

He could not find any work, so to keep from starving, he sat by the road-side all day, begging for money.

Just by listening, Bartimaeus could tell many things about the people passing by on the road. He could tell if they were hurrying or strolling. He could tell if they were alone or in groups. He could tell if they were excited or sad. He caught many snatches of conversation, and some of the people knew him and stopped to talk to him.

Bartimaeus had heard about Jesus and his teachings. Bartimaeus knew that Jesus loved people and did wonderful things, including healing the sick.

If only I could get to Jesus, thought

213

Bartimaeus. It seemed impossible. Every morning Bartimaeus made the long, difficult trip along the busy streets of Jericho to his begging place just outside the city gates. He had chosen that spot because so many people passed by there on their way to and from Jerusalem.

Then Bartimaeus heard that Jesus was on his way to Jerusalem. He would be coming that way.

For a moment Bartimaeus was full of excitement. Then he remembered that wherever Jesus went, there were crowds. How could a blind man possibly push his way through a crowd to find a person he couldn't see?

Disappointment flooded through him. But maybe, if he just sat there and called out to Jesus, he might be able to make himself heard.

For several long, hot, dusty days, Bartimaeus sat by the roadside and worried. Then at last he heard the sounds of an excited crowd, distant at first, but coming closer.

"What's happening?" he called to the passersby.

"Jesus of Nazareth is coming!" someone answered.

Bartimaeus's heart raced. He took a deep breath and listened for the sounds of the crowd to come even closer. He waited until he guessed Jesus was passing him, then shouted, "Jesus, help me!"

"Shhh!" People at the edge of the crowd hushed him. "Be quiet!"

Bartimaeus took no notice of them. "Jesus!" he shouted even louder. "Jesus, Son of David, help me!"

Amid all the noise and bustle, Jesus

heard Bartimaeus and turned to look for him. Jesus saw that Bartimaeus was blind and unable to make his way through the crowd.

"Bring that man to me!" Jesus said.

Now hands were urging Bartimaeus to get up. Voices said, "Come on! Jesus wants you!"

His heart pounding, Bartimaeus threw off his cloak so that it wouldn't get in his way. He scrambled to his feet and let himself be led into the middle of the crowd. The guiding hands let go of him, and he knew he must be standing in front of Jesus.

He heard Jesus ask, "What do you want me to do for you?"

"Oh," Bartimaeus replied, "if only I could see."

Jesus answered, "Then see. Your faith has healed you."

At once light dazzled Bartimaeus. He put up a hand to shade his eyes. He could see the sunshine. He could see the trees, the sky, and the faces of the crowd. He could see Jesus.

No longer would he have to sit begging by the roadside. He'd never sit there again. His sight was now perfect.

Bartimaeus was overjoyed and gave thanks to God. Then he joined the crowd following Jesus, rejoicing at every new thing he saw.

When the people saw Bartimaeus, they all praised God and were glad.

But also in Jericho, someone else was longing to see Jesus.

Zacchaeus

Zacchaeus was a chief tax collector in Jericho. He was rich, but his money had come from collecting taxes from the people. Sometimes Zacchaeus and the other collectors took more money from the people than was rightfully owed in taxes. Almost all Jews hated tax collectors for this very reason. Zacchaeus had few friends, and he was very lonely.

One day as he sat by himself, he heard the sounds of many people passing by his house. What could be going on? Zacchaeus went outside and saw that the road was filled with people. He listened to their excited voices. "Jesus is coming this way!" they were saying.

Zacchaeus had heard of Jesus. He had heard that Jesus was friendly, even toward tax collectors.

Zacchaeus longed to see what Jesus looked like. But Zacchaeus was a very short man, and he was standing at the very back of the crowd now lining the road. When he tried to squeeze to the front, the people looked down at Zacchaeus in disgust, then they moved even closer together.

Zacchaeus was desperate. He could tell by the sounds of the crowd that Jesus was getting closer. It appeared that Jesus would pass by without Zacchaeus getting even a glimpse of him.

Then Zacchaeus had an idea. Farther down the road was a sycamore tree. Zacchaeus ran to the tree and began to climb it as quickly as he could. He was out of breath when he reached the top, and he hoped he wouldn't be too late to see Jesus.

Once the wealthy tax collector was perched in the branches of the tree, he had a perfect view of the road. He could see the crowd coming toward him, and in the midst of the people, he could see Jesus. Somehow Zacchaeus knew at once which one was Jesus.

Zacchaeus watched the crowd getting closer and closer. Now they were passing by the sycamore tree. Some of them were right underneath him. Jesus was almost there.

Suddenly Jesus stopped and looked straight up at Zacchaeus. Jesus said to him, "Zacchaeus, come down. Today I must stay at your house."

It was a moment or two before Zacchaeus realized what Jesus had said. Then filled with excitement and joy, he came scrambling down. Jesus wanted to stay with him.

"You are very welcome in my house," Zacchaeus replied. "It's just a short distance from here. Let me show you the way."

Now Zacchaeus was not squeezed

to the back of the crowd. He was leading the way with Jesus beside him. When the people saw what Jesus did, they began to mutter, ''Look at that! Jesus is actually going to visit the house of a sinner!''

When Zacchaeus heard these words, he stopped. ''Master,'' he said, ''I'll give half of my belongings to the poor. And if I've cheated anyone, I'll give him back four times as much.''

There was a gasp of surprise from the people. Jesus said to them, ''Salvation has come to this house today, for this man is also a son of Abraham. Remember, the Son of Man has come to seek out and save those who have strayed from God.''

Zacchaeus heard Jesus's words, and he felt happier than he had ever been before. Gladly Zacchaeus led the way into his house.

After Jesus had visited Zacchaeus, he continued on his way toward Jerusalem.

The people thought about the many things Jesus had taught them.

The Sermon on the Mount

One day when Jesus saw the crowds following him, he went up on a mountainside and sat down. The people gathered all around Jesus, and he taught them. Here are some of the things he said that day:

"Happy and blessed are those who know they must trust in God, for the Kingdom of Heaven shall be theirs.

"Blessed are those who mourn and are sad, for they shall be comforted.

"Blessed are those who are not proud but humble, for they shall inherit the whole earth.

"Blessed are those who greatly desire to do right, for they shall be satisfied.

"Blessed are those who are merciful, for mercy shall be shown to them.

"Blessed are those whose thoughts are pure, for they shall see God.

"Blessed are those who make peace, for they shall be called the children of God.

"Blessed are those who suffer for what they know to be right, for theirs is the Kingdom of Heaven.

"If men persecute you, call you names, and tell lies about you because you love me, rejoice and be glad, for your reward in heaven will be great.

"If you are my followers, you are like salt which gives flavor to food. Or you are like a light for the whole world. So don't hide your light where it can't be seen. When you do good, people will see it, and they will give praise to God your Father.

"You have been told, 'You shall not kill.' But I say to you, thoughts which make you feel like murdering someone are also wrong.

"You have been told, 'An eye for an eye, and a tooth for a tooth.' But I say to you, do not take revenge on anyone who acts wrongly against you.

"You have been told, 'Love your

friends, but hate your enemies.' But I say to you, love your enemies. Pray for those who do you wrong. This way you will become sons and daughters of your heavenly Father. For he makes his sun to shine and rain to fall on the good and bad alike. Why should God give you a reward for loving the people who love you? Even tax collectors do that. And if you talk only to your friends, you've done nothing special.

"If you help those who are in need, don't tell everyone about it. Your Father in heaven will see, and he will reward you.

"When you pray, talk quietly to God. He is your Father and knows what you need even before you ask him for it.

"Pray like this: Our Father, who is in heaven, hallowed be your name. Your kingdom come, your will be done, on earth as it is in heaven. Give us this day our daily bread. And forgive us our debts as we forgive our debtors. And lead us not into temptation, but deliver us from evil. For yours is the kingdom, the power, and the glory, forever. Amen.

"And don't worry. Your heavenly Father knows what you need. Put his kingdom first, try to do as he wants, and everything you need will be given to you. Don't worry about tomorrow. Tomorrow will have enough worries of its own.

"Don't judge other people, saying they are right or wrong. If you judge them, you will be judged yourselves. It's as if you saw a speck of sawdust in someone else's eye and never noticed a huge plank of wood in your own eye.

"If your son asked for bread, would you give him a stone? Or if he asked you for a fish, would you give him a snake? If you know how to give good gifts to your children, just think of how much more your heavenly Father will give to those who ask him.

"Always treat other people the way you would like them to treat you. This is what the law is about."

As they listened, the people were amazed because Jesus taught them with authority, but not in the usual way of the teachers of the law.

He finished his teaching that day, as he often did, by telling a parable, a story with a special meaning.

Matthew 7:24-27; Luke 6:47-49

The House on the Rock

Jesus had been speaking to a crowd on a hillside. At the end of his sermon, he told them this parable.

"There were two men. Each one wanted to build a house. The first man understood how important it was for his house to have a good, firm foundation. So he dug deep into the ground until he came to solid rock. He laid the foundation on the rock and built his house there.

"Soon afterward a storm began to blow. The wind howled and the rain poured down. Rivers overflowed their banks, flooding the land and beating against the walls of the house.

"But the house was built on a strong foundation, and it did not fall.

"Anyone who hears my words and lives by them is like the wise man who built his house on the rock. When troubles come, that person will not give in, but will stand firm.

"The second man cared nothing about having a strong foundation for his house. He built it on sand.

"When the storm came, the flood-waters rose and the wind hurled itself against the house. Without a strong foundation, the house had no chance. It fell down with a mighty crash.

"Anyone who hears my words and does not live by them is like the foolish man who built his house upon the sand. When troubles come, that person will be crushed by them because he does not have anything strong on which to stand."

The Sower

Wherever Jesus went, crowds of people gathered around him, wanting to hear him. He often told parables, or stories with special meanings, for the people to think about. This is one of the parables Jesus told.

"A farmer went out to sow some seed. As he walked up and down his field, he scattered handfuls of grain from the basket slung over his shoulder.

"Some seed fell on the path, and the birds swooped down and ate it.

"Some seed fell on rock, where there was little soil. The seeds sprouted, but the young plants could not put down roots. They soon withered and died in the hot sun.

"Some seed fell among thorn bushes. The seed grew, but the thorns grew faster, choking out the tender plants.

"But some seed fell on the good, rich earth. The plants put down deep, strong roots. The crop grew tall and ripened in the sun. By the time of the harvest, the plants had produced a hundred times more grain than the farmer had sown."

Jesus's disciples didn't understand the meaning of this parable, so they asked him to explain it.

Jesus replied, "The seed stands for God's Word. Some people listen to God's Word carelessly. Satan can easily make them forget what they've heard. That is the seed which fell on the path.

"Some people listen gladly and believe for a short time. But as soon as trouble comes, they stop believing. That is the seed which fell on the rock and had no roots.

"Some people hear the message, but their minds are so full of other thoughts, worries, and desires that there is no room for God's Word to grow. That is the seed which fell among thorns.

"But some people listen to God's Word and believe it. They make his message part of their hearts, and their lives show that they love and obey God. That is the seed which fell on rich soil and produced a fine harvest."

223

The Good Samaritan

A teacher of the law tried to test Jesus with a difficult question.

"Master," he said, "what must I do so that I can live forever in God's kingdom?"

Jesus knew the lawyer wanted to trap him, so he answered with a question. "What does the law tell you about this?"

The lawyer answered, "I must love the Lord my God with all my heart and with all my soul and with all my strength, and I must love my neighbor as much as I love myself."

"That's right," said Jesus. "If you do that, you will live."

But the lawyer was not satisfied, and he asked another question. "Who is my neighbor?"

Jesus answered with a parable.

"Once a man was going from Jerusalem to Jericho. The road was lonely and dangerous. Bands of thieves often hid among the rocks, waiting to pounce upon unwary travelers.

"The man hurried along, hoping to avoid any trouble. But it was no use. A band of thieves suddenly sprang out and attacked the man, stripping him of his clothes and all that he had been carrying. Then they disappeared among the rocks, leaving the man half-dead by the roadside.

"For a long time, the man lay in the hot sun, too weak and injured to move, hoping desperately that someone would come and help him.

"At last he heard footsteps approaching. Feebly he raised his head to see who was coming.

"It was a priest. The man thought that surely a priest would help him. But as the injured man watched helplessly, the priest walked by on the other side of the road without giving the man a second glance.

"The man's head throbbed more painfully than ever. He knew that he desperately needed help. He weakly closed his eyes.

"He heard more footsteps, and as they neared, he opened his eyes and saw that a Levite was coming. Levites were servants of the Temple. Surely someone who served God in the Temple would help. The Levite came over, bent down, and looked at the man.

"Then the Levite straightened up and walked on.

"The injured man groaned in despair. He would die there by the roadside.

"Once again the man heard the sounds of another traveler approaching. He painfully opened his eyes and saw that the traveler was a Samaritan. The man sank back with a groan. The Jews and Samaritans had been enemies for years. It was certainly no use expecting this

Samaritan to help him. The man closed his eyes, all hope gone.

"But the sounds of footsteps and the clip-clop of the donkey's hooves slowed to a stop. The injured man felt gentle hands touching him. He looked up and saw that the Samaritan was helping him. The Samaritan bathed his wounds with soothing oil and poured wine on them as an antiseptic. He bandaged the injuries as well as he could and gently held a drink of cool, clear water to the injured man's lips, supporting the man's head as he drank.

"The Samaritan refused to leave the man lying by the roadside. When the injured man tried to stand, his head spun and he would have fallen if the Samaritan had not supported him carefully.

"Seeing that the man was too weak to walk, the Samaritan led him to the donkey and helped him onto its back. Then slowly and carefully, the Samaritan led the donkey along the stony road until they came to an inn.

" 'We'll rest here for the night,' said the Samaritan.

"He led the man inside and took care of him, attending to his wounds once more and bringing him food and drink.

"When morning came, the Samaritan could tell that the injured man was still not well enough to continue with his journey.

" 'It doesn't matter,' said the Samaritan. 'You must stay here until you are fit to travel.'

"And knowing the robbers had stolen all the man's money, the Samaritan spoke to the innkeeper.

" 'Here are two pieces of silver,' he said. 'Take care of this man. If it costs more than this, I'll pay you the rest when I come back this way.' "

The lawyer had been listening intently to the story.

"Now," said Jesus, "which one of those three was a neighbor to the man who was robbed and beaten?"

The lawyer answered, "The one who was kind to him and helped him."

And Jesus said, "Go and follow his example."

The Lost Sheep and the Lost Coin

The Pharisees and the scribes were muttering among themselves. "Just look at that! Jesus is talking to tax collectors and people who don't obey God's laws. He even eats with those people!"

Jesus heard what they were saying, and he told them this parable.

"Imagine a shepherd who has a hundred sheep. When he counts them one evening, he finds that only ninety-nine are safely in the fold. One of his sheep is lost. What does he do? He leaves the other ninety-nine sheep in a safe place and goes in search of the one that is missing.

"He searches all over the countryside and does not give up. When he finally finds his lost sheep, the shepherd is full of joy. He tenderly picks up the weary sheep and carries it home on his shoulders. Then he calls to his friends and neighbors and says, 'Look, be glad with me! I've found my sheep that was lost!' "

Jesus looked at the Pharisees and the scribes.

"I say to you that God is like this shepherd. There is more joy in heaven over one person who realizes that he has been doing wrong and changes his ways than over ninety-nine good people who have been doing right all the time."

The Pharisees and scribes who were listening frowned and were not pleased with Jesus's words. Then Jesus told another parable to make his meaning clear.

229

"Imagine a woman who has ten pieces of silver. Suddenly she realizes that she has lost one of the coins. She is very upset because each coin is worth a great deal of money. What does she do? Anxiously, she lights the lamp and places it so that its light shines into every corner of her house. Then the woman gets her broom and sweeps carefully.

"She searches everywhere until at last she sees her coin, shining in the light of the lamp. She joyfully picks up her coin and calls to her friends and neighbors, 'Come here, let's celebrate! I lost my coin, but now I've found it. Be happy with me.' "

Jesus said to his listeners, "I tell you, there is joy among the angels over one sinner who repents."

The Prodigal Son

Jesus told another parable for the benefit of the Pharisees and the scribes.

"There was once a man who had two sons. The older son was hard-working and obedient. But the younger son did not want to work. He didn't like being told what to do and was never content.

"'It's so boring at home!' he complained.

"The younger son knew his father was rich and owned a lot of property. He also knew that when his father died, everything would be divided between himself and his brother. But it could be years before he inherited his part of the estate. Why should he have to wait for his father to die before he could enjoy himself?

"So without thinking about his father's feelings at all, the younger son demanded, 'Give me my share of everything now!'

"The father loved his son very much but guessed the lad would want to leave home as soon as he had enough money. Even though the father knew how much he would miss his son, he didn't want to force his son to stay by keeping him short of money.

"So the father divided the family estate fairly between his two sons.

"As soon as he received his share, the younger son collected everything he owned and went off to a distant land.

"People soon found out he had a lot of money. They came to his parties, accepted his presents, and pretended to be his friends.

"For a while the young man enjoyed himself. He bought whatever he wanted and did just as he liked. But soon the money was gone, and when his new 'friends' found out, they went too. To make things worse, there was a severe famine in the land.

"Now the young man was alone in a strange country with no money, no food, no friends, and no family. He tried to get a job, but no one would employ him. Finally a man hired him to look after his pigs.

"The young man took the job. He had no home, no money, and no one to care whether he lived or died. His once fine clothes were now dirty rags, and he was so hungry he wished he could share the pigs' food.

"One day as he sat watching the pigs, he thought about home. He realized that while he was starving to death, his father's servants had more than enough to eat.

"'I don't deserve to be called a son anymore,' he said to himself, 'but perhaps my father would give me a job. I'll go back and ask him to make me one of his servants.'

"So the son set out on the long walk home. Weary, half-starved, and footsore, he trudged along the road. He wondered if his father would let him into the house at all. Maybe his father had forgotten all about him by now.

"But far from forgetting, his father had never stopped watching for him. His father looked down the road every day, hoping his son would return.

"Now in the distance, a thin, shabby figure appeared, limping along. Could it be? The father strained his eyes, shading them against the sun.

"Even though the figure looked nothing like the finely dressed young man who'd gone marching off many months ago, the father recognized his son at once.

"With a cry of joy, the father ran down the road to meet his son.

"The youth could hardly believe it. Instead of refusing to see him, his father threw his arms around his son and kissed him.

"The son tried to say how sorry he was that he'd done wrong, and he tried to explain that he was no longer worthy to be called his father's son.

"But his father was already calling to the servants. 'Hurry, bring my son the finest clothes! Put a ring on his finger and kill the fattened calf we've been saving. We must celebrate! It was as if my son were dead, but now he's alive again!'

"When the elder son came in from the fields, he heard the music and laughter coming from the party. He called to a servant, 'What's happening?'

"The servant explained, 'Your brother has returned, and your father is having a great celebration!'

"The older brother grew very angry and refused to go inside the house.

"The father came hurrying out to him, because he loved both his sons. 'Come to the party!' he pleaded.

"The older son answered angrily. 'I've stayed here and worked hard for you all these years, and you've never even given me a young goat so I could have a party with my friends. But this son took half your money and wasted it. Then when he had nothing left, he came home, and you killed the best calf for a grand celebration!'

" 'Son,' said his father, 'you have always been with me, and everything I have is yours! But we should still be glad and celebrate, because your brother was lost to us and now he's found.' "

Jesus explained that God is like the father in the story. He never stops loving us. He's ready to forgive anyone who is sorry for what he has done wrong, and he is overjoyed when everything is well again.

The Midnight Visitor

Jesus was explaining more about prayer to his disciples when he told them this parable.

"It's midnight. You are at home when suddenly there's a knock on the door. You open it, and standing there is a friend of yours. He's on a journey, and he's stopped at your house to rest and have a meal. You welcome him gladly and invite him in. Then you realize that you don't have anything for him to eat. It's the middle of the night. Where can you get food at this hour?

"You think desperately, and you remember your friend down the road.

"Quickly you run to his house. The house is dark, but you bang on the door anyway. You call out to him. 'Please, will you lend me three loaves of bread? A friend of mine has turned up unexpectedly, and I haven't got any food for him.'

"You wait. After a moment you hear a sleepy voice from inside the house.

"'Go away, stop bothering me! The door's locked for the night. I'm in bed, and so is my family. I can't get up now and give you bread.'

"What will you do?

"You don't go away. You keep on knocking and calling to him. At last you hear him stumbling about in the darkness inside his home. He lights the lamp and comes to the door. Then he gives you the bread because you wouldn't stop asking."

Jesus's disciples listened to the story and wondered about its meaning. Jesus said to them, "In your prayers, ask and keep on asking. If you, being ordinary human beings, know how to give good things to him that asks, how much more will God give good gifts to you. Ask, and if it is something God knows will be good for you, you will receive it."

The Talents

Jesus told another parable to his disciples.

"A rich man was going on a journey. It wasn't practical to take his money with him, so he called his three servants to him to leave the money in their charge.

"To the first servant, he handed five talents of money. To the second, he handed two talents. Finally to the third, he handed one talent. Each talent was worth a very large amount of money. The rich man divided up his money according to how he thought each servant would be able to manage it.

"Then the rich man went off on his journey.

"The first servant took the five talents and invested them. He did so well that he soon doubled the amount of money entrusted to him.

"The second servant also invested the money. He too doubled the amount.

"But the third servant thought, Suppose I try to invest this money? I might lose it all. My master would be furious with me. Anyway, I didn't get as large an amount as the others received. It can't matter much what I do with the money, as long as I don't lose it. I'll just keep it safe. I'll hide it.

"The third servant secretly dug a hole in the ground and buried his talent there.

"After a long time, the rich man came back from his travels. His three servants came to him. The first said, 'Master, I invested the five talents you entrusted to me. I made five more. Here are the ten talents.'

"The rich man said, 'Well done, good and faithful servant. You've been trustworthy over a few things. Now I will put you in charge of many. Come and share my happiness.'

"Then the second servant said, 'Master, I took the two talents you entrusted to me, and I made two more. Here are the four talents.'

"And the rich man said, 'Well done, good and faithful servant. You've been trustworthy over a few things. Now I will put you in charge of many. Come and share my happiness.'

"The third servant had been watching. Now reluctantly he came forward. He could see he had to make some excuse.

"'Master,' he said. 'I know that you are a hard man. You gather harvests which you haven't sown. I was afraid to do anything with the money, in case I lost it. So I kept it safe in a hole in the ground. Here it is.'

"The rich man was furious. 'You wicked, lazy servant! In all this time, you have done no work for me at all! If you knew I reaped where I hadn't sown, why didn't you at least put my money in the bank, where it would have earned interest for me? You should have been braver and used your chance to serve me.'

"Then he ordered, 'Take that talent away from him and give it to the servant who has ten. For to every person who has something, more will be given, until he has plenty. A person who uses his opportunities will find his life growing richer and richer. But a person who wastes his chances will have nothing. His life will grow even poorer than it was before. Now take this useless servant and send him away.'"

When Jesus told this parable, he was telling his disciples of their responsibility. Jesus was like the master in the story, leaving his followers to continue the work of increasing God's kingdom on earth.

Jesus as the Good Shepherd

Jesus moved steadily on toward Jerusalem even though he knew what would happen to him there. On the way he explained more about himself to his disciples.

They were used to seeing shepherds caring for sheep. They knew that if danger from a lion or a bear threatened the flock, a good shepherd would protect his animals. He would be ready to die in the attempt rather than leave them to be killed.

The disciples had seen shepherds searching for fresh pastures for their flocks and for cool streams where they could drink in safety. The disciples had seen shepherds searching for lost lambs and watching tenderly over the ewes. A good shepherd would know each animal individually.

So the disciples understood something of Jesus's love and care for them when he said, "I am the Good Shepherd. The Good Shepherd gives his life for his sheep. I am the Good Shepherd; I know my sheep, and they know me. As God the Father knows me, so I know the Father. And I lay down my life for the sheep.

"No man takes it from me. I lay it down myself. I have the power to lay it down, and I have the power to take it up. This is what I have been told to do by my Father."

Many people heard the words Jesus said. They argued among themselves over what he meant, and some of the people grew angry.

"He is speaking blasphemy!" they said. "He is making himself out to be God!"

The angry people wanted to stone him.

But Jesus slipped away from them. He left Judea and went back across the River Jordan. Many of the people there believed in him.

But he did not stay long.

Mary, Martha, and Lazarus

In the village of Bethany, about two miles from Jerusalem on the side of the Mount of Olives, there lived three friends of Jesus: Mary, Martha, and their brother Lazarus.

Martha had often invited Jesus to stay at their house. During one of his visits, she busied herself with the preparation of the meal, trying to make everything especially nice for him.

Martha was becoming flustered and cross because her sister Mary wasn't helping at all. Mary was just sitting there, listening to Jesus. It wasn't fair.

For a while Martha worked alone. Then words burst from her. "Lord, my sister is leaving me to do all the work! Don't you care? She should be helping me. You tell her!"

Jesus answered gently, "Martha, you're worrying about many things. But they're not really as important as what Mary has chosen to do. I won't take it from her."

Then Martha realized that listening to Jesus was more important than getting special meals ready or being fussy about the housework.

Jesus thought of Mary, Martha, and Lazarus as his good friends. Now as he walked with his disciples, a man rushed up to him.

"There's a message for you from Mary and Martha," the man said urgently. "Your friend Lazarus is very ill."

Jesus said quietly, "The end of this sickness is not death. God's glory will be shown because of it."

Though he loved all three of them

very much, Jesus did not set off at once for Bethany. Instead, he remained where he was for two more days. Then he said to his disciples, "Let's go back to Judea."

They answered in alarm, "The people there want to stone you!"

But Jesus replied, "Our friend Lazarus is asleep and I am going to wake him."

The disciples were puzzled. Surely, if someone were ill, sleep would be good for them.

"Lord, if he sleeps, he'll get better," they said.

Jesus saw they didn't understand, so he spoke plainly. "Lazarus is dead. And because of what you will now see, I'm glad I wasn't there. Because now you will believe."

The disciples looked at one another. Thomas was absolutely certain Jesus would be stoned to death if they went. Even so, he said, "Come on! Let's all go, so that we can die there with him."

By the time they neared Bethany, Lazarus had been buried for four days. Many of the Jews had come to comfort Mary and Martha. Some of them saw Jesus and his disciples approaching the village and rushed to announce their arrival.

When Martha heard that Jesus was coming, she hurried out of the house to meet him. Mary remained sitting, quiet and still. As soon as Martha reached him, she said, "Lord, if you'd been here, my brother wouldn't have died!"

Then she added, "But I know that God will do whatever you ask him, even now."

Jesus's eyes were full of sympathy and understanding. "Your brother will rise to life again," he said.

Martha faltered. "I know he will rise to life in the resurrection on the last day," she answered.

Quietly but clearly Jesus said, "I am the resurrection and the life. He who believes in me, though he were dead, yet will he live. And whoever lives and believes in me will never die. Do you believe this?"

Martha met his eyes. Quietly and calmly she replied, "Yes, Lord, I believe you are the Christ, the Son of God, who has come into the world."

When she had said this, she slipped back to the house.

"Mary," she whispered, "Jesus is here. He wants to see you."

There was something different about Martha, a kind of excitement. Mary stirred herself from her grief and hurried out to meet Jesus. The Jews who had been in the house comforting her said, "See how quickly she moved! She must have gone to mourn at Lazarus's grave. We'd better go after her."

So they followed.

Mary almost ran along the road toward Jesus. When she reached him, she tearfully threw herself down at his feet. Mary used exactly the same words as Martha had used.

"Lord, if you'd been here, my brother wouldn't have died!"

When Jesus saw how she wept and that her friends wept also, he was distressed. "Where have you buried Lazarus?" he asked.

"Come and see," they answered. As they led him to the place, Jesus wept. Some of the watching Jews said, "Jesus must have loved Lazarus very much." But others said, "He could make blind men see. Couldn't he have prevented Lazarus from dying?"

Jesus reached the tomb, a cave whose entrance was blocked by a large stone.

Jesus said to the people watching, "Take away the stone."

There was a pause. Then Martha said, "Lord, by now the body will smell. Lazarus has been dead for four days."

Jesus answered her, "Didn't I say that if you believed, you would see God's glory?"

So hesitantly at first, not quite knowing what to expect, the people moved the stone away.

Jesus then spoke to God. "Father, I thank you because you have heard my prayer. I know that you hear me always, but I am saying this so that all these people may know that you have sent me."

Jesus finished his prayer, then called loudly, "Lazarus, come out here!"

And the man that had been dead came out. His hands and feet were still wrapped in grave clothes, and his face was still covered by a cloth.

The people stood silent and completely awestruck.

"Help him remove those grave clothes," Jesus said. "And let him go free."

Then the people did as Jesus told them to do.

Many of the Jews who had seen all this believed that Jesus was indeed the Messiah, the Son of God.

But some of them went to the chief priests and the Pharisees and reported these events to them.

The chief priests and the Pharisees called an urgent meeting to discuss what had happened.

"He's got to be stopped!" they said. "If we let him go on like this, everyone will believe in him! The Romans will come and destroy us, our Temple, and our whole nation."

"It is better for one man to die than for the nation to perish," said Caiaphas, the high priest.

From that day on, the chief priests and the Pharisees plotted to kill Jesus.

Knowing of their plan, Jesus went secretly to the village of Ephraim and stayed there until the time was right for what he knew must happen.

Matthew 21:1-11; Mark 11:1-11; Luke 19:28-40; John 11:55-57; 12:12-19

Palm Sunday

It was nearly time for the Festival of the Passover. Many people were traveling to Jerusalem to join in the celebration during this great time of praise to God. The favorite topic of most conversations was speculation about Jesus. Would he stay away from Jerusalem for fear of the Jewish leaders? Would he come to Jerusalem as all good Jews were supposed to? If he came, would he sneak into town? They kept looking for Jesus among the crowds in the Temple.

"Do you think Jesus will come?" they would ask each other. "Probably not. He must know about the order from the Pharisees and the chief priests that anyone who knows where Jesus is must report him. They are waiting for the right moment to arrest him."

Jesus did indeed know of the order. But it did not change his mind. He set out from Ephraim with his disciples.

As they came near to Bethphage, a village on the Mount of Olives, he said to two of them, "Go into the village. You'll see a donkey tied up there. You'll know which donkey I mean because she'll have a young colt beside her, a colt which no one has ridden yet. I want you to untie the colt and bring it here to me."

241

The disciples nodded in agreement. They thought it was better for Jesus to stay out of sight.

Jesus went on, "If anyone asks you what you're doing, just say, 'The Lord needs the colt and will send it back again soon.'"

The disciples nodded again. But they were puzzled. Why did Jesus need the donkey's colt?

Later they remembered the words which the prophets had spoken. The prophets foretold that the king of the Jews would come to his people humbly, riding on the colt of a donkey.

But now they went into Bethphage, as Jesus asked them. Sure enough, there was the colt tied up exactly as Jesus said. They untied it.

Some people who had been watching them suspiciously called out, "Hey, what are you doing with that colt?"

The disciples answered, "The Lord needs it and will send it back soon."

Immediately the people became silent and stepped back to allow the disciples to lead the colt away.

Jesus was waiting for them. When the disciples realized he was going to ride the colt, they spread their garments on its back to make a saddle.

Word spread quickly, and a crowd gathered near the road.

"Jesus is coming!"

People threw their garments down in the road so that Jesus might ride over them. Some people cut branches from the palm trees and spread them on the road. Some people waved the branches like banners.

As Jesus and his disciples traveled toward Jerusalem with Jesus riding on the donkey, they were completely surrounded by the crowd. People were shouting, "Hosanna to the Son of David! Blessed is he that comes in the name of the Lord! Hosanna in the highest!"

Many people in the crowd were there only because they'd heard about how Jesus raised Lazarus from the dead. In spite of all Jesus's attempts to teach them about himself and about God's kingdom, the people still didn't understand.

So Jesus did not sneak quietly into Jerusalem, fearful of the plots made by the chief priests and the Pharisees. Instead he returned to the city openly and courageously in the middle of a cheering crowd.

As Jesus and his followers entered the city streets, the people who were already there asked, "Who is this?"

Jesus's followers proudly replied, "This is Jesus, Jesus of Nazareth!"

And Jesus went directly to the Temple.

Matthew 21:12-17; 26:4; Mark 11:15-19; Luke 19:45, 46

Cleansing the Temple

When Jesus reached the Temple, he stopped. Anger rose within him as he saw what was happening there.

Young goats and lambs waiting to be bought and used as sacrifices stood trembling in their pens and bleated in distress. Also, there were caged doves and pigeons, terrified by the noise and bustle of the crowds. People flooding in from all over the country were in need of sacrifices. Here at the Temple, they could buy a sacrifice acceptable to the priests. The Temple looked like a marketplace.

There were moneychangers as well. Because Roman coins could not be used in the Temple, men sat at tables with piles of coins in front of them, ready to make change for the people who wanted to buy sacrifices.

As Jesus watched, he saw that the moneychangers were making a profit. They were making a profit in God's Temple. They were lining their pockets with money the people were bringing to give to God.

Jesus was furious. He picked up a piece of rope which lay on the ground

nearby and slammed it down like a whip on a pile of coins. The coins scattered, rolling everywhere. Jesus overturned all the tables, and as the moneychangers sprang to their feet, Jesus also overturned their stools.

Now he went to the animals, kicking away the bars of the pens so that the lambs and baby goats could run free. He scattered the cages, and the birds soared into the air. Then Jesus looked at the sellers of birds and animals and at the moneychangers and said, "It is written in the Scriptures, 'My house shall be called a house of prayer.' But you have made it a den of thieves!"

The Temple was filled with confusion and with the noise of fleeing animals, of people diving for money, and of angry and excited voices. But above all the uproar, some of the children who had been following Jesus could be heard shouting, "Hosanna! Hosanna to the Son of David!"

244

The disciples stood and watched, unable to move. They tried to understand Jesus's actions. Jesus, their beloved Lord, was already in danger of death. Instead of appeasing the chief priests and the Pharisees, he was condemning the way the Temple was being run. Jesus's enemies were sure to be more angry than ever.

The blind and lame people came to Jesus, begging to be healed. And Jesus healed them, right there in the Temple. Even though the chief priests and Pharisees had Jesus in their grasp, they dared not touch him. They were afraid that the crowd would turn against them.

The children were still shouting, "Hosanna to the Son of David!" The Pharisees could no longer suppress their anger.

"Don't you hear what they're saying?" they demanded.

"Certainly I hear them," Jesus replied. "Haven't you read the Scriptures where this was foretold? 'Out of the mouths of babies and children you shall hear perfect praise.'"

Again Jesus was correcting them, the experts on the Scripture. He continued, "If the people hadn't called out, even the stones would have taken up the cry."

The Pharisees and chief priests said among themselves, "It's no use. It's as we said before. We're not succeeding in stopping him. Next he'll be leading the people to revolt. He must be stopped. We'll have to capture him secretly."

It was getting late in the day. Jesus took his twelve disciples, and they left the noise and bustle of Jerusalem to go to the village of Bethany for the night.

And a few days later in a house in Bethany, a beautiful thing happened.

Supper at Bethany

One evening when Jesus and his disciples were in Bethany, Simon, who had been a leper, invited them to supper at his house. Some of Jesus's other friends were there also.

As the guests reclined at the table, a woman came into the room. In her hands she held an alabaster jar of precious perfume. Everyone stopped talking to watch her. There was something about the way she looked and the sorrow on her face.

Quietly the woman went over to Jesus. Gently and reverently she poured the perfume over his head and his feet. Then she dried his feet with her hair.

The lovely scent of the perfume filled the room. The guests looked at her silently and were puzzled.

Then Judas Iscariot, who was in charge of the disciples' money, spoke sharply. "What a waste. That perfume was worth more than a year's wages. It could have been sold, and the money could have been given to the poor."

Some of the other disciples agreed. The woman shrank back. She had tried to tell Jesus that she knew of the sorrow and suffering that was to come to him and that she cared deeply. But her action of love had been misunderstood. She'd been stupid and wasteful.

But Jesus had not misunderstood. "Leave her alone!" he said. "What she has done is beautiful. There will always be poor people among you whom you can help. But you will not always have me. She poured this perfume over me to prepare my body for the burial which is to come. And I tell you that wherever the Gospel is preached throughout the whole world, her love revealed here will also be told. Her action will never be forgotten."

The woman knew Jesus understood her as he protected her from the disciples' harsh words, and she loved him more than ever.

But Judas was furious. In his anger and disappointment, Judas went secretly to the chief priests and officers of the Temple.

"I know where Jesus is," he told them. "I will tell you where he goes, and you will be able to capture him in a quiet place away from the sight of the crowds who follow him."

The chief priests rubbed their hands together in delight. They thought they were to be rid of Jesus at last.

They promised Judas Iscariot thirty pieces of silver as a reward, and Judas began watching for a chance to hand Jesus over to them.

Matthew 21:18-22; Mark 11:12-14, 20-25

The Withered Fig Tree

Early one morning Jesus and his disciples set out from Bethany to walk to Jerusalem.

On the way Jesus felt hungry. He noticed a fig tree growing by the road-side. It seemed to be a good, strong tree with plenty of leaves. It looked as if it would be full of fruit, just as Jerusalem appeared to be full of people who were ready to follow him.

But when Jesus went over to the tree and seached among its branches, he couldn't find a single fig. What it had promised wasn't there at all, just as the people in Jerusalem would soon show how little they really cared about Jesus.

Jesus said to the tree, ''You will never bear fruit again,'' and the fig tree withered up in the sunshine.

The disciples were amazed. ''Why did it wither so quickly?'' they asked.

Jesus said to them, ''If you have faith and don't doubt, you will be able to do much more than wither a fig tree. You will be able to tell this mountain to be moved, and it will be cast into the sea. When you pray and believe, you will receive. So when you ask for something in prayer, believe that you will receive it, and you will have it.''

Still talking together, Jesus and his disciples went on toward Jerusalem.

248

Mark 12:37-44; Luke 20:45-47; 21:1-4

The Widow in the Temple

When Jesus and his disciples reached Jerusalem, they went straight to the Temple. As usual, a large crowd gathered eagerly to hear Jesus's teaching.

"Beware of the teachers of the law," he warned them. "They walk around full of their own importance. They have places reserved for them in the synagogues, and they sit in the best seats whenever there is a feast. But secretly they cheat the poor and take away their homes. Then they stand where everyone can see them and recite long prayers, so that people will be impressed by how good they are. But God is not deceived. The lawyers will be punished for their deeds."

As the disciples listened, they were afraid for Jesus, for this kind of teaching would anger the authorities still more. Yet the disciples understood that Jesus couldn't bear to see the people betrayed by the very men who should be showing them the love of God.

Now as Jesus sat there, he could see people putting money into the offering box. Many rich men came swaggering through the crowds. They dropped their silver and gold coins into the box with a loud clatter, hoping everyone would be impressed by the amount they had given.

Then a woman whose husband had died came into the Temple. It was clear that she was very poor. She was pale and shabbily dressed. Humbly she walked to the offering box. Hoping no one would notice her, she quietly dropped in two small copper coins.

As she moved away, she was ashamed because her offering was so small. Jesus spoke to the listening crowd. "I tell you that this poor widow has given more than any of those rich people gave."

The crowd gaped at him. How could he say that? Hadn't he seen the two tiny coins?

Jesus explained. "The rich men gave out of their plenty. It was such a small proportion of their wealth that they won't even notice it has gone. But this woman has given God all the money she had, because she loves him. She gave her all. No one can ever give more than that."

Now the crowd understood. The widow hurried away, but there was a warm glow in her heart.

Judas stood back and watched. He was still waiting for a chance to betray Jesus.

Preparing for the Last Supper

It was the first day of the Festival of the Passover. Jesus's disciples asked him, ''Where shall we eat the Passover meal?'' They were wondering if there was a safe place anywhere in Jerusalem.

Jesus took Peter and John to one side. ''Go into Jerusalem,'' he said. ''As you enter the city, you will meet a man carrying a pitcher of water. Follow him. He will lead you to a house. Say to the owner of the house, 'The Teacher asks where he may eat the Passover meal with his disciples.'

''He will show you to a large, upper room. That is where you must make everything ready.''

Peter and John set out. Sure enough, they met the man carrying the pitcher of water. To see a man carry water was very unusual because carrying water was normally work for women.

There was no need to speak. Peter and John anxiously followed the man, keeping well behind him so they wouldn't attract suspicion.

The man led the disciples safely to the house. The owner showed them to the upstairs room, just as Jesus had promised. Peter and John began the preparations.

When they had finished preparing for the Passover meal, the two disciples returned to Jesus and the others. Later that evening the twelve went with Jesus to the upper room.

In that hot, dusty country, it was the custom for a servant to wash the feet of anyone coming into a house.

But the disciples went straight to the table. None of them intended to be a servant to the others.

So as the meal was being served, Jesus stood up and took off his outer robe, wrapping a towel around his waist.

The disciples watched, first in amazement, then with shame. Jesus poured water into a basin and washed their feet, drying them with the towel around his waist.

Jesus began to wash Peter. Peter resisted him, saying, ''Lord, do you mean to wash my feet?''

''You don't understand now what I'm doing,'' Jesus replied, ''but you'll understand later.''

''You'll never wash my feet!'' Peter said, feeling he couldn't bear to have Jesus serve him.

''If I don't wash you, you'll have no part of my kingdom,'' Jesus answered.

Then Peter cried, ''Lord, wash not

only my feet but my hands and my head as well!''

Jesus answered, ''Anyone who has had a bath only needs to wash his feet. You are clean.''

Then he said, ''All my disciples are clean, except one.''

Jesus knew that Judas meant to betray him that night.

When Jesus had washed all the disciples' feet, he took off the towel and put his robe on again. Then he sat once more at the table.

''Do you understand?'' he asked. ''You call me 'Teacher' and 'Lord,' and you are correct because that is what I am. But since I, your Lord and Teacher, have washed your feet, you should be ready to wash one another's feet. I did this so that you could copy me. Don't be ashamed to carry out such tasks. No servant is greater than his master, nor is any messenger more important than the one who sent him. If you serve one another, you will be happy and blessed. And whoever is kind to any messenger of mine is being kind to me and to the one who sent me.''

Now they were ready to start their meal.

Matthew 26:21-35; Mark 14:17-31; Luke 22:14-23, 31-34;
John 13:21-38; 14:1-31; 18:1, 2

The Last Supper

It was their last supper together. Jesus was very troubled. ''I tell you truly,'' he said, ''one of you who sits at the table with me will betray me.''

Only Judas knew exactly what he meant. Judas had already secretly agreed to betray Jesus to the Jewish authorities. But the other disciples were not aware of what had happened, and Jesus's statement con-

fused them. They were upset, fearing that they might indeed betray him in a moment of carelessness or doubt.

''Is it I, Lord?'' they asked.

John was sitting next to Jesus. Peter whispered to John, ''Ask him which one of us he means.''

John moved very close to Jesus. ''Lord,'' he pleaded in a low voice, ''who is it?''

Jesus answered, "It is he to whom I give this bread."

He dipped some bread into the sauce and handed it to Judas.

"The Son of Man will die as it has been foretold," said Jesus. "But it will be terrible for the man who betrays him. It would be better for that man if he had never been born."

Judas met Jesus's eyes and tried to bluff his way out. "Surely you don't mean me!" he said.

But Jesus knew. "Go and do what you have to do," he replied.

Judas got up and went out into the night.

None of the other disciples realized what was happening. They knew Judas was in charge of the money. So they thought Jesus had told him to go and buy something they needed.

During the meal Jesus took the bread and gave thanks to God for it. Then he broke the bread and gave it

to the eleven, saying, "Take this and eat it. It is my body, broken for you. Do this in memory of me."

The disciples were puzzled and stared at him. Jesus took the wine, and when he had given thanks to God, he poured the wine for the disciples. He said, "Drink all of it. This is the cup of the New Covenant in my blood which is shed for you. I will drink no more of the fruit of the vine until the day I drink it once again in the Kingdom of God."

Still the disciples looked distressed. "God's glory will be revealed," Jesus said. "My beloved friends, I shall not be with you much longer. So I give you a new commandment. Love one another as I have loved you."

"Lord, where are you going?" they asked. "We will come with you!"

"You cannot come with me now," Jesus answered gently. "Later you will follow me."

"Why can't we come with you now?" Peter demanded. "I would die for you!"

"All of you will desert me and run away," said Jesus. "And Peter, before the rooster crows today, you will say three times that you never knew me."

"I'll never deny knowing you!" Peter cried, deeply distressed.

Jesus continued to comfort his special group of friends. "Don't let your hearts be troubled! You believe in God, so believe in me also. In my Father's house there are many rooms. If it wasn't so, I would have told you. I go to prepare a place for you. And if I go to prepare a place for you, I will come again and take you there, so that where I am, there you may be also. You know where I am going, and you know the way."

Thomas said, "Lord, we don't know where you are going, so how can we know the way?"

Jesus answered, "I am the way, the truth, and the life. No one comes to the Father, except by me. If you had known me, you would have known the Father."

Then Philip said, "Lord, show us the Father! Then we will know!"

Jesus replied, "Philip, have I been so long with you, and yet you still haven't known me? If you have seen me, you have seen the Father."

He looked around at their troubled faces. "If you love me, obey my words. I will ask the Father to send you another comforter, who will be able to stay with you forever. I will not leave you like orphans; I will come to you. Soon the world shall see me no more. But you will see me. And because I live, you will live also. Peace I leave with you; my peace I give to you. Do not let your heart be troubled, neither let it be afraid."

After Jesus and the disciples had talked a while longer, they sang a hymn and went out into the night.

They walked in the darkness until they came to the Garden of Gethsemane.

And Judas knew exactly where they had gone.

In the Garden of Gethsemane

The Garden of Gethsemane was dark and shadowy in the moonlight. Jesus said to his disciples, "Sit here while I go over there and pray. Peter, James, and John, come a little further with me."

Peter, James, and John went with Jesus. They could see he was very distressed.

"Keep watch," said Jesus. "My sorrow is so great—it almost crushes me."

Jesus went a little way apart from them and knelt on the ground. He prayed, "Father, if it is your will, take this cup of suffering from me. But let your will be done, not mine."

Then Jesus came back to Peter, James, and John. Instead of keeping watch as he had asked, they had fallen asleep because they were weary after the long, hard day.

Jesus said, "Simon Peter, are you asleep also? Couldn't you keep watch for just one hour?"

The three disciples woke up very ashamed. They felt terrible that they had let him down when he was in such distress.

"Keep watch," he said again. "And pray that you may not give in to temptation." Then he looked at them with gentleness and compassion. "Your spirits are truly willing, but your bodies are weak," he said.

He went away again to pray. In

agony, he said, "Father, if this cup of suffering is the only way, your will be done."

He came back to the three. Once more they had fallen asleep. Once more he woke them up. They could find no words to say to him.

A third time Jesus prayed. A third time he returned and found them sleeping. This time he said, "Are you still asleep? Look, the hour has come. Let's go. Here comes the one who will betray me."

The disciples awoke, suddenly aware of the light of torches and lanterns in the garden. They saw an approaching crowd carrying sticks and swords. Sent by the chief priests, the mob was accompanied by soldiers of the Temple.

The disciples struggled to their feet. But Jesus was not trying to escape.

He stepped forward calmly and quietly, facing the rabble. "Who are you looking for?" he asked.

"Jesus of Nazareth," answered the people.

"I am he," Jesus replied.

Judas pushed his way to the front. He went to Jesus.

"Do what you have to do," said Jesus.

Then Judas kissed Jesus and called him "Rabbi," for this was the secret sign that had been arranged with the chief priests.

"Do you betray the Son of Man with a kiss?" Jesus asked him.

The soldiers moved forward to arrest Jesus. Peter was furious and seized a sword, cutting off the ear of the servant of Caiaphas, the high priest.

But Jesus touched the man's ear and healed him.

"Put down your swords," he said to his followers. "For he who lives by the sword shall die by the sword. Don't you think I could ask my Father for help? He could send legions of angels to defend me. But if I do, the scriptures will not be fulfilled. Do you think I will not obey my Father's will?"

Jesus spoke to the crowd. "Am I leading a revolt? Is that why you come to capture me with sticks and swords? Didn't you see me every day, teaching in the Temple? You didn't arrest me then."

Finally, he said to the soldiers, "I am Jesus of Nazareth whom you have come to arrest. Let these others go."

His disciples, seeing what was going to happen next, deserted Jesus and fled.

The Trials of Jesus

Now Jesus was in the hands of his enemies. They bound him and led him away. Because the disciples were afraid for their own lives, they deserted him. But Peter and John were tormented by love, fear, and sorrow and couldn't bear not knowing what was happening. So they stopped running and turned to follow Jesus. They kept well back and remained hidden in the darkness.

The chief priests, the elders, and the temple guards took Jesus to the house of Caiaphas, the high priest. First Jesus was questioned by Annas, father-in-law of Caiaphas. Then he was taken before Caiaphas himself to be put on trial by the Sanhedrin, the Jewish high court.

Peter and John waited outside in the courtyard. It was a cold night, and the servants had made a fire. Shivering from the cold, Peter moved closer toward the fire. He saw people being taken into the house. These people were prepared to tell lies about Jesus, and the chief priests were determined to have Jesus killed, even though he had done nothing which deserved death.

Jesus listened to the many lies which were told, but he remained silent until at last Caiaphas spoke. "Tell us. Are you the Son of God?"

There was a hushed pause as everyone waited for the answer. Jesus said, "Yes, as you have said. And you will see the Son of Man sitting at the right hand of God and coming in the clouds of heaven."

"He speaks blasphemy!" announced Caiaphas. "We do not need to hear any more!" And he tore his cloak, as was the custom with the Jews when they believed someone was speaking against God. "What do you think should happen to him?"

"He must be put to death!" shouted the chief priests and the elders. Then they began to strike Jesus.

Outside, Peter heard the shouts. As he shivered in cold and fear, one of the maids noticed him. "You!" she said. "You were with that man."

"No!" Peter said in fear. Hastily he left the fire and went out to the gateway.

Another girl saw him and said, "This man was with Jesus."

"I don't know what you're talking about!" protested Peter.

But later other people standing nearby said, "You are one of them. We can tell you come from Galilee by the way you talk."

Peter was desperate. "I tell you *I don't know him!*" he shouted. And then,

as the people looked at him with hard, unfriendly eyes, Peter heard a rooster crow.

He remembered what Jesus had said to him. ''Before the rooster crows today, you will say three times that you never knew me.''

Then Peter rushed outside and cried bitterly in sorrow and shame.

It was dawn. The chief priests and the elders took Jesus under guard to Pilate, the Roman governor of that district. Judas saw this. He realized Jesus had been condemned to death by the Jews, and he couldn't bear it. He took the thirty pieces of silver which had been his reward for betraying Jesus and hurried to the chief priests and elders. ''I was wrong,'' he said. ''I've betrayed an innocent man.''

They answered cruelly, ''Why should we care? What you did was up to you.''

Judas threw the money at them. Then, unable to live with the thought of what he had done to Jesus, he went out and hanged himself.

Now Jesus stood silently while Pilate questioned him. ''They say you have been calling yourself a king. Are you king of the Jews?''

''You say that I am,'' said Jesus.

The chief priests and elders accused him of many things, but Jesus answered not one word.

Pilate was puzzled. ''Don't you hear what they're saying against you?'' he asked. Still Jesus remained silent.

Stirred up by the Jewish leaders, a crowd of people had collected. Pilate addressed the crowd. ''I can't find anything to charge this man with,'' he said.

The chief priests and the elders thought quickly. They had to charge Jesus with something which Pilate would think was a crime.

"He has been trying to start a riot in Galilee!" they shouted.

"So he's from Galilee," said Pilate. "Then this has nothing to do with me. You must take him to Herod. Herod rules in Galilee."

At that time Herod was in Jerusalem for the Feast of the Passover.

So Jesus was taken to stand yet another trial.

At first Herod was pleased to see Jesus. He'd heard about the miracles Jesus had done, and he wanted to see some now. He asked many questions, but Jesus would not say one word, although the chief priests and elders continued their lies. Herod finally grew angry. He and his soldiers dressed Jesus in a beautiful robe, cruelly making fun of him. Then they sent him back to Pilate.

The crowd followed. Some people were jeering, but some were friends of Jesus. His friends followed silently, overwhelmed with sorrow.

Pilate was faced once more with the decision.

"No one has found anything to accuse this man of," he stated. "I'll have him whipped, and then I'll let him go."

But by now many people in the crowd had worked themselves into a kind of madness.

"No, no, free Barabbas instead!" they howled. Pilate knew that at this feast, one prisoner was always released. He had hoped to release Jesus. But the crowd howled for Barabbas, a murderer. Pilate was afraid. He didn't want a riot.

As he stood there, wondering what to do with Jesus, a message came to him from his wife. It said, "I've had terrible dreams because of this innocent man. Don't have anything to do with him."

The crowds were still shouting. Pilate tried once more to save Jesus. "Which of the two do you want me to free? Jesus or Barabbas?"

"Barabbas!" they yelled.

"Then what shall I do with Jesus?" asked Pilate.

"Crucify him!" they yelled.

"Why? What wrong has he done?" pleaded Pilate.

But they shouted even louder. "Crucify! Crucify!"

Pilate sent for a basin of water. In front of them all he washed his hands as a sign that he wasn't making the decision.

"This is your responsibility," he declared.

"Yes!" screamed the mob. "His blood be on our heads and on our children's heads! Crucify! Crucify!"

So Barabbas was freed, and Jesus was whipped. Then he was handed over to be crucified.

Matthew 27:27-51, 54-56; Luke 23:26-48; John 19:1-30

The Crucifixion

The Roman soldiers stripped Jesus of his clothes. They dressed him in a purple robe and put a crown of thorns on his head. Then they put a staff in his hand and cruelly made fun of him by kneeling down and saying, "Hail, king of the Jews!"

Then they took the staff and struck him with it.

Once more Pilate took Jesus out to show him to the people. Surely now they would have pity on him. But still the crowds shouted, "Crucify! He says he is the Son of God! By our law he must die!"

Pilate took Jesus to one side and tried to question him again. But Jesus would not answer.

Pilate had never met anyone like this before. "Don't you know I can either set you free or have you crucified?" he asked.

Then Jesus answered, "You would have no power at all if it wasn't given to you by God."

The crowd was shouting at Pilate again. "If you let this man go, you are no friend of Caesar's. Anyone who says he is king is in opposition to Caesar."

Pilate was very much afraid of Caesar. So he finally handed Jesus over to be crucified.

The soldiers put Jesus's own clothes on him again. Then they forced him to carry a heavy cross to the place called Golgotha.

Weakened by the beatings, Jesus fainted on the way up the hill. A man named Simon of Cyrene was called out from the crowd to carry the cross for Jesus.

At the place of execution, Jesus's friends watched helplessly as the

261

soldiers nailed Jesus to the cross with one nail through each hand and foot.

The hammer blows fell. Jesus was in great pain, but he prayed to God, ''Father, forgive them, for they know not what they do.''

The cross was lifted and set into place. Then the soldiers sat down and began to divide up Jesus's clothes among them. They threw dice to see who would win his robe.

As he hung on the cross, many people jeered at him. The chief priests and elders mocked him, saying, ''Let him come down from the cross now and we will believe him!'' But Jesus was intent on carrying out God's plan, and he would not answer them.

Jesus's friends, especially the women, stood nearby. They hoped it would comfort Jesus to see them there. Even when most of the crowd had gone, they remained.

Two thieves were crucified on either side of Jesus. One thief was sorry for the wrong he had done and asked Jesus to think of him. To him Jesus said, "Today you will be with me in paradise."

As Jesus looked down from the cross, he saw his mother, Mary, and his disciple John. He said, "Woman, here is your son. Son, here is your mother." They realized that Jesus wanted them to be as mother and son to one another and to comfort each other.

Now Jesus was in very great pain. He called out to God, fulfilling the prophecy of the psalmist. "My God, my God, why have you forsaken me?"

After a while he said, "I am thirsty." So the people below soaked a sponge in vinegar and held it up to his lips.

Soon Jesus said, "It is finished. Father, into your hands I commit my spirit." And he died.

For the last three hours that Jesus was on the cross, there was darkness over all the land. As he died, there was a great earthquake, and the curtain which hung in the Temple was ripped in two.

The people were very afraid. The Roman soldiers who had helped crucify him were terrified. When they saw these things, they said, "Surely, this was the Son of God."

The Burial of Jesus

Jesus and the two thieves were crucified on Friday. The next day was the Jewish Sabbath, so that Friday afternoon, the Jewish rulers went to Pilate and asked that the bodies be taken down from the crosses. They did not wish them to be hanging there on a holy day.

First the soldiers broke the legs of the two thieves so that they died at once. But when they went to break the legs of Jesus, they found he was already dead. So as the Scriptures had foretold, none of his bones were broken. To be certain of his death, one of the soldiers pierced Jesus's side with a spear. Blood and water flowed from the wound.

Some friends of Jesus wanted his body so they could bury it properly and with care. One of them was Joseph from Arimathea, a wealthy member of the Sanhedrin who had secretly believed in Jesus.

He went boldly to Pilate and asked for the body.

Pilate turned to the Roman soldiers. "Is Jesus dead already?" he asked in surprise.

The soldier reported that he was, so Pilate gave Joseph permission to bury Jesus.

Joseph went to Golgotha, the place where Jesus had been crucified. Nicodemus, another member of the Sanhedrin who had also been a secret follower of Jesus, went with him.

Reverently they took the body and wrapped it with spices in a new linen cloth, as was the burial custom of the Jews.

Then they placed Jesus's body in the tomb which Joseph had intended to be his own when he died. The new tomb, which had been freshly cut out of solid rock, was in a garden close to the place where Jesus had been crucified.

The women who had been with Jesus at the cross followed Joseph and Nicodemus as they moved the body and took note of the location of the tomb.

Then Joseph rolled a large stone across the entrance of the tomb to close it. The men walked off, leaving Mary Magdalene and Mary, the mother of James and Joseph, still sitting across from the tomb.

Grieving bitterly, the women also left the garden.

It was now the Sabbath, and the chief priests and the Pharisees went back to Pilate because they were still anxious.

"Sir," they said, "we remember that while this liar was still alive he said, 'In three days I will be raised from the dead.' Command that a guard watch over the tomb until the third day has passed. Otherwise his disciples may steal the body and then spread the rumor that he is alive. The last lie would be more troublesome than the first."

"Very well," said Pilate. "Go and make the tomb as secure as possible. You may take a guard."

So the chief priests and the Phari-sees went to the garden, taking Roman soldiers with them. They put a seal on the stone so that it would be impossible to move it without the seal being broken. They also left well-drilled and highly disciplined Roman soldiers on guard.

Then they left the tomb believing that they were finished with Jesus and his teaching for good.

Matthew 28:1-10; Mark 16:1-8; Luke 24:1-12; John 20:1-25

The Resurrection

At sunrise on Sunday morning, Mary Magdalene and some of the other women set out to go to the tomb, taking more spices with them so they could anoint the body of Jesus. The women were grieving deeply and longed to show their love for Jesus by continuing to serve him, even in death.

On their way to the tomb, the women remembered the huge stone that had been rolled across the entrance. How would they ever be able to move it?

As they worried, a violent earthquake shook the ground, and in the garden an angel of the Lord came down, rolled away the stone, and sat on it. The angel's appearance was like a flash of lightning, and his clothes shone brilliantly white. When the Roman guards saw him, they fainted in terror.

Before the women reached the tomb, the angel had gone and the soldiers had awakened and fled in fear. Mary Magdalene hastened along in front of the others and saw that the stone had been rolled away. In great distress she ran back to find Peter and John.

The other women arrived at the tomb. Fearfully, they crept inside and gazed around. But the body of Jesus was no longer there. Suddenly, two angels in shining white clothes stood beside them. The women were terrified.

"Don't be afraid," said the angels. "You are looking for Jesus, who was crucified. But why are you looking for the living among the dead? He is not here. He is risen! See, this is where his body was laid. Remember what he told you.

"Now, go and give this message to Peter and the other disciples. Tell them that he is going before you into Galilee and you will see him there."

And the women remembered that Jesus had said he would rise on the third day.

They turned and ran as fast as they could to deliver the news to the disciples.

But Mary Magdalene had already reached Peter and John. "They have taken him away!" she sobbed. "And we don't know what they've done with his body!"

Stricken with fear and grief, Peter and John ran to the tomb. John arrived first and paused at the entrance. Peering in, he saw the cloths that had been used to wrap the body of Jesus.

Then Peter arrived, panting and breathless. He didn't stop at the entrance, but instead he went straight into the tomb.

Peter saw the linen cloth and wrappings which had bound Jesus's head. The cloths were lying separately and were neatly folded.

And Peter believed.

Then John also entered the tomb. He and Peter looked at each other in amazement. Puzzled and not fully understanding, they returned to the house where the other disciples were waiting.

But Mary Magdalene had not gone all the way back to the tomb with them. Instead she stood alone in the garden, weeping.

Now she stumbled forward and looked into the tomb. There she saw two angels sitting where the body of Jesus had been laid—one at the foot and the other at the head. But Mary did not realize they were angels.

"Woman, why are you crying?" they asked.

"Because they have taken away my Lord and I don't know where they have put him," she sobbed.

Mary then turned around and saw someone standing there, but she did not recognize him.

"Woman, why are you weeping?" the person asked. "Who is it that you are looking for?"

Nearly blinded by her tears, Mary thought he must be the gardener. "Sir, if you took him away, please tell me where you have put him!" she begged. "I will go and get him!"

Then Jesus said, "Mary."

She turned fully toward him and cried, "Rabboni!" which means "Teacher."

"Don't touch me," Jesus said. "I haven't yet gone back to my Father. But go to my friends and tell them I am returning to my Father and your Father. I am returning to God."

Mary was overjoyed and hastened back to the group of disciples. "I have seen the Lord!" she cried. Then she gave them his message.

But the disciples could not accept the good news. In spite of all the times Jesus had tried to explain what was to happen, now that it had occurred, they couldn't believe he had risen.

Late that same Sunday evening, the disciples were gathered in the room of a house. All the doors were locked tightly because the disciples were afraid. They were terrified that the Jewish authorities would find them and arrest them.

Suddenly, Jesus was standing in the room among them.

"Peace be with you!" he greeted them. The disciples gazed at him in fear, thinking he was a ghost. He held out his hands so that they could see the marks left by the nails. Then Jesus showed them where his side had been pierced by the Roman soldier's spear.

At last the disciples could accept the truth. This was no ghost. It was their master, risen and alive. They were full of joy.

Again Jesus said to his disciples, "Peace be unto you. As the Father has sent me, I also send you."

Thomas, who was not there when Jesus appeared to the disciples, returned some time later. The disciples excitedly told him, "We have seen the Lord!"

But Thomas shook his head. "Unless I can see and touch the marks of the nails and put my hand into the wound in his side, I won't believe!" he said.

And Thomas continued to grieve deeply.

The Roman Guards Talk to the Chief Priests

Some of the guards who had been at the tomb when the stone was rolled away went to the chief priests and told them everything that had happened.

The chief priests, pale and trembling, went to the other Jewish leaders. The guards' story could not be allowed to spread.

Together the Jewish leaders worked out a plan.

"Listen," they said to the guards, "you must say that Jesus's disciples came in the night and stole his body while you were asleep."

Then they offered the soldiers a large sum of money as a bribe. The soldiers hesitated. They did not like the idea of claiming to be asleep on duty.

The chief priests became more agitated. "If Pilate hears about all this, we'll make him believe you were completely blameless," they urged. "You've no need to worry."

So the guards took the bribe and spread a false story. Many of the Jews believed it.

But more of Jesus's disciples were beginning to learn the truth.

Luke 24:13-35; John 20:24-29

The Walk to Emmaus and Thomas Is Convinced

That Sunday evening, two of Jesus's followers were walking sadly to Emmaus from Jerusalem. Jesus himself drew near and walked alongside them.

Buried in their grief, the two didn't recognize Jesus. As they traveled together, Jesus asked them what they were talking about that made them so unhappy. One of the men, Cleopas, said, ''How can you not know what's been happening in Jerusalem these last few days? Everyone knows.''

''About what?'' asked Jesus.

''About Jesus of Nazareth,'' said Cleopas. ''He was a prophet, powerful in words and actions before God and all the people. The chief priests and rulers demanded that he be crucified. But we believed that he was the one who would set Israel free from the Romans. Now some of our women say that angels have told them that Jesus is alive. When some of us went to the tomb, the body was gone, but Jesus was not to be seen.''

Jesus answered, ''You are so slow to believe. It was necessary that all those things should happen.''

Then he began to explain the prophecies about the Messiah, beginning with the books of Moses.

As they walked and talked, the two followers began to feel happier. They became excited.

When they reached Emmaus, Jesus said he was going to walk farther. But Cleopas said, ''It's getting very late. It will soon be dark. Spend the night here with us.''

So Jesus went into the house with them. A meal was prepared, and they sat down to eat. Jesus took the bread and blessed it. Then he broke the bread and handed it to them. There was something familiar in the way he did this.

They recognized him immediately, and in that moment he disappeared from their sight. The two looked at each other, their faces ablaze with joy.

"It was Jesus! The stories the women told were true!" they cried. Then they rushed all the way back to Jerusalem to tell the other disciples.

But it was seven more days before Thomas was convinced.

Once again the disciples were in the room with the doors shut and locked. It was just as before, except this time Thomas was present with the others. Suddenly Jesus was there with them.

"Peace be with you," he greeted them. As they gazed at him, he held out his hands. Gently he spoke to Thomas. "Put your finger in the marks of the nails, and put your hand into the wound in my side. And do not doubt, but believe."

Thomas did not need to touch the nail prints nor put his hand into the wound. Filled with a mixture of awe, love, and almost overwhelming joy, he whispered reverently, "My Lord and my God."

Jesus said, "You believe because you see me. Blessed are those who have not seen me and yet have believed."

John 21:1-20; Matthew 28:16-20

Breakfast on the Shore

Jesus had said he would go before his disciples into Galilee. Now seven of the twelve waited there for him near the shores of the Sea of Galilee. Peter was one of the seven. He longed to see Jesus again; yet he was desperately upset about having denied knowing him three times.

After a while Peter felt that he could no longer bear to sit there doing nothing. He sprang to his feet. ''I'm going fishing,'' he said. It would be like the old days before he'd even met Jesus.

''We'll come with you,'' said the others. Anything was better than this waiting.

So they got into a boat and cast off. All night they fished, but they caught nothing. Dejectedly they began to sail toward the shore.

The sun had just begun to rise as the boat approached the land. The disciples could see a man standing on the beach, but they did not recognize him.

The man called to them from the shore, "Have you caught any fish, my children?"

"No," they answered.

He said, "Throw your net on the right side of the boat. You'll find some fish there."

James, John, and Peter looked at one another. Once before, someone had told them to do that.

They let the net down, and immediately it was full of fish. The net was so heavy with fish that the disciples couldn't haul it in. John said, "It is the Lord!"

Peter waited no longer. He put on his robe and waded to the shore. He splashed and stumbled through the water in his eagerness to get to Jesus. They were only about three hundred feet from the bank, so the others stayed behind to row the boat to the shore and haul in the net.

When they landed on the beach, a fire was already burning with fish cooking on it. There was bread waiting for them as well.

Jesus said, "Bring over some of the fish you've just caught."

While the others stood gazing at him, Peter dragged the net ashore by himself. There were one hundred and fifty-three fish altogether, yet the net was not torn.

"Come and have breakfast," Jesus invited them.

Still none of the disciples ventured to ask, "Who are you?" They were sure it was him. He was the same, yet he was different.

Jesus took the bread and gave it to them, as he had done so often before. Then he gave them each a portion of the fish.

When the meal was over, Jesus said, "Simon Peter, do you love me?"

"Yes, Lord," Peter replied. "You know I love you."

"Then feed my lambs," said Jesus. "Simon, do you truly love me?"

Peter answered again, "Lord, you know I love you."

Jesus said, "Care for my sheep."

And a third time Jesus asked, "Simon Peter, do you love me?"

Now Peter was hurt. "Lord," he answered, "You know everything. You know I love you."

Jesus said, "Feed my sheep." And he added, "Peter, truly I say to you, when you were young, you dressed yourself and went wherever you wanted to go. But when you are old, you will stretch out your hands, and another will dress you and carry you where you don't want to go."

It wasn't until much later that Peter realized those words foretold his own death in God's service. All he knew now was that he had been given the chance to say three times that he loved Jesus. Peter knew that Jesus had forgiven him for those three times that Peter had declared he didn't even know Jesus. And even more wonderful, Jesus had commanded Peter to care for his followers.

Some days later, the other disciples were also entrusted with the task of continuing Jesus's work on earth. They gathered on a mountain in Galilee, as Jesus had instructed them to do. When he appeared to them there, they worshiped him, although some of them doubted it was really him. Then Jesus came closer and spoke to them.

"All authority in heaven and on earth is given to me," he said. "Go and make disciples everywhere, baptizing them in name of the Father and of the Son and of the Holy Spirit. Teach them to obey all the commands I have given you. And lo, I am with you always, even to the end of the world."

Soon the disciples were to start this task. But first they were to see something marvelous.

The Ascension

For forty days after his crucifixion, Jesus appeared at different times to his disciples. Some of his followers had doubted, but by now the eleven were absolutely convinced of the truth of his resurrection.

As they ate their last meal together, Jesus said to them, "You must wait here in Jerusalem for the gift which my Father will send to you—the gift of the Holy Spirit."

But the disciples still didn't fully understand. There were many questions they wanted to ask. Jesus knew he could no longer remain on earth with them. He led them outside the city to the Mount of Olives.

"When the Holy Spirit comes to you, you will receive power," he promised them. "You will speak of me in Jerusalem, in all Judea and Samaria, and to the end of the earth."

He lifted up his hands to bless them, and even as he did so, he was taken up from them and received into the skies. Then a cloud hid him so that they could see him no longer.

As they gazed upward, two men dressed in shining white garments appeared beside the disciples and spoke to them.

"Men of Galilee, why do you stand gazing upward into the sky? This Jesus, whom you have seen taken up into heaven, will one day return in the same manner."

Filled with joy, the disciples went back to Jerusalem. There they prayed in the upper room.

And while they were waiting for the gift that Jesus had promised them, they spent much of their time in the Temple, praising God.

The Gift of the Holy Spirit

Fifty days after the Feast of the Passover came the Feast of Pentecost. Only ten days earlier, Jesus had ascended into heaven, and the disciples were still waiting for the gift of the Holy Spirit which Jesus had promised to them.

They chose Matthias to be one of the twelve in place of Judas Iscariot, and they became known as the apostles. On the day of Pentecost, they were all gathered together in the room of a house in Jerusalem.

Suddenly there came a sound from heaven like a rushing, mighty wind. It filled the whole house, and as the apostles looked at each other in fear, they saw what seemed to be tongues of fire. The fire divided so that a flame rested above each one of them.

The apostles were filled with the Holy Spirit of God, as Jesus had promised them.

As they spoke to each other, they found that they were talking in different languages, guided by the power of the Holy Spirit.

Jews from many nations were staying in Jerusalem to worship God at the Feast of Pentecost. When the news about the apostles spread, a crowd of these people came to listen. The visiting Jews were utterly amazed, because each one of them heard the apostles speaking in his own language—languages which the apostles had never spoken before.

"Aren't all of these men from Galilee?" they asked one another.

"How is it we can hear them talking about God in our own languages? What does it mean?"

Some of the listening crowd began to laugh and jeered, "They're drunk! That's what it is."

But Peter stood up boldly in front of them all, and the other apostles stood with him. No longer were they hiding in a locked room. Inspired and strengthened by the Holy Spirit, they were about to tackle the whole might of the Roman Empire and their own Jewish authorities.

"Listen to me," said Peter. "These men aren't drunk."

Then he told them how the Scriptures said God's Holy Spirit would be poured out on men, that their sons and daughters would prophesy and their old men would dream dreams. Then Peter told them the story of Jesus.

Around three thousand people heard, believed, and were baptized. Many miraculous signs and wonders were performed at that time in Jerusalem.

Now all of the believers shared everything they had. They gave each other what was needed. They met every day in the Temple and in each other's homes. They ate together, prayed together, and learned together.

They were happy and they praised God. Each day more and more people believed.

But the authorities were watching.

The Lame Man at the Beautiful Gate

In Jerusalem there lived a man who was unable to walk because he had been born lame. Because there was no work he could do, he was forced to beg for money.

Every day he was carried to the gate which was called Beautiful, and there he was left to beg for the remainder of the day. Many people passed by

the man on their way to and from the Temple, and often they gave him money.

One afternoon soon after the Holy Spirit came upon the apostles during the Feast of Pentecost, the lame man was in his usual place at the gate when he saw Peter and John coming toward him. They were on their way to the Temple to pray.

''Please!'' he called out. ''Give me whatever you can spare!''

Peter and John stopped. ''Look at us!'' said Peter.

They're going to give me some money, thought the lame man expectantly.

Then Peter spoke. ''I don't have any silver or gold,'' he said, ''but I will give you what I do have. In the name of Jesus Christ of Nazareth, get up and walk!''

The lame man was astonished and stared at Peter. Then Peter stretched out a hand to the man. Bravely, he clasped Peter's hand and struggled to

stand. Immediately the man felt new strength flow into his ankles and then into his feet. Cautiously, he let go of Peter.

He could stand.

He took a few steps, testing his new ability. He could walk. He could run. He could jump.

Peter and John went on into the Temple, and the man went with them, walking, leaping, and praising God.

People already in the Temple saw him, and they were amazed. "Isn't that the lame man who sits at the Beautiful Gate asking for money?" they asked one another. "What has happened to him?"

The people crowded around, all trying to get a better look. The man was afraid and held onto Peter and John tightly.

Peter spoke to the people. "Men of Israel, why are you so surprised? Why are you staring at us as if we'd made this man walk by our own power?"

Then Peter told the people about Jesus.

The people listened, and so did the Sadducees, the priests, and the captain of the temple guard.

"Jesus was the Christ!" Peter declared. "He was sent from God, as the Scriptures had foretold. And after he died on the cross, he rose to life again. He came to bring everlasting life to us all."

The priests, the Sadducees, and the captain of the temple guard were furious. Again someone was preaching this message of resurrection.

The temple guard pushed through the spellbound crowd and arrested Peter and John.

By now it was late in the evening, so the two apostles were thrown into prison for the night.

"You can wait here until morning," the captain of the guard told them menacingly. "Then the court will decide what should be done with the two of you."

But in spite of the arrest, many of the people who had been in the Temple that day believed the message preached by Peter and John. Now the number of believers in Jerusalem had grown to five thousand men and many more women and children. The Jewish authorities were becoming very worried indeed.

Acts 4:5-37

Peter and John on Trial

The next morning Peter and John were brought from prison and put on trial before the Sanhedrin, the Jewish court. Caiaphas, the high priest who had tried Jesus, was in charge of the proceedings. He ordered that the lame man also be brought to the court.

"Stand in front of us," Caiaphas ordered Peter and John sternly. They willingly obeyed and met the eyes of their accusers bravely, even after spending the night in prison. Annas, who was Caiaphas's father-in-law and formerly high priest himself, began the questioning.

"Tell us, by what authority or power did you do this?" he asked.

Then Peter was filled with the power of the Holy Spirit and replied without hesitation, "If you have called us here to answer for our good deed of yesterday, the healing of this lame man, then you and all the people of Israel should know. It was by the power of Jesus Christ, the one whom you rejected. He is the only one with the power to save."

The council members were amazed. Peter and John were just ordinary men. Yet they had courage and spoke with such boldness. Truly these men had been with Jesus.

"Wait outside," ordered Caiaphas.

Peter and John obeyed, still under guard.

Then the members of the Sanhedrin anxiously discussed what could be done.

"Everyone in Jerusalem knows they have performed this miracle," they said. "It's no use trying to deny it. But we must tell them that they dare not speak again in the name of Jesus. Otherwise this belief is going to spread."

So Peter and John were called back. Once more they stood in front of the Sanhedrin.

"In the future, you are not to speak or teach in the name of Jesus," ordered Caiaphas.

Courageously Peter and John replied, "Decide for yourselves if it is right for us to obey you instead of God. We must tell everyone of the miraculous things we have seen and heard."

The council members became even more furious. They made many threats of what would happen to Peter and John if the two apostles continued to preach.

But in the end, Peter and John were released. As before, the Jewish leaders were afraid to act because of the people. They knew that at that very minute, crowds were praising God for the miracle of the healing of the lame man, a miracle made even more remarkable now that the people had learned he was over forty years old.

Peter and John were freed and went back to the house where they staying. Soberly they told the others what had happened.

Then all the believers there joined together in prayer. "God, who made the heavens and the earth and the sea and all living creatures, you know how Herod and Pontius Pilate plotted together against Jesus. But they did only what you had already decided must be done.

"Please hear the threats now being made against us. Give us boldness so that we can continue to preach your message unafraid. And please continue to work miracles through the name of Jesus. Amen."

After they had prayed, their courage was restored. They knew themselves to be filled with the power of the Holy Spirit, and they were not afraid to speak God's message.

The believers continued to share everything they had. If they sold their land or their homes, they brought the money from the sale and gave it to the apostles to divide among the people as it was needed.

But one man and his wife didn't want to give all the money from the sale of their land.

Ananias and Sapphira

Ananias, one of the believers, sold some of his land and received a fair price for it. He watched the other believers handing their money over to the apostles, but he wanted to keep some for himself. Who knew when he might need it? He discussed it with his wife, Sapphira, and together they agreed not to tell anyone the exact price of the land.

So Ananias hid part of the money and took the rest to Peter. Solemnly he laid it down at the apostle's feet.

But Peter said sternly, "Ananias, why have you done this? You've let Satan make you lie to the Holy Spirit. You've kept for yourself some of the money from the sale of your land. You haven't lied to me. You've lied to God!"

When Ananias heard these words, he fell to the ground and died.

Some of the young men in the group carried him outside and buried him.

Soon afterward, Sapphira came into the house where the believers were. She was quite unaware of what had happened to her husband. Peter showed her the money Ananias had brought.

"Sapphira," he said, "is this truly the price your husband was given for the land?"

Sapphira nodded. "Yes," she lied. "That's the full amount."

Then Peter said, "How could you both agree to test the Holy Spirit? Your husband is dead. Here come the young men who carried him out and buried him. And they will carry you out as well."

Sapphira was so overcome that she also fell down and died and was buried beside her husband. Everyone who heard this story was full of fear.

But the twelve apostles were performing many miracles of healing and doing other wonderful things.

The believers met regularly together in Solomon's Porch. Those who didn't belong were afraid to join them there, although the believers were held in high regard. More and more believers were being added to the group all the time.

And sick people were carried out into the streets and laid on beds, so that as Peter walked by, at least his shadow might fall on them. People came from all the towns around Jerusalem and brought with them those in need of healing, and every sick person was made well.

The Apostles Imprisoned

As the number of believers increased and as the people flocked to hear the apostles, the high priest and the Sadducees grew very jealous. Once more they had Peter and John arrested and imprisoned, this time along with the other apostles.

But that night as the apostles tried to sleep, an angel appeared to them. The angel unlocked the prison doors and let them out.

"Go!" said the angel. "Return to the Temple. Tell the people more about this new life you have found."

The apostles, hardly believing what was happening, hurried silently away from the prison and made their way through the dark streets.

At daybreak they were once more in the Temple, teaching the people.

The high priest and his associates

had called a full meeting of the Sanhedrin for that morning. When the Jewish leaders arrived, they sent officers to the prison, ordering that the prisoners be brought before the council.

The officers soon returned, obviously shaken. "Sirs," they said, "the jail was locked securely. The guards stood outside the doors. All seemed to be in order. But when we went inside, the jail was empty! The prisoners were gone!"

"What?" cried the chief priests and the captain of the temple guard. And as they looked at one another and wondered exactly what could have happened and what they were going to do about it, a messenger came before them.

"Those men you arrested yesterday are in the Temple. They are teaching the people," he said.

"Leave this to me!" said the captain of the guard.

He went to the Temple, taking some of his men with him. But when they reached the Temple, the crowd was so large that the soldiers dared not seize the apostles by force. The people might have turned against the soldiers and stoned them.

So forcing himself to be polite, the captain asked the apostles to accompany him to the Sanhedrin. The apostles agreed to go. Soon they stood once more before the high priest and the Sadducees.

Caiaphas shouted, "We have forbidden you to speak in the name of Jesus of Nazareth or to continue preaching about him! Yet you are still doing so! What is more, you're trying to make us guilty of having killed him!"

Peter and the others replied calmly, "We must obey God rather than men. It was God who raised Jesus from the dead. We must tell the people about this and about the Holy Spirit, who has been given by God to all who obey him."

When they saw that Peter would not be silenced, the Sanhedrin called for the apostles to be put to death immediately. There was an uproar.

But a Pharisee named Gamaliel shouted, "Wait!"

As the noise died down, he ordered the guard, "Take the followers of Jesus outside for the moment."

When this had been done, Gamaliel spoke earnestly to the court. "Think! Many other rebellions have started, but when the leaders were killed, their followers went back to their own homes. The rebellions were over. So I say in this case, leave these men alone. If their actions are only from men, the whole thing will fizzle out, as usual. But if this movement should be from God, nothing you do will stop it, and you will be fighting against God himself."

There was silence in the room. Gamaliel's words rang true. The Sanhedrin hesitated now about insisting on a death sentence.

So instead, the council had the apostles beaten and ordered them never to preach about Jesus again. Then the apostles were released.

As the apostles left the court, they were not frightened or overcome by the beating, but joyful, because God had thought them important enough to allow them to suffer in the cause of their beloved Lord.

Wherever they went, they continued to tell people about Jesus. But more trouble was bound to come from the authorities.

Acts 6:1-15; 7:1, 2, 51-60; 8:1-5

Stephen

The number of believers was growing every day. They were still trying to share everything, but some of them had begun to grumble.

"The widows of the Greek believers aren't being given as much food as the widows of the Hebrews," the Greeks complained.

So the twelve apostles called a meeting. "Listen," they said, "we can't stop preaching God's message just to wait on you at the table. Choose seven men whom you know to be wise and fair. They can take over the task of distributing things among you. Then we can continue with our special work of prayer and teaching the people."

So the believers chose seven men. They were presented to the apostles, who blessed them.

Among the seven was Stephen, a man full of faith and the Holy Spirit. He was a great preacher and also performed many miracles.

The Jewish leaders were frightened. This new gospel of Christ was spreading too far and too fast. Even a great number of priests believed. The people were taking less and less notice of the Law of Moses.

When Stephen started to preach, certain members of the synagogue were among the crowd listening to him. They argued with him. But Stephen was filled with the Holy Spirit and wisely avoided their traps.

Then the members of the synagogue bribed men to tell lies about Stephen. They stirred up the elders and other leaders against him and had him brought before the Sanhedrin, where they continued their false accusations.

As the members of the Sanhedrin listened, they watched Stephen intently. To their amazement, they saw that instead of showing fear or distress, his face was like an angel's.

"What do you have to say to these charges?" the high priest asked him angrily.

Then Stephen seized his chance. He replied fully, beginning with the lives of Abraham and Moses and finishing with an accusation against the Jews themselves. "You are all the same," he said. "Your fathers killed the prophets of the Christ, and now you have murdered the Christ himself."

His listeners were so furious that

they could not contain themselves. But Stephen looked upward. "I see the heavens opened and the Son of Man, standing at the right hand of God!" he said.

The people in the court put their hands over their ears, so they could not hear any more. Then screaming and shouting, they rushed toward Stephen. The angry crowd seized him, dragged him out of the city, and began to stone him.

Some of the men who had falsely accused Stephen now slipped off their outer robes, so they could throw better. They laid their robes at the feet of a young man named Saul.

As the stones rained down on him, Stephen prayed openly, "Lord Jesus, receive my spirit." When he could no longer stand, he fell to his knees and cried out, "Lord, do not hold this sin against them."

So Stephen died. And Saul watched with approval.

That same day a great persecution began against all the believers in Jerusalem, and many of them fled.

Stephen was buried by some of his fellow believers, who mourned his death deeply.

Saul was so determined to destroy all the believers that he searched for them from home to home in Jerusalem, dragging any believers that he found off to prison.

The believers who had fled were now scattered throughout Judea and Samaria, but wherever they went, they preached about Jesus. So the gospel of the Kingdom of God began to spread.

Philip, one of the seven selected by the believers, went to the city of Samaria and began to preach about Jesus there.

Philip and the Ethiopian

Crowds came to listen to Philip as he preached in Samaria, and he healed many sick people. There was much happiness in the city.

Then one day an angel appeared to him with a message from God. "Philip, you must go south to the desert road that goes from Jerusalem to Gaza."

Leave the city where things were going so well and travel to a desert road which practically no one used? Philip was puzzled.

But he obeyed, and after he reached his destination, Philip stood at the roadside. Why had God sent him there?

Then in the distance, he saw a chariot. It was coming toward him from Jerusalem and would soon pass the spot where he was standing.

The Holy Spirit spoke to Philip. "Go across to that chariot and stay close to it."

So as the chariot passed, Philip caught up with it and ran alongside. He saw that inside the chariot sat a man from the country of Ethiopia.

To Philip's surprise, the Ethiopian was reading aloud from the book of Isaiah, part of the Scriptures. He had come to the words, "He was led as a sheep to the slaughter; and like a lamb silent before his shearer, so he opened not his mouth."

Panting, Philip called out to the man, "Do you understand what you are reading?"

Startled, the Ethiopian looked up and saw Philip. "How can I understand if no one explains it to me?" he asked.

"I can explain," said Philip.

"Really?" Delighted, the Ethiopian ordered his driver to pull up. "Will you come and sit with me?" he asked Philip.

Thankfully, Philip accepted his invitation.

As the chariot drove on, the Ethiopian explained that he was an official in charge of the treasury of the Queen of Ethiopia. He'd been to Jerusalem to worship God, and now he was on his way home.

The Ethiopian turned back to the words of Isaiah. "Who is the writer talking about?" he asked. "Does he mean that he is the sheep led to the slaughter? Or is he speaking of someone else?''

Then Philip told him the story of Jesus. The Ethiopian listened closely, and as he listened, he believed.

As they passed beside some water along the roadside, the Ethiopian cried out, ''Look! Can I be baptized here at once?''

Philip nodded. ''If you believe with all your heart, you may.''

The Ethiopian said, ''I believe that Jesus is the Son of God.''

Then he ordered his driver to stop. Philip and the Ethiopian climbed down to the dusty road. Then they both went into the water, and Philip baptized the Ethiopian.

When they came out of the water, the Holy Spirit suddenly took Philip away. His work in that place was finished, and the Ethiopian could see him no longer. Rejoicing, the Ethiopian continued happily on his journey home.

Philip found himself at Azotus and journeyed on to Caesarea, preaching as he went.

But back in Jerusalem, Saul was still violently persecuting the believers.

Saul on the Road to Damascus

Saul wasn't satisfied with persecuting only the believers in Jerusalem. He went to the high priest.

"Give me letters of introduction to the rulers of the synagogues in Damascus," he said. "I will go there. And if I find any followers of Jesus among the worshipers, I'll arrest them, men or women, and bring them back here to Jerusalem. They must all be killed! This talk about Jesus of Nazareth must be stopped!"

The high priest gave the letters to Saul, and the young man set off grimly, taking with him others who would help him wipe out the followers of Jesus.

But as he traveled along the road to the city of Damascus, Saul was suddenly surrounded by a light of unearthly brilliance.

Saul fell to the ground. He heard a voice speaking to him. "Saul, Saul, why do you persecute me?"

Trembling, Saul whispered, "Who are you, Lord?"

The answer came. "I am Jesus, whom you are persecuting."

Jesus? The one who believers kept saying was alive? Could it be that Saul had been wrong?

Still trembling, he asked, "Lord, what do you want me to do?"

"Get up," Jesus answered. "Go into Damascus. There you will soon receive your instructions."

The men who were traveling with Saul stood silent and fearful. They could hear the voice, but they could see no one.

Saul stumbled to his feet. He put a hand to his eyes. He couldn't see. He was blind.

One of the men took Saul's hand. "Come," he said. "We'll lead you the rest of the way to Damascus."

Saul went with them, terrified by what had happened. They took him to the house of Judas. For three days he could not see, and during that time he refused to eat or drink. But Saul did pray.

Living in Damascus was a believer named Ananias. The Lord Jesus appeared to him in a vision and said, "Ananias."

Ananias was startled for a moment. Then he answered, "I am here, Lord."

"You must get up and go to the street called Straight, to the house of Judas," said the Lord. "There you must ask for Saul of Tarsus. He has been blinded, and now he is praying. He has had a vision in which a man named Ananias comes to him and places his hands on him, restoring his sight."

Ananias was fearful. "But, Lord, I've heard about this man. He's done terrible things to the believers in Jerusalem, and he's come here to arrest all who are believers. He's brought letters of authority from the high priest himself."

Jesus answered quietly, "Ananias, go to him. I have chosen him to be my messenger both to the Jews and to the people of other nations. I will speak to him myself and show him how much he must suffer in my name."

Ananias nervously set out for the street called Straight. But there he hesitated. Suppose Saul was waiting to trap him?

He forced himself to knock on the door. At once he was admitted and was shown into the room where Saul was waiting.

For a moment Ananias stood and stared at him. This man who had been so cruel and so harsh now sat blind and helpless, praying to God in distress.

Ananias went forward and placed his hands on Saul, as Jesus had told him to. "Saul, my brother," he said

gently, "Jesus himself has sent me to you—the same Jesus who met you on the road to Damascus. He sent me so that you might be able to see again and be full of the Holy Spirit."

At that moment it seemed as if something like fish scales fell from Saul's eyes. His face began to shine with joy.

"I can see!" he cried excitedly. "I can see!"

Weak from his three days of fasting, Saul shakily stood up. Quietly, he spoke. "I believe," he said. "And I want to be baptized."

So Saul was baptized immediately. And as soon as he had eaten something, his strength quickly returned to him.

But soon Saul was to be in grave danger.

Saul's Escape from Damascus

Saul stayed with the believers in Damascus for a while. He used as much energy in helping them as he had previously used in having them killed. He preached in the synagogues, and everyone who heard him was utterly amazed.

"Isn't this the same Saul who persecuted the followers of Jesus in Jerusalem?" they asked one another. "Listen to him now! He's claiming that Jesus is the Son of God!"

Saul's preaching grew so powerful that the rulers of the synagogues in Damascus were not able to answer his arguments. Frightened and angry, the rulers decided Saul must be killed.

"He'll be leaving the city soon," they said. "To get outside, he will have to go through one of the gates. If we post guards at all of them, we'll be bound to catch him when he tries to leave."

But Saul's friends heard of the plot and warned him.

"There must be a way to get you safely out of Damascus," they said anxiously. "If you can't go through the gates, you'll have to go over the wall."

But the walls around Damascus were strong and very high in order to protect the city in case of attack.

"I know!" said one of the believers. "We'll get a basket and some strong ropes. Then when it's dark, Saul can sit in the basket, and we will be able to lower him down through an opening in the wall."

It would be very risky, but no one could think of a better plan.

That night a group of believers moved quietly to the place they had chosen. They fastened the ropes securely to the basket and let it hang through an opening in the wall. Bravely Saul climbed into it.

They paused for a moment and listened. If anyone should discover them, it was possible they would all be killed.

But there was silence everywhere. As quickly as they could, Saul's new friends let out the ropes. Down went the basket, bumping against the wall and swinging back and forth. More believers were waiting at the bottom. They looked upward, holding their breath.

Saul landed safely and was rapidly helped out of the basket. Losing no time, he quickly thanked his friends and set out on the road back to Jerusalem.

When he arrived, Saul went to find the believers there. But they were terrified of him because of the way he'd persecuted the believers. They wouldn't accept that he too was a believer now.

Then Barnabas said, "Saul, I trust you. I will take you to see the apostles."

Barnabas told the apostles how Saul had met Jesus on the Damascus road and how he had been preaching about Jesus in the synagogues of Damascus.

The apostles then accepted the word of Barnabas, and the believers in Jerusalem made Saul welcome and invited him to stay.

Just as he had done in Damascus, Saul began to preach powerfully in the synagogues. He also talked with the Greek-speaking Jews, but they became angry and plotted against his life.

When the believers discovered this, they took Saul to Caesarea, then sent him on to Tarsus, where he would be safe.

For a while, the persecution of the churches throughout Judea, Galilee, and Samaria stopped. Through the fear of the Lord and with the comfort of the Holy Spirit, the churches grew in number.

Meanwhile, Peter traveled around the countryside, preaching to the people about Jesus and healing any who were sick.

Dorcas of Joppa

In Joppa there lived a lady called Tabitha, or Dorcas. She was one of the believers, and all the people in the church in Joppa loved her. She was always thinking of kind things she could do for others, and she was always making new clothes for people, especially those who were poor and in need.

One day Dorcas became ill and died. The people were very distressed. They felt they couldn't bear to part with her until they'd had time to get used to the idea. So instead of burying her body at once, as was the custom, they washed it with loving care and placed it in an upstairs room.

As they grieved, one of them said, "If Peter were here, he might be able to help."

Then another said, "But he is!

He's in Lydda. And when he arrived there, he healed Aeneas, who hadn't been able to get out of bed for the last eight years!"

The believers looked at each other with growing hope. Lydda was only a few miles from Joppa.

Two of them set out immediately. They found Peter and begged him to come back with them. Peter agreed to their request.

As soon as they reached Joppa, the believers took him to the upstairs room. There the widows whom Dorcas had helped so much were weeping. They showed Peter the clothes she had made for them while she was alive.

Peter gently asked them all to leave the room. When they had gone, he knelt down and prayed. Then he turned toward the body. "Dorcas, stand up!" he said.

She opened her eyes and looked at him. When she saw it was Peter, she sat up. He held out his hand and helped her to her feet. Then he opened the door of the room and showed her to all the people who had been waiting outside. They had been afraid to hope, but now they saw that she was alive again.

There was great rejoicing as the story spread all over Joppa, and many more people became believers in the Lord Jesus.

A tanner, or leather worker, named Simon invited Peter to stay at his house. While he stayed there, Peter had a vision from God.

Peter Meets Cornelius

It was almost midday, and Peter had gone up to pray on the flat roof of Simon the tanner's house.

He grew very hungry. While he was waiting for a meal to be prepared, he had a vision about food.

Peter saw something that looked like a large sheet. It was being lowered down to the earth by its four corners. In the sheet were all kinds of creatures: animals, birds, and reptiles. And a voice said, "Get up, Peter. Kill and eat!"

Peter was very hungry. But ac-

cording to the Law of Moses, these animals were unclean. They were not to be eaten by the Jews. Peter answered, "Oh no, Lord! I've never broken the law by eating anything which is common or unclean."

The voice spoke again. "You must not call unclean that which God has cleansed."

This happened three times. Then the sheet rose again into the sky.

Peter sat there, wondering. What

did the vision mean? Was it really about food? Or was there more to it than that?

As he thought, he heard a loud knocking on the door of the house. Someone shouted, "Is Simon Peter staying here?"

The Holy Spirit spoke to Peter. "Do you hear those three men? They're looking for you. I have sent them to you. Go with them."

The men had come from Caesarea with a message from Cornelius, a Roman centurion. Peter invited them in for a meal and a night's rest. Then he and some of the other believers from Joppa accompanied them back to Caesarea. The journey took almost two days.

At last they arrived at Cornelius's house. It was full of people. Cornelius had asked his close friends and relatives to come and listen to what Peter would say.

When Peter reached the doorway, Cornelius knelt to worship him.

"Get up!" said Peter. "I'm only a man, not a god."

As they went into the house, Peter began to understand the meaning of his vision. Jews had always been forbidden to visit anyone of a different nationality because foreigners were thought to be ritually unclean. They didn't keep the Jewish religious laws. But now Peter realized that no one made by God could be called "unclean."

He explained this to Cornelius and then said, "Now, why did you send for me?"

Cornelius said, "An angel told me to do so. He knew exactly where you were to be found, so I obeyed him. Please, tell us what God has commanded you to say."

Peter nodded. "I realize now that God's kingdom is not just for Jews, as we thought. Anyone of any nation who believes in him and obeys his words is acceptable to God."

Then Peter told Cornelius and his friends and relatives about Jesus. He finished, "The sins of everyone who believes in Jesus will be forgiven through his name."

As Peter spoke, the Holy Spirit came down on everyone who was listening, and they all began to praise God in many different languages, or tongues.

Some of the Jews from Joppa were amazed. How could God pour out his Holy Spirit on Gentiles, people of other nations? But Peter said, "These people have received the Holy Spirit just as we did. So who can refuse to let them also be baptized?"

No one could refuse. They were baptized in the name of Jesus, and a Roman centurion became a follower of Jesus Christ.

When Peter went back to Jerusalem, the believers there said, "How could you stay in the house of Gentiles? And eat with them?"

So Peter told them the whole story. After telling about his vision, he said, "God gave these people the Holy Spirit, just as he gave the Holy Spirit to us. How could I possibly stand against God?"

Then the believers understood and praised God. But the time of peace for them was ending.

Peter in Prison

King Herod was beginning to persecute the believers again. He arrested John's brother James and had him killed by the sword.

The Jews were pleased, and Herod, seeing this, had Peter thrown into prison. He intended to have him put on trial and killed as soon as the Festival of the Passover ended.

Remembering the last time Peter had been arrested, Herod thought to himself, I'll make certain he doesn't escape this time! And he gave orders that Peter be heavily guarded day and night.

The believers in Jerusalem were greatly upset. James had been killed. Were they to lose Peter also?

They began to pray. They pleaded with God to spare Peter. Day and night the believers prayed. Finally, on the night before his trial, they were still praying. They knew that night could be Peter's last if he were sentenced to death.

In prison Peter was asleep. He was chained hand and foot, and the door was locked. Two soldiers were in the cell with him to guard him and more soldiers stood outside guarding the iron gate. Surely escape was impossible.

But suddenly, Peter felt someone gently shaking his shoulder. Startled, he woke up. Then he rubbed his eyes in disbelief. An angel stood in the cell beside him, and a light was shining in the darkness. "Quick, get up!" said the angel.

Get up? Couldn't the angel see the heavy chains? But even as Peter thought about them, the chains fell off. Yet the loud, sudden clanking did not disturb the guards. They seemed to be fast asleep.

Amazed, Peter quickly scrambled to his feet.

"Get dressed and put on your sandals," the angel said. "Then pull your garment around you and follow me."

As quickly as he could, Peter obeyed. Was this really happening? Or was it a dream?

The angel silently opened the cell door. Peter went with him. They passed the sleeping guards and came to the huge iron gate. To Peter's utter amazement, the gate swung open by itself, and they passed through into the night.

As they walked along the street, the angel suddenly left Peter.

Alone in the starlight, Peter looked around. It was true. He really was out of prison. God had sent the angel to rescue him. Peter hurried along the road to the house of Mary, John Mark's mother.

Inside the house the believers were praying desperately for Peter to be released. Suddenly, they heard a loud knocking at the outer door.

A young woman named Rhoda went to answer the knock.

Guessing that whoever answered the door would be alarmed, Peter called out, "It's me, Peter!"

Peter! Rhoda was overjoyed. Not stopping to open the door, she ran straight back to the believers.

"Peter's here!" she interrupted. "He's at the door!"

Although they had been praying for this very thing, they didn't believe her. "You must be mad," they said.

"No!" she insisted. "It's him. Really it is!"

"It can't be him," they said. "It's his angel."

Meanwhile Peter was desperately afraid that someone would come along the road and discover him. He continued to knock. At last the believers went together to open the door, and they saw him.

"Shhh!" Peter held up his hand. In their excitement they were likely to cry out and betray his presence. They took him inside and listened eagerly as he told them what had happened. "Tell James and the other believers about this," said Peter. Then he quietly left.

In the morning there was a great commotion at the prison. None of the soldiers could explain how Peter had completely disappeared. No one had seen anything or heard anything or remembered anything.

Herod was furious. He ordered that Peter be found. A thorough search was made, but Peter seemed to have vanished. Then Herod sent for the guards and questioned them himself. Discovering that they had no satisfactory explanation, Herod commanded that all of the guards be executed.

Then Herod left Judea and went to Caesarea. There he made a speech to the people. Hoping to gain favor with Herod, the people shouted, "Surely he speaks not as a man, but as a god!"

Herod listened proudly, doing nothing to stop them or to give honor to the true God. An angel struck Herod down, and he died.

But the good news of the Gospel continued to spread.

Saul's First Journey

When the believers scattered after the killing of Stephen, some of them went to Antioch. There they spread the good news of the Gospel. Many people in Antioch believed and joined the church.

Barnabas came from Jerusalem to Antioch to learn more of what was happening there. He was delighted and encouraged the new believers in the faith, and many were added to their number.

Barnabas had been wondering about Saul, so he went to Tarsus, found Saul, and invited him to come to Antioch to help with the new church. Saul came. And it was at Antioch that the believers were first called Christians, followers of Jesus Christ.

One day the Holy Spirit said to the members of the church there, "Set Saul and Barnabas apart. There is special work for them to do." The people realized that God wanted Saul and Barnabas to leave Antioch and take the good news to other places.

So when they had prayed and fasted together, the believers blessed the two men and watched as they set off on their journey. John Mark, a young cousin of Barnabas, went with them as a helper.

After various exciting adventures, including a meeting with a sorcerer on the island of Cyprus, the three came to Pamphylia. There John left the group and went home. But Saul, now known as Paul, traveled on with Barnabas.

They reached another Antioch, this one in Pisidia. The Jews there asked Paul to preach in their synagogue. His sermon was so powerful that he was invited to preach again the following week.

When Paul and Barnabas went to the synagogue on the next Sabbath day, they found crowds waiting outside. Gentiles as well as Jews had come to listen. Practically the whole town was there.

But the Jews were jealous. They didn't want to share the good news about Jesus with the Gentiles. They argued with Paul and contradicted him angrily.

Paul preached even more boldly. "It was necessary that God's Word should first be spoken to you," he said. "But you have refused to accept it. So we now take the message to the Gentiles."

The Gentiles were pleased when they heard this, and many of them became believers. The Jews became furious, and they made trouble in the town for Paul and Barnabas, so the two men left Antioch and went to Iconium.

There much the same thing happened. Soon the whole town was divided between those who were for Paul and those who were against him. Some of those against Paul plotted to stone the apostles, but Paul and Barnabus were warned in time. They got away and went to visit the towns of Lystra and Derbe and the surrounding area.

In Lystra there was a man who had never been able to walk. As Paul preached, he noticed the intent look on the man's face. This man had the faith to be healed.

Looking straight at him, Paul commanded loudly, "Stand up on your feet!"

The man jumped up and walked. Everyone who saw it happen was utterly amazed. The news spread rapidly and hundreds of people came rushing to see the lame man walk and to see Paul and Barnabas.

"They are gods!" shouted the people, and they called Barnabas "Zeus" and Paul "Hermes." The priest of the temple of Zeus hurried to bring bulls and garlands of flowers so that a sacrifice could be made.

But Paul and Barnabas were horrified. "No!" they shouted. "We're not gods! We're not gods! We're men like yourselves. We came to tell you about the living God."

At last the people were restrained. The noise died down, and the priest went back to his temple. Then some travelers from Antioch in Pisidia and from Iconium arrived. They immediately recognized Paul and Barnabas.

The crowd was already disappointed. Now the newcomers turned the people against the apostles. Soon the crowd had become a howling mob. "Stone them! Stone them!" they cried furiously.

Barnabas escaped, but Paul was stoned.

Thinking he was dead, the people dragged Paul outside the city and left him there.

The believers found Paul and gathered sadly around him. Then to their joy, he opened his eyes. He had only been stunned. Courageously, Paul returned to Lystra.

The next morning he and Barnabas continued their travels, encouraging new believers and establishing more churches.

At last they arrived back at Antioch, the town from which they had begun their journey. The believers there listened as Paul and Barnabas told of their adventures.

And the two apostles stayed a long time in Antioch.

A Letter to the Churches

Some men arrived in Antioch from Jerusalem and started to teach that the Gentiles had to keep Jewish customs if they wanted to be Christians. Paul and Barnabas disagreed very strongly with this, so they and some other believers set off for Jerusalem to argue the question with the apostles there.

On the journey Paul and Barnabas stopped at various churches, telling people that Gentiles were now entering the kingdom. Everyone received the news with joy.

But in Jerusalem several of the church members insisted that before Gentiles could become Christians, they must agree to keep all the laws given by Moses to the Israelites.

The apostles and elders called a special meeting. After they had argued for a while, Peter stood up. He told them about his vision and about the way God had sent the Holy Spirit to the Gentiles in the house of Cornelius.

Then Paul and Barnabas spoke, telling especially about the wonderful things they had seen God do among the Gentiles.

Finally James stood up. Firmly he said, "I think we should write to the Gentiles. We shouldn't make it unnecessarily difficult for them to be Christians.

"We should simply tell them that no food offered to idols should be eaten, that men and women must behave honorably toward one another, and that they must not drink blood nor eat anything that has been strangled."

This was agreed on. A very important decision had been made. The Christian church was for everybody who loved and trusted God.

The letter was written, and Judas and Silas, along with some of the other believers in Jerusalem, were chosen to return to Antioch with Paul and Barnabas to deliver it.

The people at Antioch listened gladly to the message of the letter. Judas and Silas gave them much encouragement.

Silas remained in Antioch with Paul and Barnabas, but they were beginning to feel restless.

Paul and Silas

Paul said to Barnabas, "Let's go back to the cities where we preached and see how they're doing."

"Great!" said Barnabas. "We'll take John Mark with us."

"No, we won't!" replied Paul. "He left us last time. I'm not taking him again."

A fierce argument followed. Barnabas absolutely refused to leave his young cousin behind. So the apostles agreed to split up. Barnabas and John Mark sailed for Cyprus. John Mark soon proved to be very trustworthy, and Paul himself said he was a valuable fellow worker and a comfort to him.

But for the moment, Paul asked Silas to join him. Soon after they started their journey, they asked a young believer named Timothy to join them.

They traveled through Syria and Cilicia, visiting the young churches and encouraging them. Paul wanted to go to other parts of Asia Minor to tell the people there about Jesus, but something always happened to stop him from going.

The three had gone as far as Troas when Paul had a vision. A man from Macedonia stood before him, begging, "Come and help us!"

When Paul woke up, he described his vision to his companions. They agreed that the vision was a message from God. Troas was a sea port, so they went down to the docks and booked passage on a ship sailing for Neapolis.

Arriving at Neapolis, they disembarked and traveled to Philippi, the chief city of the region.

On the Sabbath they went down to the river bank which they knew was used as a place of worship by the religious women of the town. There they preached, telling the story of Jesus. One of the women who listened to them was Lydia, a seller of purple cloth. And as she listened, she believed.

She and all the members of her household were baptized, and she invited Paul and Silas to stay at her house. They accepted the invitation.

One day as they were on their way to a prayer meeting, a slave girl met them. Because she could tell fortunes, she made a great deal of money for her owners. Now she followed the two apostles, calling out, "These men are servants of the Most High God. They

are telling you how you can be saved!''

After the girl had behaved in this way for many days, Paul became very troubled about her. ''She must be possessed by an evil spirit,'' he said. He stopped and turned around to face the girl. Firmly, he said, ''Evil spirit, in the name of Jesus Christ, I command you to come out of her!'' And the spirit obeyed.

The girl immediately regained her senses. She was happy, but her owners were not. They realized that they would no longer be able to make money with her. Furiously they grabbed Paul and Silas and dragged them before the magistrates in the local marketplace.

''These men are Jews!'' they declared loudly. ''They're upsetting the whole town by teaching customs which are illegal for us Romans to practice.''

There was no proper trial. Soon the marketplace was crowded with people shouting insults and accusations at Paul and Silas. Without giving them any chance to defend themselves, the magistrates declared them to be guilty. They were to be stripped, then beaten and thrown into prison.

The sentence was carried out immediately. The jailer was told to take special care that the two men did not escape. So he put them into the innermost cell and fastened their feet securely in the stocks.

Acts 16:25-40; 17; 18; 20:1-2

The Earthquake

In prison that night, Paul and Silas couldn't sleep, so they began to pray and sing hymns.

The other prisoners listened in amazement.

At about midnight a sudden earthquake shook the foundation of the prison. The doors of the cells swung open, and everyone's chains were loosened.

The jailer awoke startled and ran from his house to find out what had happened at the prison. When he arrived, he could see that every door was wide open.

The prisoners must have escaped, the jailer thought desperately. Knowing he could expect no mercy from the authorities, he pulled out his sword to kill himself.

But Paul called out, "It's all right. We're all here."

The jailer shouted to his servants, "Quickly, bring lights."

In the flickering light of the torches, he knelt in front of Paul and Silas. "Sirs," he asked, trembling, "what must I do to be saved?"

This was an extraordinary question for a jailer to ask, but Paul replied instantly. "Believe in the Lord Jesus Christ, and you will be saved—you and all your household."

The jailer and his household knew very little about Jesus, and he asked if they could hear more.

Gladly Paul and Silas told the story. Then the jailer washed their wounds and did what he could to make them more comfortable. He and all his household were baptized.

He then invited the two apostles into his house for a meal, overjoyed because he and his whole family had come to believe in Jesus.

At dawn the magistrates sent officers to the prison to order that Paul and Silas be released.

The jailer hurried to Paul and Silas. "You're free!" he said. "You can go!"

"No," said Paul. The bewildered jailer looked at him. Paul faced the officers. "We were beaten in public without a fair trial, even though we are Roman citizens. Now the magistrates want us to leave quietly without fuss. No, if they want us to leave, they can come here and tell us so themselves."

The officers were astounded. They reported back to the magistrates, and the magistrates became very worried. They hadn't realized Paul and Silas were Roman citizens. Beating a Roman citizen without first allowing him a proper trial was a serious offense.

Anxiously the magistrates came to the prison. They humbly led the two men out of the prison gates and requested politely that they leave Philippi.

But Paul and Silas were not ready to go yet. First they returned to Lydia's house to tell her what had happened and to encourage the other believers.

Then when they were ready, Paul, Silas, and Timothy set off again.

After many adventures, including having to split up for a while, they all reached Corinth. Here Paul grew discouraged. But God sent him a vision, saying, "Don't give up, Paul. And don't be afraid. I am with you. I have many followers in this city, and no one will harm you."

No one in Corinth harmed Paul, and it was eighteen months before he left Corinth to continue his journey.

The Boy Who Fell Asleep

On a warm Saturday evening in an upstairs room in Troas, Paul was speaking to the believers. He had much to say, for he was leaving the next day. When midnight came, Paul was still talking.

In the room a boy named Eutychus had perched himself on a window ledge to listen. Now as Paul spoke on and on, Eutychus dozed off.

He fell out of the window, and he hit the ground with a thud, three floors below.

There was a great commotion. Everyone rushed downstairs and outside. Eutychus lay very still on the ground.

Somebody lifted the boy up. "He's dead!" they whispered.

Gently they laid him down again. Paul pressed his way to the front and threw himself on top of Eutychus and hugged him. "It's all right," he said. "Don't be afraid. He's alive."

While the boy was attended to, Paul and most of the others went back upstairs. There they broke bread together, and Paul continued talking until daybreak. Then Paul set off once more on his journeys.

After the meeting was concluded, Eutychus was brought in very much alive. Everyone was amazed and comforted.

Paul in Trouble

Paul had gone to visit the Temple in Jerusalem. There he was recognized by some of the Jews who had opposed him when he had visited their cities. They cried out, "Men of Israel, help! This is the man who teaches everyone against the people of Israel and against our law. He's also brought Gentiles into this Temple, defiling this holy place!"

The accusations were not true, but they started a riot. People came running from all sides, seized Paul, and dragged him out of the Temple. The mob hastily shut the doors behind them, then tried to kill Paul.

A messenger rushed to inform the commander of the Roman soldiers whose job it was to keep peace in the city. Gathering some of his men, the commander ran quickly to the place where the crowd was. When they saw the soldiers coming, the mob stopped beating Paul.

The commander arrested Paul and ordered that chains be put on him. Then he said, "Who is this man? What has he done?" Immediately there was an uproar and everyone shouted different accusations.

311

"Take him to the barracks," the commander ordered his men. "We'll never find out the truth here."

The soldiers tried to obey, but when they reached the barracks, the crowd became so violent that Paul had to be carried inside.

Above the uproar Paul shouted to the commander, "May I say something?"

"Do you speak our language? Aren't you the foreign leader of a band of terrorists?" asked the commander.

"No, I'm not," said Paul. "I'm a Jew, born in Tarsus, a city in Cilicia. Please, commander, let me speak to these people."

The commander looked at Paul, then at the mob. "You can try," he answered.

Upright and unafraid, Paul stood on the steps of the barracks and motioned with his hands for the crowd to be quiet. Amazingly, the noise died down. Paul waited until there was absolute silence. Then he spoke in Hebrew, and the crowd listened.

Paul told them that he had persecuted the Christians until he met Jesus on the Damascus road. When he began to tell the crowd how God had told him to take the message to the Gentiles, they grew furious.

There was such an outcry from the crowd that Paul could no longer be heard.

Fearing a riot, the commander ordered that Paul be taken inside the barracks. "Flog him and question him. Find out the truth."

As the flogging was about to start,

Paul asked the centurion standing there, "Is it lawful for you to flog a Roman citizen when nothing has been proved against him?"

The centurion thought for a moment. Then he went to the commander. "Sir, this man says he is a Roman citizen. What will you do?"

They both knew the danger of flogging a Roman citizen without first having a trial and finding him guilty.

The commander went to question Paul. "Are you a Roman?" he asked.

"I am," said Paul.

"I had to pay a large amount of money for my citizenship," said the commander.

"I was born a citizen," Paul answered.

Hearing this, the men who were going to question Paul backed away. The commander himself was worried when he discovered that he'd had a Roman citizen put into chains. But he still wanted to find out why the Jews were accusing Paul so angrily.

So the commander ordered an assembly of the Sanhedrin and brought Paul to stand before them. But a great dissension arose between the Pharisees and the Sadducees, and the commander had Paul returned to the barracks.

The Shipwreck and the Snake

Paul was disappointed because he felt that he'd lost a chance to speak to the Jewish leaders. But God spoke to him in a vision. "Take heart, Paul! You have witnessed for me in Jerusalem. Now you will witness for me in Rome."

Paul was encouraged. He longed to see Rome, and he realized that God could use what had just happened to fulfill his divine purpose.

That night, to save Paul from yet another attempt on his life, the commander sent him under a large guard to Caesarea. Felix, the governor there, could arrange the trial.

Felix had Paul imprisoned in Herod's palace until a new trial could be arranged. Then once more Paul stood before the Sanhedrin and the high priest, Ananias. This time he was allowed to speak. But Felix made no judgment.

"We'll wait until the commander arrives," he said. "Meanwhile, Paul is to be kept under guard. Allow his friends to take care of him."

So Paul was imprisoned again. Felix and his wife Drusilla often came to talk to him. Felix was hoping Paul would bribe him in order to obtain freedom. After two years Felix was transferred, but he left Paul in prison because he wanted to please the Jews.

Festus, the new governor, wanted to know why Paul was in prison. He treated Paul with kindness by asking if he would like to go back to Jerusalem for a retrial.

"No," said Paul. "I want to be tried by Caesar in a Roman court."

Festus asked his counselors for advice. Then he replied to Paul, "Very well. You have appealed to Caesar. To Caesar you shall go."

Before arrangements could be made, King Agrippa arrived in Caesarea. Because Paul was such a famous prisoner, the king wanted to speak to him. So Paul again told the story of Jesus. King Agrippa listened closely. "You almost persuade me to be a Christian," he said. And to Festus he remarked, "If this man hadn't insisted on being tried by Caesar, he would have been set free."

But Paul had insisted, and it was decided to send him to Caesar. Paul and some other prisoners were placed on a ship bound for Italy.

The ship's passage had been delayed very much by bad weather. Now as it lay at anchor in Crete, Paul warned the centurion in charge of the danger of sailing on.

But instead the centurion took the advice of the captain, who was unwilling to stay where they were for the winter. They set sail, hoping they could get as far as Phoenix before winter fully set in.

At first there was a fair wind. But soon a fierce storm came up, and the ship was driven helplessly before it. The situation became desperate.

Shouting above the noise of the wind and the waves, the captain ordered that the cargo be thrown overboard in an effort to lighten the ship. The next day the tackle was also thrown over the side. Still the storm raged, and the ship tossed up and down.

The crew and the prisoners gave up all hope of being saved. Then Paul stood up to address them. "Men, if you'd taken my advice not to leave Crete, we wouldn't be in this trouble now. Even so, take heart.

"For an angel of my God came to me this night and said, 'Don't be afraid, Paul! You will stand trial in front of Caesar. God will save the lives of everyone who sails with you in this ship.' I trust God that it will happen exactly as he has said. But be warned, we will run aground on an island."

Sure enough, on the fourteenth night of the voyage, the sailors could tell that the ship was nearing land. They dropped four anchors, hoping to hold the ship off the rocks. Some of the sailors became terrified and began to lower a lifeboat, pretending they were going to drop more anchors. Ac-tually, they were attempting to save themselves.

But Paul yelled to the centurion, "Unless those men stay with the ship, they will be drowned!"

So the soldiers cut the ropes that held the lifeboat, and it fell away empty.

As they waited for dawn, Paul urged, "Eat! You will need all the strength you can get. I tell you, not one of you will be lost." And to encourage them, he took some bread, gave thanks for it, and ate it in front of them. Then they all took heart, and they too ate some food.

When daylight came, they saw they were near a sandy bay. They tried to beach the ship there, but it ran aground. Huge waves began to break the ship apart. "Kill the prisoners before they escape!" shouted the soldiers.

"No," responded the centurion. "Jump overboard, all of you. Swim or grab a plank. Get yourselves to land somehow."

They obeyed his order, and every one of them reached the shore in safety.

They were cold and wet. The islanders built a huge campfire to warm them, and Paul collected firewood. As he put it on the fire, a poisonous snake driven out by the heat fastened itself onto his hand. The watching islanders thought he would die immediately, but Paul simply shook the snake off. Everyone waited and watched. After a long wait, Paul was still obviously unharmed, and the islanders decided that Paul had to be a god.

Publius, the chief official of the island, provided food and shelter for the shipwrecked men. When Paul learned that Publius's father was sick, Paul went to him and healed him. Afterward many sick people came for healing.

It was three months before the shipwrecked men set sail again in a different ship. But finally, Paul arrived at his destination—the city of Rome.

The Letters to Christians

In Rome Paul was allowed to rent a private home with only one soldier to guard him. He was under house arrest and could not leave, so the people came to him. Paul continued to preach fearlessly.

But in A.D. 64, there was a huge fire in Rome. The Emperor Nero blamed the Jews for the fire, and a relentless persecution of Jews and Christians began.

During that time many of the Christians who refused to give up their faith were killed. Paul is believed to be one of those put to death at that time.

But through his words, Paul continued to influence the church. While imprisoned, he had spent much of his time writing letters to new Christians. Many of his letters were saved and read over and over again.

These letters are in the Bible, along with letters from James, Peter, John, and Jude. They are full of encouragement, instruction, and wisdom; and they are still treasured by Christians today.

John's Vision

God sent John a vision of the future.

John wrote, "After the judgment, I saw a new heaven and a new earth. I heard a voice out of heaven saying, 'Behold! God is with men, and he will dwell with them. God shall wipe away all tears from their eyes; and there shall be no more death, nor sorrow, nor crying; there shall be no more pain, for these things have passed away.' The holy city shall be very beautiful, for the glory of God shall be its light. Then Jesus said, 'Behold! I am coming soon!' The grace of our Lord Jesus Christ be with you all."